P9-APK-613

GREAT
CONTEMPORARIES

Great Contemporaries

BY

Winston S. Churchill

The University of Chicago Press

Chicago and London

Originally published in 1937 by
Thornton Butterworth Ltd., London

The University of Chicago Press, Chicago 60637
Published 1973. Printed in the United States of America
International Standard Book Number: 0-226-10630-6 (clothbound)
81 80 79 78 77   9 8 7 6 5 4 3 2

CONTENTS

LIST OF ILLUSTRATIONS

PREFACE

THESE essays on Great Men of our age have been written by me at intervals during the last eight years. Although each is self-contained, they throw from various angles, a light upon the main course of the events through which we have lived. I hope they will be found to illustrate some of its less well-known aspects. Taken together they should present not only the actors but the scene. In their sequence they may perhaps be the stepping-stones of historical narrative.

I have preferred not to include any of the British political or military figures who are with us to-day. This does not imply lack either of material or appreciation. There is greater freedom in dealing with the past. The central theme is of course the group of British statesmen who shone at the end of the last century and the beginning of this—Balfour, Chamberlain, Rosebery, Morley, Asquith and Curzon. All lived, worked and disputed for so many years together, knew each other well, and esteemed each other highly. It was my privilege as a far younger man to be admitted to their society and their kindness. Reading again these chapters has brought them back to me, and made me feel how much has changed in our political life. Perhaps this is but the illusion which comes upon us all as we grow older. Each succeeding generation will sing with conviction the Harrow song 'There were wonderful giants of old.' Certainly we must all hope this may prove to be so. In the meantime those to whom these great men are but names —that is to say the vast majority of my readers—may

9

perhaps be glad to gain from these notes some acquaintance with them.

Though I have made very large additions, I have in almost every case left the text as I originally wrote it. Here and there it has been necessary, in these swiftly-moving times, to bring the story up to date. I have also softened a few judgments or expressions before admitting them to a permanent record. In particular I have rewritten the story of the resignations from Mr. Balfour's Cabinet in 1903, and it now presents to the public what is I believe for the first time a correct account. I am also indebted to a friend for the detail of the events attending Mr. Bonar Law's resignation and the choice of Mr. Baldwin as his successor by King George.

WINSTON SPENCER CHURCHILL.

August 13, 1937.

THE EARL
OF ROSEBERY

Elliott & Fry, Ltd

THE EARL OF ROSEBERY AS PRIME MINISTER

THE EARL OF ROSEBERY

IT might be said that Lord Rosebery outlived his future by ten years and his past by more than twenty. The brilliant prospects which had shone before him until he became Prime Minister in 1894 were dispersed by the break-up of his Government and the decisive defeat of the Liberal Party in 1895. The part he took as an Imperialist and a patriot in supporting, four years later, the South African War destroyed his hold upon the regard and confidence of a large section of the Radical masses. His resignation of the Leadership of the Liberal Party had already released them from their allegiance. By his definite declaration against Home Rule when Mr. Balfour's fall in 1905 was approaching, he cut himself off deliberately and resolutely from all share in the impending Liberal triumph and long reign of power. He severed himself by purposeful action from his friends and followers. 'Content to let occasion die,' he withdrew from all competition for leadership in the political arena; he erected barriers against his return which he meant to be insurmountable; he isolated himself in cool and unaffectedly disdainful detachment. It was known only too well that overtures would be useless. By 1905 his political career was closed for ever. It was only in 1929 that his long life ended.

Dwelling in his wide and beautiful estates, moving frequently from one delightful house and one capacious library to another, he lived to sustain the burden of an eightieth birthday, lighted by the refinements of profound and astonishingly wide-ranging literary knowledge, amused by the Turf, and cheered and companioned by his children and his grandchildren. The afflictions of old age fell successively with gathering weight upon him in his ever-deepening retirement ; and when he died his name and actions had faded entirely from the public mind, and were only revived and presented to the eyes of a new generation by the obituary notices. But those actions, and still more the character and personality which lay behind them, are worthy of most careful study, not only for the sake of their high merit, but at least as much for their limitations.

Lord Rosebery was probably my father's greatest friend. They were contemporaries at Eton and at Oxford. Although apparently divided by party, they moved in the same society, had many friends in common, and pursued the same pleasures and sports—of which racing was ever the sovereign. Their correspondence was sparkling and continuous, and their intimate personal relations were never affected by the fierce political struggles of the 'eighties, or by any vicissitudes of fortune.

I inherited this friendship, or rather the possibility of renewing it in another generation. I was anxious to cultivate it for many reasons, of which the first was to learn more about my father from his contemporary, his equal and his companion. With some at least of those feelings of awe and attraction which led Boswell to Dr. Johnson, I sought occasions to develop the acquaintance of childhood into a grown-up friendship. At first he did not seem to approve of me : but after the South African War, when I had at least become well known and was a young M.P., he began to show me marked kindness. The biography of my father by which I was soon absorbed opened a wide and fertile field of common interest. He assisted actively in the enterprise, drew richly upon his fund of choice reminiscence, collected letters and documents, read proofs, criticized sympathetically but penetratingly both the subject and the work. This formed a theme of common interest between us and built a bridge across the gulf of a different generation.

During the years of my literary task, from 1900 to 1905,

I was often his guest in all his houses, at Mentmore, in Berkeley Square, at the Durdans hard by Epsom Downs, on the Firth of Forth at Dalmeny, at his shooting lodge, Rosebery ; and we also met year after year on long visits to common friends in the delicious autumn of the Scottish Highlands. Politics provided additional links and ties ; for we were both adrift from our parties. He was out of sympathy with the Liberals : I was soon quarrelling with the Tories. We could both toy with the dream of some new system and grouping of men and ideas, in which one could be an Imperialist without swallowing Protection, and a social reformer without Little Englandism or class bitterness. We had certainly that solid basis of agreement and harmony of outlook upon middle courses, which is shared by many sensible people and was in those days abhorrent to party machines. Need one add that the party machines always prove the stronger ?

Over the biography one awkwardness arose. Lord Rosebery's interest was so strong and his desire to help delineate his friend so keen, that he took the trouble to write a considerable appreciation of Lord Randolph, which he suggested I should incorporate textually in my account. I was deeply touched, and at the same time embarrassed : for after all I had my own way of doing things, and the literary integrity of a work is capital. Moreover, his picture of Randolph Churchill's school days contained the word ' scug,' an Eton slang term which I considered derogatory and unsuited to a biography written by a son. I therefore deferentially but obstinately resisted this expression. He stuck to it and explained its harmless Etonian significance. In the end he wrote that I had rejected his contribution and that it was withdrawn. A few years later it appeared as the widely-read and deeply-interesting monograph on Lord Randolph and my book about him, in which Lord Rosebery drew with admiration and affection the ' brilliant being ' who had so compulsively cheered, charmed, directed, and startled his youth and prime. The incident, though it distressed me at the time, did not seem in any way to rankle in my illustrious friend. He had all the grand comprehensions, and though sensitive to a degree, did not take my recalcitrance amiss. On the contrary, I think he liked me the better for my filial prudery.

It is difficult to convey the pleasure I derived from his conversation as it ranged easily and spontaneously upon all kinds of topics ' from grave to gay, from lively to severe.' Its peculiar quality was the unexpected depths or suggestive turns which revealed the size of the subject and his own background of knowledge and reflection. At the same time he was full of fun. He made many things not only arresting, but merry. He seemed as much a master of trifles and gossip as of weighty matters. He was keenly curious about every aspect of life. Sportsman, epicure, bookworm, literary critic, magpie collector of historical relics, appreciative owner of veritable museums of art treasures, he never needed to tear a theme to tatters. In lighter vein he flitted jauntily from flower to flower like a glittering insect, by no means unprovided with a sting. And then in contrast, out would come his wise, matured judgments upon the great men and events of the past. But these treats were not always given. He was at his best with two or three and on his day ; and sometimes in larger company he seemed shy and ill at ease. When he was out of humour, he could cast a chill over all, and did not hesitate to freeze and snub. On these occasions his face became expressionless, almost a slab, and his eyes lost their light and fire. One saw an altogether different person. But after a bit one knew the real man was there all the time, hiding perversely behind a curtain. And all the more agreeable was it when he came out.

Hardest of all is it to revive the impression which he produced upon his hearers when dealing with the greatest affairs. His life was set in an atmosphere of tradition. The Past stood ever at his elbow and was the counsellor upon whom he most relied. He seemed to be attended by

Learning and History, and to carry into current events an air of ancient majesty. His voice was melodious and deep, and often, when listening, one felt in living contact with the centuries which are gone, and perceived the long continuity of our island tale.

Lord Rosebery was the first Prime Minister for many years who had never served in the House of Commons. He will very likely be the last. Whatever one may think about democratic government, it is just as well to have practical experience of its rough and slatternly foundations. No part of the education of a politician is more indispensable than the fighting of elections. Here you come in contact with all sorts of persons and every current of national life. You feel the Constitution at work in its primary processes. Dignity may suffer, the superfine gloss is soon worn away ; nice particularisms and special private policies are scraped off ; much has to be accepted with a shrug, a sigh or a smile ; but at any rate in the end one knows a good deal about what happens and why.

Rosebery had none of this. He addressed and captivated great meetings ; he gained the plaudits of tumultuous crowds ; he followed Mr. Gladstone through all the immense popular enthusiasms of the Midlothian campaign. But these were the show occasions, where ardent supporters were marshalled in overwhelming strength. They were very different from the bustling experience of a Parliamentary candidature, with its disorderly gatherings, its organized oppositions, its hostile little meetings, its jeering throng, its stream of disagreeable and often silly questions.

Rosebery's Eton tutor in something of a spirit of prophecy said of him that he ' sought the palm without the dust.' This was not true in the sense in which the phrase is often used—that of avoiding hard work. Rosebery was capable of very hard work and of long hours of daily concentration both on politics and literature. He sought indeed the palm, but the dust had never come his way ; and when in high station the compromises, the accommodations, the inevitable acquiescence in inferior solutions, were forced upon him, he was not toughened against these petty vexations, or trained to see them in their true light. Although equipped with capacious knowledge of the part of a modern Statesman, he was essentially a survival from a vanished age, when great Lords ruled with general acceptance and strove, however fiercely, only with others like themselves. While he stood under the ægis of Mr. Gladstone, the Radical masses presented themselves as devoted, loyal, enthusiastic adherents. It was not until the Gladstonian spell had passed away that he realized how very imperfect was his contact with them. He did not think as they thought, or feel as they felt, or understand the means of winning their unselfish and unbounded allegiance. He understood the hard conditions of their lives, and was intellectually indignant at their wrongs and sufferings. His mind ranged back across centuries of their history, and selected with shrewd and wise judgment the steps required to sustain their progress and welfare. But actually to handle them, to wrestle with, them, to express their passion and win their confidence this he could not do.

Professor Goldwin Smith, with whom he was on terms of intimate acquaintance and correspondence, said of him to me in Toronto in 1900, ' Rosebery feels about Democracy as if he were holding a wolf by the ears.' This was a harsh judgment, and probably beyond the truth ; but it was not opposed to the truth. As the franchise broadened and the elegant, glittering, imposing trappings faded from British Parliamentary and public life, Lord Rosebery was conscious of an ever-widening gap between himself and the Radical electorate. The great principles ' for which Hampden died in the field and Sidney on the scaffold,' the economics and philosophy of Mill, the venerable inspiration of Gladstonian memories, were no longer enough. One had to face the caucus, the wire-puller and the soap-box ; one had to stand on platforms built of planks of all descriptions. He did not like it. He could not do it. He would not try.

He knew what was wise and fair and true. He would not go through the laborious, vexatious and at times humiliating processes necessary under modern conditions to bring about these great ends. He would not stoop ; he did not conquer.

Let us test these general comments by his career. The milestones of Rosebery's public life stand forth abruptly along the track. He was one of the first Whig nobles who as a young man embraced the Liberal and democratic conceptions of the later nineteenth century. The stir and enthusiasm of Mr. Gladstone's Midlothian campaign carried him into politics. There he was, on the spot, a gifted, bright figure in Edinburgh and Scotland, thirty-one or thirty-two, with all that rank and fortune could bestow. And here was the Grand Old Man, to listen to whose words rich and poor travelled for days and stood in rain and mist for hours, fighting in Rosebery's own Scottish domain for what seemed to be a world cause. Rosebery plunged into politics as ' a chivalrous adventure.' ' When I found myself in this evil-smelling bog, I was always trying to extricate myself. That is the secret of what people used to call my lost opportunities and so forth.'

These rather bitter words written in the years of eclipse did not in any way represent the effort, the industry, the resolution, or the robust citizenship which Rosebery contributed for a quarter of a century to British and Imperial affairs. He was an earnest, painstaking man whose heart beat the faster for any cause touching the honour or the greatness of Britain or which concerned the well-being and progress of the mass of the people. He served an apprenticeship of some years in minor offices. He pressed for Scottish legislation more advanced than any for which Mr. Gladstone's Cabinet of 1880 was prepared. He became at a bound amid general applause Foreign Secretary in Mr. Gladstone's government of 1886. Here came the second milestone. Home Rule split the Liberal party to the roots. Every man had to choose which way he would go. Rosebery had no sentimental liking for the Irish. But although in his historical writings he repressed his bias, he had latent in him all the Whig scorn for Tories. He stood up to them. He adhered to Mr. Gladstone. He went into the wilderness with him.

The favour or frown of Society contacts in those days played a part in public life incomprehensible to the present generation. But Rosebery stood so high in the land that he could look down upon the cuts and resentments of the London governing class. He was upon occasion as stiff a Radical as John Morley. He had at times a large though indefinite following among Trade Unionists and labouring men. The spectacle of this eloquent, magnificent personage separating himself from the bulk of his class, ' biding by the Buff and the Blue,' excited the hostility of the Unionist party, and filled the Liberals in the cool shade with a sense of hope and expectancy for his future. It clung to him through years of misunderstanding and disappointment. At first they said ' He will come.' Then for years ' If only he would come.' And finally, long after he had renounced politics for ever, ' If only he would come back.'

Out of office, by birth debarred from the experience of electioneering and of House of Commons rough-and-tumble, he found in the London County Council the most lively substitute open to a peer. He was the first and greatest chairman of the London County Council. For nearly three years he guided, impelled and adorned its activities. He raised the status of the municipal life of London to the level of ministerial office. At the centre of twenty-two committees he laid strong, keen hands upon every aspect of London government. When, sorely smitten by the Parnell divorce and other Irish difficulties, Mr. Gladstone and the Liberal party returned to power at the election of 1892 with a majority of only forty, dependent upon the Irish vote, Rosebery was for the second time the widely-acclaimed Foreign Secretary of the new administration. More than ever he was ' the man of the future.'

He seemed at this time to represent in a Liberal guise the Disraelian idea of Tory Democracy, revived by Lord Randolph Churchill, and also the cruder but far more effective form of Radical-Imperialism embodied in his final phase by Joseph Chamberlain. In the main the differences between all these three men were questions of emphasis and style. Rosebery expressed the spirit of the modern British Empire with a foresight and precision which make him in retrospect the immediate spiritual successor of Disraeli. The discordances of his culminating period arose from the fact that he became the ministerial successor of Mr. Gladstone. Now that I reflect upon his conversation and re-read his speeches in Lord Crewe's deeply-informed biography, I realize that he responded spontaneously to the same stimuli which actuated Disraeli. Indeed he often seems to march out of the pages of ' Coningsby '—the aristocrat-champion of the poor and depressed classes—' I would make these great slum-landlords skip.'

And at the same time to dream of a glorious and abiding British Empire, freed to the utmost possible degree from European entanglements, was at all times his indulgence, and to achieve it his aim. He carried the story of Empire forward into a chapter only read with comprehension after he had long ceased to be an actor on the political stage. Who can dispute these somewhat unfashionable assertions in the light of his message to Australia delivered at Adelaide on January 18, 1883 : ' . . . These are no longer colonies in the ordinary sense of the term ; but I claim that this is a country which has established itself a nation, and that its nationality is now and will be henceforward recognized by the world. . . . But there is a further question ; does this fact of your being a nation imply separation from the Empire ? God forbid ! There is no need for any nation, however great, leaving the Empire, because *the Empire is a Commonwealth of Nations.*' Rosebery lived to see this phrase, which fell from the prescient lips of genius, become fifty years later the accepted statutory law which now to-day alone encircles the most numerous, the most diverse, the most wide-spread, voluntary, but none the less habitual, association of states and nations of which there is record.

The disharmonies and the eventual rupture of his political career sprang from his proud and at times supercilious inability to subject himself to the mechanism of modern democracy and to the exigencies of the party caucus. Had he possessed Mr. Baldwin's phlegmatic capacity of putting up with a score of unpleasant and even humbling situations, in order to be master of something very big at the end of a blue moon, he would indeed have been not only a Prophet but a Judge in Israel. He was far too sensitive, too highly strung, for these compromises and submissions. He was a child and brilliant survivor of the old vanishing, and now vanished, oligarchic world which across the centuries had built the might and the freedom of Britain. He was often palpably out of touch with his environment ; perhaps that is no censure upon him. It must however be emphasized that physically he did not stand the stresses well. In times of crisis and responsibility his active, fertile mind and imagination preyed upon him. He was bereft of sleep. He magnified trifles. He failed to separate the awkward incidents of the hour from the long swing of events, which he so clearly understood. Toughness when nothing particular was happening was not the form of fortitude in which he excelled. He was unduly attracted by the dramatic, and by the pleasure of making a fine gesture. He would not join Mr. Gladstone's Government in 1880, for that might seem to be the direct reward of his share in the Midlothian campaign. He volunteered to join after the death of General Gordon at Khartoum, because then it was a case of 'all hands to the pumps.' In a wearing ordeal his thoughts strayed to the fine speech he could make on resignation. And then he was of course never given the chance of wielding real power. He never held office with a large, loyal, solid majority behind him. He never had a united party at his back, and could never plan ahead for two or three years at a time.

How these Victorians busied themselves and contended about minor things! What long, brilliant, impassioned letters they wrote each other about refined personal and political issues of which the modern Juggernaut progression takes no account! They never had to face, as we have done, and still do, the possibility of national ruin. Their main foundations were never shaken. They dwelt in an age of British splendour and unchallenged leadership. The art of government was exercised within a limited sphere. World-revolution, mortal defeat, national subjugation, chaotic degeneration, or even national bankruptcy, had not laid steel claws upon their sedate, serene, complacent life. Rosebery flourished in an age of great men and small events.

The third milestone at the top of his life marked his Prime Ministership—'First Minister of the Crown' as he would call it. This indeed was a strangely-lighted episode. Early in 1894 Mr. Gladstone, eighty-four years old, resigned his leadership of Her Majesty's Government and the Liberal party in protest against the Navy estimates and what he called 'the increasing militarism of the times.' Two men stood forth to succeed him—Rosebery and Harcourt. Rosebery was in the Lords, Harcourt in the Commons. Sir William Harcourt was a genial, accomplished Parliamentarian, a party man, ambitious in a calculating style, a Falstaffian figure, with an eye fixed earnestly, but by no means unerringly, upon the main chance. The Liberal Government, holding office by the Irish vote, assailed vehemently by the far more solid Unionist array, was struggling along under the freely-used veto of the House of Lords, by majorities which sometimes fell below twenty, towards an ugly election. It was a bleak, precarious, wasting inheritance.

It was at this time that he most felt the need of his wife, who had died some years before. With all her almost

23

excessive adoration of Rosebery, she was ever a pacifying and composing element in his life, which he was never able to find again, because he never could give full confidences to anyone else. She was a remarkable woman on whom he had leaned, and without her he was maimed.

The Cabinet were all agreed that they would not serve under Harcourt. The party were pretty sure he would not fill the bill. Rosebery became Prime Minister, but Harcourt as Chancellor of the Exchequer and Leader of the House of Commons held the real power. He stipulated for special conditions. He was to decide in a Parliamentary emergency upon the action of the Government in the House of Commons. He must be informed of every detail of Foreign Affairs. He must have the Cabinet called whenever he chose. He must have a share in patronage. In so far as these claims were not unreasonable, there was no need to prefer them. They must in practice have been conceded from day to day. But a formal contract was novel. Rosebery said quite simply that he did not want to be Prime Minister at all, but if he were, he must be a real Prime Minister. However, in the end Harcourt exacted his conditions. The gravamen against him is that he did not keep his side of the pact. Rosebery did not receive fair play from him. On the contrary, he used all his frequent and potent opportunities to torment and harry the Prime Minister, and make his position intolerable. Thus Rosebery's Premiership of less than two years was a period of endless vexation. His only consolation was to win the Derby as Prime Minister twice running, with Ladas and Sir Visto, to the huge scandal of the Nonconformist conscience. Flouted, frustrated, undermined by Lobby intrigue, and finally overwhelmed by the strong surge of Unionist power, Rosebery and with him the Liberals were swept away for ten years in the summer of 1895 into the trough of disunited opposition. He never held office again.

There remained the final stroke. The Armenian massacres of 1896 excited the defeated Liberals. They clamoured for intervention and strong measures against Turkey. Rosebery with his Foreign Office outlook did not share this mood. He did not voice the party feeling. Mr. Gladstone emerged from his retirement with a tremendous speech recalling Midlothian days. Rosebery resigned the disputed leadership of the Liberal party, and resolved to retire for ever from politics. But he was still under fifty, and life rolled on.

The Boer war brought new cleavages in the Liberal party, which in those days comprised and held in suspended animation all the forces now represented by British Socialism. Rosebery unswervingly supported the war, and with him stood the ablest Liberal statesmen of the future—Asquith, Grey, and Haldane. They formed for mutual protection the Liberal Imperial League. But the spirit of the party was estranged. The rank and file wanted to attack the Tory Government and the war as well. A youngish Welshman, Lloyd George, with fiery mocking tongue said all the things they wished to hear—and even more. Years of barren internal bickering followed. Rosebery could not extricate himself from the political fight, which he now detested in all sincerity. He faced the enmity of the Irish. He bore the aversion of the Radicals and Labour men. He listened wearily to the endless remonstrances of the party press. Still at times his voice rang throughout the land. In his arresting speech at Chesterfield in December, 1901, he called for a meeting at 'a wayside inn' which should bring about peace with the valiant, desperate Boer commandos. This was a recognizable factor in bringing about the Treaty of Vereeniging. He took a prominent part in the fight to preserve the Free Trade system, and for a time in 1905 it seemed that he would take his place in a Liberal Restoration. But he lost touch with his friends, or they lost touch with him ; and always he reiterated that he would never take office again. So the great Government of 1905 was formed without him, and for nearly a quarter of a century he remained willingly, resolutely, but at the same time uneasily, the spectator of formidable and fateful events.

It was in the sphere of Foreign Affairs that Rosebery found his home. Here he was Master. He combined the knowledge of the historian or of a Foreign Office official with the practical understanding and the habit of command of a Statesman. He did not have to form his views from the files of papers set before him. He knew the whole long history about how all these nations had lived their lives for two or three hundred years, and what they had fought about, and which ones had been subjugated and were boiling with ancient wrongs under the smooth surface of modernism. He knew with pregnant conviction much that other leading men in England—and may we add the United States—only found out during and after the Peace Conference. He knew not only the British share in bygone events, but the whole European tale. Jugoslavia and Czechoslovakia—then unborn—the failings and vitalities of partitioned Poland, and the vanished Empire of Stephen Doshan, were—no doubt under other symbols—living realities to him. He felt in his bones, with his finger-tips, all that subterranean, subconscious movement whereby the vast antagonisms of the Great War were slowly, remorselessly, inexorably assembling. He had laboriously inspected the foundations of European Peace ; he saw where the cracks were, and where a subsidence would produce a crash. His heart responded instinctively to any readjustment or disturbance of the balance of power. In Rosebery's time Foreign Affairs and war dangers were invested with a false glamour and shrouded in opaque ignorance. But when some school-teacher was dismissed in Upper Silesia Rosebery said to me, ' All Prussia has been shaken.' When Delcassé was forced to resign, he said that the German Army corps were afoot. And when Lord Lansdowne signed the Anglo-French Agreement of August, 1904, with all the prestige of the Conservative Party behind him, and amid the tributes of Liberals and Pacifists all over the world, Rosebery said in public that 'it was far more likely to lead to War than to Peace.'

This last I conceive to be the greatest proof of his insight. I was a very young man at the time, but I recall the situation vividly. The Conservative reign was in its plenitude. But there was the perennial quarrel with France—gunboats at Bangkok; later the French resentments about Fashoda; all the Liberals crying out for peace, for reconciliation with France, for the lifting of a dangerous and vibrant animosity. 'Let us settle with our nearest neighbour. Let us make mutual concessions and have no more fears of war with France.' Rarely has national agreement been more complete. The Foreign Secretary moved forward amid general, nay almost universal applause. The pact between England and France was made, all the small disputes were swept away amid sincere rejoicings. Only one voice—Rosebery's—was raised in discord: in public 'Far more likely to lead to War than to Peace'; in private 'Straight to War.'

It must not be thought that I regret the decisions which were in fact taken. I do not think that any movements on the European chessboard could have prevented the challenge to world peace sooner or later of the ever-growing overweening military power and temper of Germany. The occasion would have been different, the hour might have been delayed, the grouping of Powers might not have been the same; but given the world as it was at the beginning of the Twentieth Century, I doubt if anything could have averted the hideous collision. And if it had to come, we must thank God it came in such a way that the world was with us through the conflict.

There was another sphere in which Rosebery moved with confidence and distinction. He was one of those men of affairs who add to the unsure prestige of a minister and the fleeting successes of an orator the more enduring achievements of literature. Some of his most polished work is found in his Rectorial Addresses and in his appreciations of great poets and writers like Burns and Stevenson. His private letters, of which he wrote so many, are alive with Byronic wit and colour. His style, lucid, pointed, musical and restrained, was an admirable vehicle for conveying his treasure of historical research to the world. He has enriched our language with a series of biographical studies, terse, pregnant and authoritative, which will long be read with pleasure and instruction on both sides of the Atlantic. *Pitt, Peel, Randolph Churchill,* are literary gems, and on the larger scale *Chatham* and *Napoleon* make definite contributions to the judgment of history. Yet even in this field there are some characteristic, self-imposed limitations. He never planned or executed a work of the first magnitude —a work to hold the field against all comers for a century. His taste, discernment, and learning were directed to partial tasks, and in these he attracts and stimulates the reader, only to leave his main curiosities unsatisfied. Rosebery's *Chatham* ends before the great period has begun : his *Napoleon* begins only when it has ended. We are excited ; we demand more ; we seek the climax. But the author has retired again to his solitudes. The curtain is pulled down and the gleaming lights extinguished—and now, alas, extinguished for ever.

The war he had dreaded came to pass by the paths he had foreseen, but his heart beat high for Britain. His younger son, the charming, gifted Neil, was killed in Palestine. The old man sank, bowed and broken under the blow. Years of infirmity followed, and what to an Imperial spirit must ever be a pang—powerlessness. A month before the Armistice he had a stroke. He lay unconscious or delirious in a small house in Edinburgh when the bells of victory rang through its streets. The Scots do not easily forget those who have been their leaders. Spontaneously in the joy of the hour a great crowd gathered with torches and beset his door in thousands to share their triumph with him. But he lay stricken, prostrate, paralysed.

He lived for ten years more, and all the qualities of his

mind resumed their play. He reached the age of eighty. If he enjoyed life in a mild way from week to week, he also thought of Death as a deliverance. He made one statement which should be helpful to all of us. For some time he had received a special Insulin treatment. One day by mistake the dose was doubled. He fell down in a total stupor, and his attendants were sure the end had come. He remained in this condition for many hours. His daughter, Lady Crewe, summoned from Paris, reached his bedside the next morning and to her relief and surprise found him alive with his mental faculties restored. ' If this is Death ' he said with the air of one who has been on a voyage and made a discovery, ' it is absolutely nothing.'

He was happy and at peace : but his steps became more weary. Although a religious man, a regular Church-goer, and a frequent Communicant, he made one odd, characteristic preparation for his departure. He bade his servant buy a gramophone, and told him that when Death came upon him, he was to make it play the Eton Boating Song. This was actually done, though perhaps he did not hear it. Thus he wished the gay memories of boyhood to be around him at his end, and thus he set Death in its proper place as a necessary and unalarming process.

One more trait must be recorded, his love of Scotland and his pride in the Scottish race and in their history. His words a quarter of a century earlier at the unveiling of the memorial to the officers and men of the Royal Scots Greys killed in South Africa may well form the epilogue to his own life.

' Honour to the brave who will return no more. We shall not see their faces again. In the service of their Sovereign and their country they have undergone the sharpness of death, and sleep their eternal sleep, thousands of miles away in the green solitudes of Africa. Their places, their comrades, their saddles will know them no more, for they will never return to us as we knew them. But in a nobler and higher sense, have they not returned to us to-day ? They return to us with a message of duty, of courage, of patriotism. They return to us with a memory of high duty faithfully performed ; they return to us with the inspiration of their example. Peace, then, to their dust, honour to their memory. Scotland for ever ! '

THE EX-KAISER

Keystone View Company

THE EX-KAISER AT DOORN

THE EX-KAISER

NO one should judge the career of the Emperor William II without asking the question, 'What should I have done in his position?' Imagine yourself brought up from childhood to believe that you were appointed by God to be the ruler of a mighty nation, and that the inherent virtue of your blood raised you far above ordinary mortals. Imagine succeeding in the twenties to the garnered prizes, in provinces, in power and in pride, of Bismarck's three successive victorious wars. Imagine feeling the magnificent German race bounding beneath you in ever-swelling numbers, strength, wealth and ambition ; and imagine on every side the thunderous tributes of crowd-loyalty and the skilled unceasing flattery of courtierly adulation.

'You are,' they say, 'the All-Highest. You are the Supreme War Lord, who when the next war comes will lead to battle all the German tribes, and at the head of the strongest, finest army in the world will renew on a still greater scale the martial triumphs of 1866 and 1870. It is for you to choose the Chancellor and Ministers of State ; it is for you to choose the chiefs of the Army and Navy. There is no office great or small throughout the empire from which you cannot dismiss the occupant. Each word you utter is received by all present with rapture, or at least respect. You have but to form a desire, and it is granted. Limitless wealth and splendour attend your every step. Sixty palaces and castles await their owner ; hundreds of glittering uniforms fill your wardrobes. Should you weary of the grosser forms of flattery, far more subtle methods will be applied. Statesmen, generals, admirals, judges, divines, philosophers, scientists and financiers stand eager to impart their treasured knowledge and to receive with profound gratification any remark upon their various spheres which may occur to you. Intimate friends are at hand to report day by day how deeply impressed this or that great expert was with your marvellous grasp of his subject. The General Staff seem awed by your comprehension of the higher strategy. The diplomats are wonder-struck by your manly candour or patient restraint, as the case may be. The artists gather in dutiful admiration before the allegorical picture you have painted. Foreign nations vie with your own subjects in their welcomes, and on all sides salute the " world's most glorious prince." ' And this goes on day after day and year after year for thirty years.

Are you quite sure, ' gentle reader ' (to revive an old-fashioned form), you would have withstood the treatment? Are you quite sure you would have remained a humble-minded man with no exaggerated idea of your own importance, with no undue reliance upon your own opinion, practising the virtue of humility, and striving always for peace ?

But observe, if you had done so, a discordant note would instantly have mingled with the chants of praise. ' We have a weakling on the throne. Our War Lord is a pacifist. Is the new-arrived, late-arrived German Empire with all its tremendous and expanding forces to be led by a president of the Young Men's Christian Association ? Was it for this that the immortal Frederick and the great Bismarck schemed and conquered? Was it for this the glorious leaders of the War of Liberation built round the citadel of Prussia the gigantic fortress of Teutonic power? The German states, so long divided, so long the sport of cross-currents, have at last come together, and their strength is overwhelming. With one blow they have humbled Austria, with another they have smitten France. In all the Continent we have no equal. Not any two countries combined together could overcome us. And are we then to be limited to Europe? Is the old grey sea-wolf England to enjoy the dominance of the world and of the oceans? Is decadent France, so long our persecutor, now cowering before our united force, to enjoy, gather and expand a splendid colonial empire? Are we to be barred from the Americas by a Monroe doctrine, warned off North Africa by an Anglo-French agreement, and rigidly excluded from China and the East by international concert? Is Holland to thrive upon its rich East Indies? Is even little Belgium to sprawl disreputable upon the vast Congo?

' Granted we are late arrivals, granted we have been the drudge and mercenary of Europe for centuries, now we stand erect in our strength. Hard work, hard thinking, organization, business, science, philosophy—where is our equal? And behind all, if you wish it, there is steel and flame and the trampling of innumerable hosts, who await but a signal from on high. Are we to be denied our " place in the sun ? " Are our expanding industries never to rest upon German-owned oil, tin, copper, rubber and the like? Is all this to be purveyed to us by the English, the Americans, the French and the Dutch? Is there to be no temperate region in which Germans may found the schools of a more learned Stuttgart, the exchange of a wealthier Berlin, or the well-crunched parade-ground of a new Potsdam? We are late, but we are going to have our share. Lay a place at the table for the German Empire, now at last by the grace of our trusty German God and its own strong army risen in its splendour, or if not we will thrust you from your seats and carve the joint ourselves ! At this supreme period in our history, this bright dawn of our advancing power, is our War Lord to be a softie, " with bated breath and whispering humbleness? " Not so ; he has sons. In one of these perchance God has implanted the spirit of a warrior-king.' All this expressed by gleaming eyes and tightened lips under a barrage of bows, salutes and clicking heels !

If the first lesson which was wrought into the fibre of

the young Emperor was his own importance, the second was his duty to assert the importance of the German Empire. And through a hundred channels where waters flowed with steady force, albeit under a glassy surface of respect, William II was taught that, if he would keep the love and admiration of his subjects, he must be their champion.

Moreover there were the Socialists; bad people, disaffected kerns that cared nothing for the greatness of Germany, for the endurance of the monarchy, nor even of the dynasty. They did not cheer; neither, except when undergoing their compulsory military service, did they salute. They were against the aristocracy and the landed classes, the true back-bone of the nation. They had no regard for the wonderful army by whose strength Germany had gained her freedom and daily preserved her united life. They voted steadily year after year against everything the Kaiser cared for, and against all the classes and interests which were his faithful servants and at the same time his conscious masters. Besides, how rude they were! How they mocked and derided! What lies they told, and worse still, what scandalous truths! Was he to be the representative of their sentiments? Was he to quarrel with all the strong forces that sustained his country and his throne, in order to voice the opinions of those who boasted that they had no country and that their first act in power would be to make short work of thrones. Was he to acquiesce in the foreigners' view—also the view of his Socialist enemies—while from every side the dominant martial and virile forces urged him to be true, and down through the centuries romance, tradition and ancestral incantations inspired him to be bold? Are you quite sure, then, reader, in your heart of hearts, that subjected to these pressures, feeding on this royal jelly, you would have remained a mild, humdrum, conservative or liberal statesman? I wonder!

When we measure the temptations and take account of the circumstances, the rule of life which the Emperor followed is remarkable. He is not incontinently to be condemned. For thirty years he reigned in peace. For thirty years his officers were taught to say—to foreigners at any rate—that it was part of his religion to prevent war. Opportunities came and went. Russia, the great counter-balancing Colossus, was laid low in her war with Japan. The danger of a war on two fronts vanished for three or four years. The Franco-Russian alliance was less than a scrap of paper. France was at his mercy. He reigned in peace. Provocations were not lacking. Diplomatic defeat was endured at Algeciras, and something very like humiliation after Agadir. William II sought to pave his way with his army and navy by words and gestures. 'The mailed fist,' 'glittering armour,' 'The Admiral of the Atlantic.' '*Hoc volo sic jubeo, sit pro ratione voluntas*,' he wrote in the Golden Book at Munich.

'But no war!' No long, crafty Bismarckian schemes, no Ems dispatch. Just strut about and pose and rattle the undrawn sword. All he wished was to feel like Napoleon, and be like him without having had to fight his battles. Surely less than this would not pass muster. If you are the summit of a volcano, the least you can do is to smoke. So he smoked, a pillar of cloud by day and the gleam of fire by night, to all who gazed from afar ; and slowly and surely these perturbed observers gathered and joined themselves together for mutual protection.

It was my fortune to be the Emperor's guest at the German Army manœuvres of 1906 and 1908. He was then at the height of his glory. As he sat on his horse surrounded by Kings and Princes while his legions defiled before him in what seemed to be an endless procession, he represented all that this world has to give in material things. The picture which lives the most vividly in my memory is his entry into the city of Breslau at the beginning of the manœuvres. He rode his magnificent horse at the head of a squadron of cuirassiers, wearing their white uniform and eagle-crested helmet. The streets of the Silesian capital were thronged with his enthusiastic subjects, and lined, not with soldiers, but more impressively with thousands of aged veterans in rusty black coats and stove-pipe hats, as if the great past of Germany saluted her more splendid future.

What a contrast twelve years would show ! A broken man sits hunched in a railway carriage, hour after hour, at a Dutch frontier station awaiting permission to escape as a refugee from the execration of a people whose armies he has led through measureless sacrifices to measureless defeat, and whose conquests and treasures he has squandered.

An awful fate ! Was it the wage of guilt or of incapacity ? There is, of course, a point where incapacity and levity are so flagrant that they become tantamount to guilt. Nevertheless history should incline to the more charitable view, and acquit William II of having planned and plotted the World War. But the defence which can be made will not be flattering to his self-esteem. It is, in short, rather on the lines of the defence which the eminent French counsel presented on behalf of Marshal Bazaine when he was brought to trial for treason in the surrender of Metz : ' This is no traitor. Look at him ; he is only a blunderer.'

It is indeed impossible to exaggerate the fecklessness which across a whole generation led the German Empire in successive lurches to catastrophe. The youthful sovereign who so light-heartedly dismissed Bismarck was soon to deprive Germany of all the reinsurance and safety founded upon an understanding with Russia. Russia was made to move into the opposite camp. The voluminous intimate correspondence between ' Willy ' and ' Nicky,' all the immense advantage of personal relationship, led only to a Franco-Russian alliance, and the Czar of all the Russias found it more natural to give his hand to the President of a Republic whose national anthem is the ' Marseillaise,' than to work with his brother-Emperor, his equal, his cousin, his familiar acquaintance.

Next in fatal order came the estrangement of England.

Here even stronger ties of blood, of kinship and of history had to be worn asunder. The work was lengthy and difficult, but William II accomplished it in good time. In this he was stimulated alike by his admiration of English life, style and customs, and by his personal jealousy of King Edward the Seventh. For Queen Victoria, the august Grandmamma, he always had respect ; but for Edward VII, whether as Prince of Wales or sovereign, he felt only a strange and mischievous mixture of rivalry and contempt. He wrote him presumptuous homilies about his private life. His scornful arrows shot off at random, even when they did not hit the target, were picked up and carried thither. ' Where is your King now ? ' he asked one day of an English visitor ; ' At Windsor, Sir ; ' ' Ah, I thought he was boating with his grocer.' * Thus family connections which might have cemented national friendship, became increasingly a cause of discord. Great Britain is a constitutional democracy, and the personal feelings of the monarch do not sway the policy of responsible administrations. But graver offences were not lacking. The Kaiser's impulsive telegram to President Kruger upon the Jameson Raid extorted such a growl from the British Lion as Germany had never heard before. Lastly, there was the Navy. The lord of the greatest of armies must also possess a navy which even the strongest naval power would hold in awe.

Thus England, carrying with her the whole British Empire, slowly inclined towards France, and under the repeated shocks of Algeciras (1906), of the Austrian annexation of Bosnia and Herzegovina (1908), and of Agadir (1911), became tacitly, informally, but none the less effectively, united with France and Russia. With England went Italy. A secret clause in the original Treaty of the Triple Alliance absolved Italy from participation in any war against Great Britain. The Kaiser had already in 1902 given mortal offence to Japan.

After so many years of pomp and mediaeval posturing,

* Sir Thomas Lipton.

39

the master of German policy had stripped his country of every friend but one, the weak, unwieldy, internally-torn Empire of the Hapsburgs. All that remained of Bismarck's network of securities had been destroyed ; and upon the other hand, an enormous latent coalition had been formed in the centre of which burned the quenchless flame of French revenge. Alsace ! It remained only for William II to offer Austria, in the sultry atmosphere of July 1914, a free hand to punish Serbia for the Sarajevo murders, and then to go away himself for three weeks on a yachting cruise.

The careless tourist had flung down his burning cigarette in the ante-room of the magazine which Europe had become. For a while it smouldered. He returned to find the building impenetrable with smoke—black, stifling, sulphurous smoke —while darting flames approached the powder chamber itself. At first he thought it would be easy to put it all out. Confronted with the abject Serbian submission to the Austrian ultimatum, he exclaimed, ' A brilliant diplomatic triumph ; no excuse for war ; no need to mobilize ! ' His instinct at this moment was evidently to arrest the con-flagration. Too late ! Faced with the imminent explosion, the Army has taken charge. The terrified populace, the reckless sightseers, the local fire brigades are driven helter-skelter back by the strict and strong cordons of armed men who are everywhere clearing the streets ; and amid this confusion the gilded pomp of personal rule, the obsequious courtiers, the Imperial liveries, the easy triumphs of peace are all swept indifferently away. Power and direction has passed to sterner hands. The ungovernable passions of nations have broken loose. Death for millions stalks upon the scene. All the cannons roar.

The dreaded ' war on two fronts ' is certain ; the defection of Italy from the Triple Alliance is certain ; the hostility of Japan is certain ; the violation of Belgium is inevitable ; and the armies of the Central Empires are launched against the little states upon their borders. But it is war on three fronts now. The British ultimatum has arrived. The ocean Empire, so long the ally of Germany, now joins the closing circle of fire and steel as her most implacable foe.

Then, indeed, did William the Second realize whither he had led his country, and in a passion of grief and fear he penned these striking, self-revealing words : ' So the famous circumscription of Germany has finally become a complete fact. . . . A great achievement which arouses the admiration even of him who is to be destroyed as its result. Edward VII is stronger after his death than I am—I who am still alive.'

The truth is that no human being should ever have been placed in such a position. An immense responsibility rests upon the German people for their subservience to the barbaric idea of autocracy. This is the gravamen against them in history—that, in spite of all their brains and courage, they worship Power, and let themselves be led by the nose. An hereditary monarchy without responsibility for government is for many countries the most sagacious policy. In the British Empire this system has attained perfection, the hereditary king having the pomp and glory, while black-coated, easily-changed ministers have the power and responsibility. But the union of both the pomp and the power of the State in a single office exposes a mortal to strains beyond the nature, and to tasks above the strength, even of the best and greatest men. Something may be said for dictatorships, in periods of change and storm ; but in these cases the dictator rises in true relation to the whole moving throng of events. He rides the whirlwind because he is a part of it. He is the monstrous child of emergency. He may well possess the force and quality to dominate the minds of millions and sway the course of history. He should pass with the crisis. To make a permanent system of Dictatorship, hereditary or not, is to prepare a new cataclysm.

William II had none of the qualities of the modern dictators, except their airs. He was a picturesque figurehead in the centre of the world stage, called upon to play a part far beyond the capacity of most people. He had little in common with the great princes who at intervals throughout the centuries have appeared by the accident of birth at the summit of states and empires. His undeniable cleverness and versatility, his personal grace and vivacity, only aggravated his dangers by concealing his inadequacy. He knew how to make the gestures, to utter the words, to strike the attitudes in the Imperial style. He could stamp and snort, or nod and smile with much histrionic art ; but underneath all this posing and its trappings, was a very ordinary, vain, but on the whole well-meaning man, hoping to pass himself off as a second Frederick the Great. There was no grandeur of mind or spirit in his composition. No long policy of cautious statecraft, no calculation, no deep insight, was his to bestow upon his subjects.

Finally, in his own Memoirs, written from the penitential seclusion of Doorn, he has naïvely revealed to us his true measure. No more disarming revelation of inherent triviality, lack of understanding and sense of proportion, and, incidentally, of literary capacity, can be imagined. It is shocking to reflect that upon the word or nod of a being so limited there stood attentive and obedient for thirty years the forces which, whenever released, could devastate the world. It was not his fault ; it was his fate.

Mr. Lloyd George, himself an actor. although a man of action, would, if he had had his way, have deprived us of this invaluable exposure in order to gratify the passions of victorious crowds. He would have redraped this melancholy exile in the sombre robes of more than mortal guilt and of superhuman responsibility, and led him forth to a scaffold of vicarious expiation. Upon the brow from which the diadem of empire had been smitten, he would have set a crown of martyrdom ; and Death, with an all-effacing gesture, would have re-founded the dynasty of the Hohenzollerns upon a victim's tomb.

Such grim ceremonial was not to be accorded. Prosaic

counsels prevailed. The fallen Emperor lived, comfortable, unromantic, safe. The passage of years lent dignity to his retirement. His private virtues had for the first time undistorted play. He lived to see the fierce hatreds of the victors freeze into contempt and ultimately vanish in indifference. He lived to see a great people, whom he had conducted to frightful disaster, pass through the sternest tribulations of defeat. He lived to receive at their hands millions of money which Germany had the moral strength to pay rather than be guilty of repudiation of lawful dues. He survived in excellent health, exemplary conduct, and happy domesticity, while the Fleet he had created with so much unwise labour rusted at the bottom of a Scottish harbour ; while the proud Army, the terror of the world, before which he had pranced so long in times of peace, was dispersed and abolished ; while his faithful servants, officers and veterans, languished in penury and neglect. It was perhaps a harder accountancy.

But he lived longer still ; and Time has brought him a surprising and paradoxical revenge upon his conquerors. He has reached a phase when the greater part of Europe, particularly his most powerful enemies Great Britain and France, would regard the Hohenzollern restoration they formerly abhorred beyond expression, as a comparatively hopeful event and as a sign that dangers were abating. If it were accompanied by constitutional limitations, it would be taken throughout the world as an assurance of peace abroad and toleration at home. This is not because his own personal light burns the brighter or the more steadily, but because of the increasing darkness around. The victorious democracies in driving out hereditary sovereigns, supposed they were moving on the path of progress. They have in fact gone further and fared worse. A royal dynasty looking back upon the traditions of the past, and looking forward to a continuity in the future, offers an element of security to the liberty and happiness of nations that can never come from the rule of dictators, however capable they may be. Thus, as the wheel swings full circle, the dethroned Emperor may find ironical consolation by his fireside at Doorn.

When the final collapse came on the Western Front, tempters had urged him to have an attack prepared, and fall at the head of his last remaining loyal officers. He has given us his reasons for rejecting this pagan counsel. He would not sacrifice the lives of more brave men merely to make a setting for his own exit. No one now can doubt that he was right. There is something to be said after all for going on to the end.

GEORGE
BERNARD SHAW

Elliott & Fry, Ltd

GEORGE BERNARD SHAW

GEORGE BERNARD SHAW

MR. BERNARD SHAW was one of my earliest antipathies. Indeed, almost my first literary effusion,
written when I was serving as a subaltern in India in 1897
(it never saw the light of day), was a ferocious onslaught
upon him, and upon an article which he had written disparaging and deriding the British Army in some minor war.
Four or five years passed before I made his acquaintance.
My mother, always in agreeable contact with artistic and
dramatic circles, took me to luncheon with him. I was
instantly attracted by the sparkle and gaiety of his conversation, and impressed by his eating only fruit and
vegetables, and drinking only water. I rallied him on the
latter habit, asking : ' Do you really never drink any wine
at all ? ' ' I am hard enough to keep in order as it is,' he
replied. Perhaps he had heard of my youthful prejudice
against him.

In later years, and especially after the war, I can recall
several pleasant and, to me, memorable talks on politics,
particularly about Ireland and about Socialism. I think
these encounters cannot have been displeasing to him, for
he was kind enough to give me a copy of his *Magnum Opus*,
' The Intelligent Woman's Guide to Socialism,' remarking
(subsequently and erroneously),' It is a sure way to prevent
you reading it.' At any rate, I possess a lively image of
this bright, nimble, fierce, and comprehending being, Jack
Frost dancing bespangled in the sunshine, which I should
be very sorry to lose.

*   *   *   *   *

One of his biographers, Edward Shanks, says of Bernard

Shaw : 'It is more important to remember that he began to flourish in the 'nineties, than to remember that he was born in Ireland'; and it is true that Irish influences are only found in him by those who are determined to find them. The influence of the 'nineties, on the other hand, is strong—not the pale influence of the decadents, but the eager impulsion of the New Journalism, the New Political Movements, the New Religious Movement. All the bubbling and conceit of New Movements (in capitals) took hold of him. For nine years he had been living in London under the pinch of poverty and the sharper twinges of success denied. His snuff-coloured suit, his hat turned (for some obscure economy) back to front, his black coat blending slowly into green, were becoming gradually known. But in all these years he only earned, he says, £6, of which £5 were for an advertisement. Otherwise he depended on his mother, and wrote, unrecompensed, a few mediocre novels. He was still so obscure that he had to arrest and startle even in the very first sentence of his articles. Jobs slowly came in—musical criticism, dramatic criticism, political squibs and paragraphs, but it was not until 1892 that his first play 'Widowers' Houses' appeared.

His early years in Ireland had given him a loathing of respectability and religion—partly because they were the fashionable butts of youth in those days, and Shaw has always been a child of that age ; and partly because his family, either in an effort to be worthy of their position as cousins of a baronet or to counteract their poverty, dutifully upheld them both. Being dragged to Low Church and Chapel, and forbidden to play with the tradesmen's children, gave him strong complexes from which he has never recovered, and made him utter loud outcries against 'custom-made morality,' against the tame conformity of the genteel ; in short, against all that is nowadays summed up by what Mr. Kipling called 'the fatted soul of things.' When at length he emerged it was as a herald of revolt, a disconcerter of established convictions, a merry, mischievous, rebellious Puck, posing the most awkward riddles of the Sphinx.

This energetic, groping, angry man of about thirty, poor, the author of some unsuccessful novels and of some slashing criticisms, with a good knowledge of music and painting, and a command of the high lights of indignation, meets in middle age Henry George, and at once joins the Fabian Society with eager enthusiasm. He speaks at hotels, and at street corners. He conquers his nervousness. He colours his style with a debating tinge which comes out in every preface to his plays. In 1889 he shows for the first time a little Marxian influence. Later on he throws Marx over for Mr. Sidney Webb, whom he has always acknowledged to have had more influence than anyone in forming his opinions. But these sources are not enough ; something must be found to replace religion as a binding force and a director. Mr. Shanks says : ' All his life he has suffered under a handicap, which is that he is shy of using . . . the name of God, yet cannot find any proper substitute.' Therefore he must invent the Life-Force, must twist the Saviour into a rather half-hearted Socialist, and establish Heaven in his own political image.

' Fine Art,' declares our hero in another foray, ' is the only teacher, except torture.' As usual, however, with his doctrines, he does not submit himself to this master's discipline. He never trifles with unprofitable concerns, and a few years later he writes: ' All my attempts at Art for Art's sake broke down ; it was like hammering 10d. nails into sheets of notepaper.' His versatile taste leads him to associate himself with Schopenhauer, Shelley, Goethe, Morris, and other diverse guides. In a moment when his critical faculty is evidently slumbering, he even ranks William Morris with Goethe !

Meanwhile he continues to attract all the attention he can. ' I leave,' he says in *Diabolonian Ethics*, ' the delicacies of retirement to those who are gentlemen first and literary workmen afterwards. The cart and trumpet for me ' ; and the trumpet, being used to arouse and shock, sends forth a quantity of bombinating nonsense such as (in the *Quintessence of Ibsenism*) : ' There are just as good reasons for burning a heretic at the stake as for rescuing a shipwrecked crew from drowning ; in fact, there are better.'

It was not until the late 'nineties that real, live, glowing success came, and henceforth took up her abode with Mr. Bernard Shaw. At decent intervals, and with growing assurance, his plays succeeded one another. ' Candida,' ' Major Barbara,' and ' Man and Superman ' riveted the attention of the intellectual world. Into the void left by the annihilation of Wilde he stepped armed with a keener wit, a tenser dialogue, a more challenging theme, a stronger construction, a deeper and a more natural comprehension. The characteristics and the idiosyncrasies of the Shavian drama are world-renowned. His plays are to-day more frequently presented, not only within the wide frontiers of the English language, but throughout the world, than those of any man but Shakespeare. All parties and every class, in every country, have pricked up their ears at their coming, and welcomed their return.

The plays were startling enough on their first appearance. Ibsen had broken the ' well-made play ' by making it better than ever : Mr. Shaw broke it by not ' making ' it at all. He was once told that Sir James Barrie had completely worked out the plot of ' Shall We Join the Ladies ' before he began to write it. Mr. Shaw was scandalized. ' Fancy knowing how a play is to end before you begin it ! When *I* start a play I haven't the slightest idea what is going to happen.' His other main innovation was to depend for his drama not on the interplay of character and character, or of character and circumstance, but on that of argument and argument. His ideas become personages, and fight among themselves, sometimes with intense dramatic effect, and sometimes not. His human beings, with a few exceptions, are there for what they are to say, not for what they are to be or do. Yet they live.

Recently I took my children to ' Major Barbara.' Twenty years had passed since I had seen it. They were the most terrific twenty years the world has known. Almost every human institution had undergone decisive change. The landmarks of centuries had been swept away. Science has transformed the conditions of our lives and the aspect of town and country. Silent social evolution, violent political change, a vast broadening of the social foundations, an immeasurable release from convention and restraint, a profound reshaping of national and individual opinion, have followed the trampling march of this tremendous epoch. But in ' Major Barbara ' there was not a character requiring to be re-drawn, not a sentence nor a suggestion that was out of date. My children were astounded to learn that this play, the very acme of modernity, was written more than five years before they were born.

*   *   *   *   *

Few people practise what they preach, and no one less so than Mr. Bernard Shaw. Few are more capable of having the best of everything both ways. His spiritual home is no doubt in Russia ; his native land is the Irish Free State ; but he lives in comfortable England. His dissolvent theories of life and society have been sturdily banished from his personal conduct and his home. No one has ever led a more respectable life or been a stronger seceder from his own subversive imagination. He derides the marriage vow and even at times the sentiment of love itself ; yet no one is more happily or wisely married. He indulges in all the liberties of an irresponsible Chatterbox, babbling gloriously from dawn to dusk, and at the same time advocates the abolition of Parliamentary institutions and the setting up of an Iron Dictatorship, of which he would probably be the first victim. It is another case for John Morley's comment upon Carlyle, ' the Gospel of silence in thirty volumes by Mr. Wordy '. He prattles agreeably with the tame English Socialists, and preens himself with evident satisfaction in the smiles alike of Stalin or Mussolini. He promulgates in stern decree that all incomes should be equalized and that anyone who has more than another is guilty—unconsciously perhaps—of personal meanness, if not fraud ; he has always preached the ownership of all forms of wealth by the State ; yet when the Lloyd George Budget imposed for the first time the slender beginnings of the Super-tax, no one made a louder squawk than this already wealthy Fabian. He is at once an acquisitive capitalist and a sincere Communist. He makes his characters talk blithely about killing men for the sake of an idea ; but would take great trouble not to hurt a fly.

He seems to derive equal pleasure from all these contrary habits, poses and attitudes. He has laughed his sparkling way through life, exploding by his own acts or words every argument he has ever used on either side of any question, teasing and bewildering every public he has addressed, and involving in his own mockery every cause he has ever championed. The world has long watched with tolerance and amusement the nimble antics and gyrations of this unique and double-headed chameleon, while all the time the creature was eager to be taken seriously.

*   *   *   *   *

I expect that the jesters who played so invaluable a part in the Courts of the Middle Ages saved their skins from being flayed and their necks from being wrung by the impartiality with which their bladder-blows were bestowed in all directions, and upon all alike. Before one potentate or notable could draw his sword to repay a scathing taunt, he was convulsed with laughter at the condition in which his rival or companion was left. Everyone was so busy rubbing his own shins that none had time to kick the kicker. Thus the jester survived ; thus he gained access to the most formidable circles, and indulged in antics of freedom under the dumbfounded gaze of barbarism and tyranny.

The Shavian cow—to change the illustration—has no

sooner yielded its record milking than it kicks the pail over the thirsty and admiring milker. He pays an incomparable tribute to the work of the Salvation Army, and leaves it a few minutes later ridiculous and forlorn. In ' John Bull's Other Island ' we are no sooner captivated by Irish charm and atmosphere than we see the Irish race liveried in humbug and strait-jacketed in infirmity of purpose. The Liberal Home Ruler, who so hopefully expected from Bernard Shaw, justification and approval for his cause, found himself in a trice held up as an object of satire rarely equalled upon the stage. The intense emotions aroused in our breasts by the trial and martyrdom of Joan of Arc are immediately effaced by the harlequinade which constitutes the final act. ' The Red Flag,' the international hymn of the Labour Party, is dubbed by this most brilliant of Socialist intellectuals ' the funeral march of a fried eel.' His most serious work on Socialism, a masterly piece of reasoning, the embodiment of the most solid convictions of Bernard Shaw's long and varied experience, a contribution to our thought upon which three whole years, sufficient to produce half a dozen famous plays, were lavished, is read with profit and amusement by capitalist society and banned by Labour politicians.

Everyone has been excoriated, every idea has been rattled, and everything goes on the same as before. We are in the presence of a thinker, original, suggestive, profound ; but a thinker who depends on contradiction, and deals out thought as it flashes upon his mind without troubling about its relation to what he has said before, or its results upon the convictions of others. Yet, and it is the essence of the paradox, no one can say that Bernard Shaw is not at heart sincere, or that his life's message has not been consistent.

Certainly, we are all the better for having had the Jester in our midst.

*   *   *   *   *

I was diverted some years ago by the accounts which were

published of his excursion to Russia. For his co-delegate or comrade in the trip he selected Lady Astor. The choice was happy and appropriate. Lady Astor, like Mr. Bernard Shaw, enjoys the best of all worlds. She reigns on both sides of the Atlantic in the Old World and the New, at once as a leader of fashionable society, and of advanced feminist democracy. She combines a kindly heart with a sharp and wagging tongue. She embodies the historical portent of the first woman Member of the House of Commons. She denounces the vice of gambling in unmeasured terms, and is closely associated with an almost unrivalled racing stable. She accepts Communist hospitality and flattery, and remains the Conservative member for Plymouth. She does all these opposite things so well and so naturally that the public, tired of criticizing, can only gape.

'It is now some sixteen or seventeen years ago,' to parody Burke's famous passage, 'that I first saw the present Viscountess Astor in London society, and surely never lighted on these shores, which she scarcely seemed to touch, a more delightful vision.' She had stepped out of a band-box from the United States to animate and charm the merry and still decorous circles through which she had then begun to move. Every door opened at her approach. Insular and masculine prejudices were swept aside, and forthwith the portals of the House of Commons, barred by immemorial tradition to women, always difficult of access to those of foreign birth, were thrown wide to receive her. In a trice she was escorted to her seat by Mr. Balfour and Mr. Lloyd George, was soon delivering her maiden speech, and offering a picture of the memorable scene to be preserved in the Palace of Westminster. These are indeed startling achievements.

It must have been with some trepidation that the chiefs of the Union of Socialist Soviet Republics awaited the arrival in their grim domains of a merry harlequinade. The Russians have always been fond of circuses and travel-ling shows. Since they had imprisoned, shot or starved most of their best comedians, their visitors might fill for a space a noticeable void. And here was the World's most famous intellectual Clown and Pantaloon in one, and the charming Columbine of the capitalist pantomime. So the crowds were marshalled. Multitudes of well-drilled demonstrators were served out with their red scarves and flags. The massed-bands blared. Loud cheers from sturdy proletarians rent the welkin. The nationalized railways produced their best accommodation. Commissar Lunacharsky delivered a flowery harangue. Commissar Litvinoff, unmindful of the food queues in the back-streets, prepared a sumptuous banquet ; and Arch Commissar Stalin, ' the man of steel,' flung open the closely-guarded sanctuaries of the Kremlin, and pushing aside his morning's budget of death warrants, and *lettres de cachet*, received his guests with smiles of overflowing comradeship.

Ah ! but we must not forget that the object of the visit was educational and investigatory. How important for our public figures to probe for themselves the truth about Russia : to find out by personal test how the Five Year Plan was working. How necessary to know whether Communism is really better than Capitalism, and how the broad masses of the Russian people fare in ' life, liberty and the pursuit of happiness ' under the new regime. Who can grudge a few days devoted to these arduous tasks ? To the aged Jester, with his frosty smile and safely-invested capital, it was a brilliant opportunity of dropping a series of disconcerting bricks upon the corns of his ardent hosts. And to Lady Astor whose husband, according to the newspapers, had the week before been awarded three millions sterling returned taxation by the American Courts, all these communal fraternizings and sororizings must have been a pageant of delight. But it is the brightest hours that flash away the fastest.

If I have dwelt upon the comical aspects of these scenes it is to draw a serious moral. Well was it said that the genius of comedy and tragedy are essentially the same. In

Russia we have a vast, dumb people dwelling under the discipline of a conscripted army in war-time; a people suffering in years of peace the rigours and privations of the worst campaigns; a people ruled by terror, fanaticisms, and the Secret Police. Here we have a state whose subjects are so happy, that they have to be forbidden to quit its bounds under the direst penalties; whose diplomatists and agents sent on foreign missions, have often to leave their wives and children at home as hostages to ensure their eventual return. Here we have a system whose social achievements crowd five or six persons in a single room; whose wages hardly compare in purchasing power with the British dole; where life is unsafe; where liberty is unknown; where grace and culture are dying; and where armaments and preparations for war are rife. Here is a land where God is blasphemed, and man, plunged in this world's misery, is denied the hope of mercy on both sides of the grave—his soul in the striking, protesting phrase of Robespierre, ' no more than a genial breeze dying away at the mouth of the tomb!' Here we have a power actively and ceaselessly engaged in trying to overturn existing civilizations by stealth, by propaganda, and when it dares, by bloody force. Here we have a state, three millions of whose citizens are languishing in foreign exile, whose intelligentsia have been methodically destroyed; a state nearly half-a-million of whose citizens, reduced to servitude for their political opinions, are rotting and freezing through the Arctic night; toiling to death in forests, mines and quarries, many for no more than indulging in that freedom of thought which has gradually raised man above the beast.

Decent, good-hearted British men and women ought not to be so airily detached from realities, that they have no word of honest indignation for such wantonly, callously-inflicted pain.

*　　*　　*　　*　　*

If the truth must be told, our British island has not had

much help in its troubles from Mr. Bernard Shaw. When nations are fighting for life, when the Palace in which the Jester dwells not uncomfortably, is itself assailed, and everyone from Prince to groom is fighting on the battlements, the Jester's jokes echo only through deserted halls, and his witticisms and commendations, distributed evenly between friend and foe, jar the ears of hurrying messengers, of mourning women and wounded men. The titter ill accords with the tocsin, or the motley with the bandages. But these trials are over; the island is safe, the world is quiet, and begins again to be free. Time for self-questioning returns; and wit and humour in their embroidered mantles take again their seats at a replenished board. The ruins are rebuilt; a few more harvests are gathered in. Fancy is liberated from her dungeon, and we can afford, thank God, to laugh again.* Nay more, we can be proud of our famous Jester, and in regathered security rejoice that we laugh in common with many men in many lands, and thereby renew the genial and innocent comradeship and kinship of mankind. For when all is said and done, it was not the Jester's fault there was a war. Had we all stayed beguiled by his musings and his sallies, how much better off we should be! How many faces we should not have to miss! It is a source of pride to any nation to have nursed one of those recording sprites who can illuminate to the eye of remote posterity many aspects of the age in which we live. Saint, sage, and clown; venerable, profound, and irrepressible, Bernard Shaw receives, if not the salutes, at least the hand-clappings of a generation which honours him as another link in the humanities of peoples, and as the greatest living master of letters in the English-speaking world.

* Alas, we laughed too soon.

JOSEPH
CHAMBERLAIN

Elliott & Fry, Ltd

JOSEPH CHAMBERLAIN

JOSEPH CHAMBERLAIN

ONE mark of a great man is the power of making lasting impressions upon people he meets. Another is so to have handled matters during his life that the course of after events is continuously affected by what he did. Thirty years have passed since Chamberlain was capable of public utterance, nearly twenty-five have passed since he was in his grave, and he has certainly fulfilled both these hard tests. Those who met him in his vigour and hey-day are always conscious of his keenly-cut impression ; and all our British affairs to-day are tangled, biased or inspired by his actions. He lighted beacon-fires which are still burning ; he sounded trumpet-calls whose echoes still call stubborn soldiers to the field. The fiscal controversies which Chamberlain revived are living issues not only in British but in world politics to-day. The impetus which he gave to the sense of Empire, in Britain and even more by repercussion throughout the world, is a deep score on the page of History.

His biographer, Mr. Garvin, has devoted the leisure thoughts of ten years to his task. He has evidently been keenly alive to his responsibilities as the personal historian of a remarkable man whose records have been entrusted to his hands. Although an ardent admirer of ' Joe ' Chamberlain and a warrior in his cause, Mr. Garvin has risen above party feuds and faction and has laid before us in all good faith and good will a monumental account of the life and times of his hero. It is evident that he has produced a standard work which every student of the later Victorian period must wish not only to read but to place upon his bookshelves.*

Chamberlain grew up in Birmingham in a period when world politics were the well-preserved domain of Whig and Tory aristocracies, and their counterparts in different nations. He revealed himself as the first intruder from the new democracy into these select but wide-ranging circles. All the activities of his early life had their scene in his native city. He had to make his living ; he had to establish his business ; he had to make his way. He was forty before he sat in the House of Commons. No easy road of favoured family or class preferment offered itself to him. He had to fight every march forward for himself in the city where he dwelt and among the innumerable jealousies which are aroused locally by the first steps in success. He chose the ground and the weapons necessary for such a situation. Radicalism was his war-horse ; municipal politics the stirrup by which he mounted to the saddle. Mayor of Birmingham, master of its local needs ; a Super-Mayor attending to gas and water, to public baths and wash-houses, to very early town-planning improvement schemes : efficient far beyond his compeers : forceful against all with whom he came in collision : a fish obviously the largest and certainly the fiercest in a pool comparatively small.

The career of this eminent man and strong actuator of world movements is divided between the period when he was making his way towards the world scene and the period when he acted upon it. In the first he was a ruthless Radical and, if you challenged him, a Republican ; in the second he was a Jingo Tory and Empire Builder. All followed naturally and sincerely from the particular pressures and environment affecting an exceptional being at one stage or the other of his life.

Thus we have Chamberlain the Radical Mayor—far worse than any naughty Socialist of to-day—who questioned whether he could condescend to drive as Mayor

* *The Life of Joseph Chamberlain.* Vols. I–III. J. L. Garvin.

in the carriage which received the Prince of Wales (afterwards King Edward VII) on his visit to Birmingham, and
Chamberlain who popularized or promulgated the conception of a vast Empire centreing mainly upon the golden
circle of the Crown. Thus we have Chamberlain the most
competent, the most searching, the most entirely convinced protagonist of Free Trade ; and Chamberlain who
lighted the torch of Tariff Reform and Food Taxation. An
immense force was exerted with complete sincerity in
different phases in opposite directions. We have a splendid
piebald ; first black then white ; or in political terms, first
Fiery Red, then True Blue.

The amount of energy wasted by men and women of first-
class quality in arriving at their true degree, before they
begin to play on the world stage, can never be measured.
One may say that sixty, perhaps seventy per cent of all they
have to give is expended on fights which have no other
object but to get to their battlefield. I remember to have
heard Sir Michael Hicks-Beach, high intellectual Tory Squire,
his life devoted to State service, thirty years a Minister of the
Crown, say in the Tariff Reform conflict of 1904, ' I was an
Imperialist when Mr. Chamberlain's politics did not go
beyond Birmingham.' It was true ; in the setting of the
quarrel it was just ; but it was not Chamberlain's fault that
he had only arrived at the commanding view-points in later
life. He had meant to get there all the time, but the road
was long, and every foot of it contested.

First there is the tale of ' Radical Joe.' We see this
robust, virile, aggressive champion of change and overturn
marching forward into battle against almost all the venerable, accepted institutions of the Victorian epoch. We see
him fighting now with a rapier, now with a bludgeon, to
establish quite new levels for the political and social status of
the mass of the people. In his stride he shrinks from
nothing and turns away from no antagonist. The monarchy,
the Church, the aristocracy, the House of Lords, the ' country
party,' London Society, the limited franchise, the great

vested interests and professions—all in their turn become his targets.

But this was no campaign of mere demagogy, of ranting and denouncing, of pushing and brawling. It was the hard, cold, deeply-informed effort of a man who, though removed by superior education and an adequate income from the masses, nevertheless understood their lives, the pressures under which they bent, the injustices and inequalities which rankled in their bosoms, the appetites and aspirations to which they would respond; and who, with heart-whole resolve, offered himself to them as a leader whom nothing should daunt.

Consciously or unconsciously he had prepared himself for this adventure by two separate sets of exercises and experiences, both of which have often served men as complete careers in themselves. He had built up with all the shrewd briskness of business competition a new and valuable industry capable of holding its own without favour or protection against all rivals, domestic or foreign. His business success was as sharp, hard and bright as the screws it made. He was able after twenty years of work as a Birmingham screwmaker to retire from the firm of Chamberlain and Nettlefold with £120,000 of well-earned capital. Money interested him no more. He had set himself free by his own exertions. Henceforth he was clad in a complete suit of armoured independence, and could confront face to face the strongest in the land. Nothing is more characteristic of Chamberlain's life than the measured steps by which he advanced towards expanding objectives. He always looked back with pride upon his screw-making days. When he came to speak in my support at Oldham in the full flush of the 'Khaki' election of 1900, he said to me with a twinkling eye, 'The first time I came here was to sell them screws.'

But the second phase was also preparatory. He knew Birmingham as a citizen and manufacturer. He became its civic chief. No greater municipal officer has adorned

English local government. ' By God's help,' he declared,
' the town shall not know itself.' The clearance of slums,
the boons of pure water and the light and warmth of gas
produced swift effects upon the population. The death-
rate of many streets fell by half in a few years. In June,
1876, he could write : ' The town will be parked, paved,
assized, marketed, gassed and watered, and *improved*—all
as the result of three years' active work.'

These great achievements of founding an efficient British
manufacture and the regeneration of Birmingham were
completed by his fortieth year. In spite of all the friction
which is inseparable from business-thrust and drastic reform,
the soundness and thoroughness of his work in these two
different fields made a profound impression upon the city he
loved so well. Birmingham followed him through all the
shifts and turns of politics. It laughed at every charge of
inconsistency, and changed its own political allegiance and
objectives at his command.

From his entry into municipal and national politics in 1870
to his death on the eve of the Great War—a period of more
than forty years—the loyalty of Birmingham was unbroken.
His word was law. In him—whether extreme Radical or
extreme Jingo, Free Trader or Protectionist ; the galvanizer
of Liberalism or its destroyer ; the colleague of Mr. Gladstone
or his most deadly opponent ; alike in days of peace or war—
the citizens of Birmingham saw only their Chief. And when
he died he transmitted his power in hereditary succession to
sons who have held it to this day in his name. This is
a record without compare in the political life of any of our
great cities. It carried into the crowded streets, clacking
factories and slums of Birmingham those same loyalties
which had heretofore thrived only in the Highland glens.
The romance of feudalism and the hereditary principle
were reproduced in novel trappings around the person of
a leader who had set out to abolish them both.

At forty-nine Chamberlain stood on the threshold of a
complete change. His outlook upon our national life,

which although always intense, had up to this point been narrow and short, broadened and lengthened; and he perceived that the remorseless unfolding of events had proved contrary to the expectations both of his youth and of his prime. The rest of his life was to be spent fighting against the forces he had himself so largely set in motion. In 1870 he had made a tremendous onslaught upon Forster's Education Bill. Repulsed by the Church and Mr. Gladstone at the time, he lived to support—reluctantly, no doubt—Balfour's Education Act of 1902, which finally established sectarian education as a vital element in English life. He believed in his early phase that the British monarchy was doomed; he lived to see it the lynch-pin of the entire Imperial structure to the building of which his later years were devoted. As President of the Board of Trade he delivered the most masterly condemnations of Protection and food taxes which are upon record; his memory will be ever associated with their adoption.

In wider spheres his policy led to results he had not fore-seen. He was prime mover in the events which produced the South African War, and there are some who say that that war inaugurated an era of armaments and violence which ultimately led to the supreme catastrophe. He was foremost in the denial to Ireland of Home Rule, with the result that a generation later a settlement was reached on terms from which Mr. Gladstone himself would have recoiled and after episodes among the most odious in living memory.

It will be difficult for the present generation to understand the overpowering part which the Home Rule struggle played in the lives of their fathers and grandfathers. The insurgent Ireland that we now see merely as a group of ill-mannered agricultural counties, outside the march of British affairs, in the 'eighties bestrode the Imperial Parliament. Irish passions, Irish ideals, Irish leaders, Irish crimes, swayed the whole structure of English public life. The Irish parliamentary party, with their wit, their eloquence and their malice, destroyed the ancient and characteristically English procedure of the House of Commons. They riveted world attention upon their actions. They made and unmade Governments and statesmen. Like the Prætorians of old, they put the Empire up to auction and knocked it down to the highest bidder. Thus the Irish problem was for more than twenty years the supreme issue. It was the pivot around which the whole political life of England revolved, and men rose or fell in power and fame according as they were able to comprehend how it might be solved or burked.

In this conflict Mr. Gladstone simply swept Mr. Chamberlain out of existence as a leader of Liberal and Radical democracy. It was one of the strangest and also most significant duels ever fought. The story opens with Chamberlain the champion of the Radical or, as we should now call them, the Socialist masses. No one ever in our modern history made so able an appeal to the ill-used, left-out millions. His ' Unauthorized Programme ' of the autumn of 1885 was set forth in a series of speeches which by their grip, their knowledge, their poise, their authority and their challenge, excelled any constitutional incitement of which our latter-day politics bear record. Mr. Lloyd George at Limehouse went much farther in a period when travelling was much easier, and many will remember how startled they were by that. But Chamberlain had a tenacity of argument, a thoroughness, a sharpness beyond the later and far more creative reformer under the modern franchise.

Mr. Gladstone reigned in majesty over Liberal Britain. Unapproachable in glamour, tradition, and oratory, he towered at seventy-seven above the stormy scene. He was a giant from a bygone epoch. He had little sympathy with the practical demands of the working class for betterment. All those questions of social reform, of labour, housing, health, light, pure water, aroused in him only a cool, though benevolent interest. He dwelt upon a plane of world issues, and he knew that the heart of Britain is stirred by sentiment rather than by self-interest, by causes rather than by gains. The great Liberal Party, of whose soul he had so long been the interpreter, should not be wrested from its allegiance by an upstart from Birmingham, however competent, however popular, however adapted to the New Age. So while Mr. Chamberlain talked bread-and-butter politics to the working classes, the Grand Old Man thought of generous liberating crusades abroad or across the Irish Channel, and disdained the material side of things.

It was little enough that Chamberlain demanded. All his reforms, then thought so shocking, have been achieved and left far behind us in our hurried journey. It is now the axiom of the Tory Party that the well-being of the people, the happiness of the cottage home, is the first duty of the ruler, once the preservation of the State is secured. But in 1886 Mr. Gladstone beat ' Joe ' on his own Radical ground. He beat him, and he broke him. He drove him into the wilderness. Never again during the Old Man's political career did Chamberlain hold public office. The battle was grim, and though Mr. Gladstone conquered in his party, he was mortally wounded in the Imperial sphere, and he too was driven from power. In less than six months Chamberlain brought the temporarily towering alliance of Gladstone and Parnell to defeat in Parliament and disaster in the constituencies. The Grand Old Man expelled the rival from the Liberal household only at the cost of in-augurating what was virtually twenty years of Tory and Unionist rule.

Chamberlain never understood the Irish Nationalist movement, and its personalities were always antipathetic to him. All ambitious politicians wanted to establish contacts with Parnell. The home of Captain O'Shea, an obscure Irish member, presented the spectacle known as ' the eternal triangle.' Parnell was Mrs. O'Shea's lover, and O'Shea, alternately threatening and complaisant, basked in the forced smiles and grudged political patronage of the Irish leader. Chamberlain was for a long time in touch with Parnell through the captain. Gladstone, when he required to be informed, had a surer means of communication through the lady. Similarly Chamberlain offered Ireland extremely well-conceived schemes of local government linked to the idea of a Federal system. Gladstone, when he finally struck, flung down a ' Parliament on College Green.' In both cases he went to the heart of the business. But Gladstone himself only saw part of the problem. He was blind to the claims and cause of Protestant Ulster. He refused to face the fact of Ulster resistance. He inculcated an indifference to the rights of the population of Northern Ireland which dominated the Liberal mind for a whole generation. He elevated this myopia to the level of a doctrinal principle. In the end we all reached together a broken Ireland and a broken United Kingdom.

The struggle against Home Rule was none the less the finest of Chamberlain's career. As is usual in life, neither side had a clear position. Chamberlain had tried hard to woo Irish nationalism, and had been repulsed. Gladstone had estranged Ireland by coercion, and won them back again with a complete contempt of consistency. There were ample grounds against both for taunts and mockery. Yet at this distance of time, and with the tale told in all its refinement, we can see that both men were natural and sincere. Their points of view could never have been adjusted. In Hartington's pithy phrase, they ' did not mean the same thing.' Gladstone never knew Chamberlain's power till he faced him in this deadly grapple. ' He never spoke like this for us,' he complained, after one of Chamberlain's merciless attacks upon the Home Rule Bill. Often must Gladstone have reproached himself that he had not taken more personal pains to carry his revolted lieutenant with him. But we can now see that it would have been no use. At the root the split was flat and utter.

Between the winters of 1885 and 1886 Chamberlain sustained a succession of staggering blows such as have rarely fallen in our country to the lot of a public man. All the political work of his life was swept away. All his hold upon Radical democracy was destroyed. His most intimate friends and comrades became henceforward his life-long opponents. The political rupture with John Morley, the tragedy of Charles Dilke, broke the circle not only of his public but of his private life and thought. His friendship with Morley had to be preserved across the gulf of party antagonism. His friendship with Dilke was valiantly but vainly extended above the abyss of personal disaster. He had to make friends and work for long bleak years in a narrow grouping with that same Hartington and those same Whigs he had been about to drive from the parliamentary scene. He had to learn the language of those very Tories against whom he had sought to rouse the new electorate.

The Irish were his most persistent foes. They added to British politics a stream of hatred all their own and belonging to centuries from which England has happily escaped. They knew that more than any other man he had broken Mr. Gladstone and frustrated Home Rule. The malignity of their resentment was unsurpassed by anything I have ever seen in this confused world. He retorted with scorn and long, slow, patient antagonism. He made them feel they had been right to hate him.

All these trials show Chamberlain at his best. His warm heart, his constancy, his perfect self-control, his ' genius for friendship,' as Morley years afterwards called it, all shine amid these stresses. He was a faithful friend. No one differed from him more, or resisted him more consistently, than his comrade and colleague, John Morley. Home Rule, Free Trade, the South African War, furnished ever fresh causes of public strife between them. Yet they preserved their private relation. There never was a year in which they could not find opportunities of meeting, and when they met, they talked with all the freedom and zest of old confederates. Morley had an affection for him which the tumults of politics and the pangs of blows and injuries given and taken in the arena were powerless to affect. No such feeling ever subsisted between Chamberlain and Gladstone. All

Gladstone's profound Tory instincts and upbringing ran counter to this challenging figure from the Midlands and the middle classes. The Grand Old Man did not like being outbid in his appeal to the working masses. He admitted him grudgingly to his Cabinet; he denied him the confidences and close association which he offered to other far less formidable colleagues. He never really understood the personal force and power of ' Joe ' until he was matched against him in irreconcilable war. Perhaps it was just as well. I often used to sit next to Mr. ' Jim ' Lowther when I first came into the House. He had sat in Cabinet with Disraeli. He was a real survival of old times, the perfect specimen of the Tory Diehard, and a great gentleman and sportsman to boot. ' We have much to be thankful for,' he remarked one day. ' If those two had stuck together, they'd have had the shirts off our backs before now.'

When the Home Rule Bill was killed, and the long Tory reign began, Chamberlain found only one personal contact with the ascendant regime. Lord Randolph Churchill had led Tory Democracy against the whole seven seats of Birmingham in the election of 1885. Crowds of working men, denouncing ' Majuba ' and ' the murder of Gordon,' and filled with patriotic enthusiasm, had confronted and almost mastered the efficient thorough-paced Radicalism of Chamberlain's domestic city. But in '86 these hostile forces became his main prop. Lord Randolph Churchill's authority among the Birmingham Tories was in the crisis absolute. He wrote to Chamberlain (June 19) : ' We shall give all our support to the Liberal-Unionists, asking for no return, making no boast nor taunt. I will engage that all your Unionist candidates have the full support of our party.' Discipline was faultless. Throughout Birmingham, Tory Democracy marched to the aid of all the men they most abhorred, and returned by solid majorities those it had been so recently the object of their political existence to quell.

But a long harsh interval followed. From '86 to '92

Chamberlain sat first with Hartington, then (after the latter became Duke of Devonshire) alone, on the front Opposition bench, amid the muttered reproaches of the ruined Gladstonians and the implacable hatred of Irish Nationalism. There he sat and kept the Unionist Government in power. He never wavered. Lord Randolph's resignation, occuring almost at the outset seemed to deprive Chamberlain of his only link with the Cabinet. He was an example of ' splendid isolation.' The Salisbury Administration, through many blunders, plodded obstinately on. Immense patience and self-control were required. Chamberlain was not found wanting. It was not till 1895 that he entered upon his final and now most famous period as Colonial Secretary and as the great Imperialist.

I have many vivid memories of the famous ' Joe.' He was always very good to me. He had been the friend, foe, and friend again of my father. He was sometimes a foe in my father's days of triumph and sometimes a friend in his days of adversity ; but always there had subsisted between them a quarrelsome comradeship and a personal liking. At the time when I looked out of my regimental cradle and was thrilled by politics, Mr. Chamberlain was incomparably the most live, sparkling, insurgent, compulsive figure in British affairs. Above him in the House of Lords reigned venerable, august Lord Salisbury, Prime Minister since God knew when. Beside him on the Government Bench, wise, cautious, polished, comprehending, airily fearless, Arthur Balfour led the House of Commons. But ' Joe ' was the one who made the weather. He was the man the masses knew. He it was who had solutions for social problems ; who was ready to advance, sword in hand if need be, upon the foes of Britain ; and whose accents rang in the ears of all the young peoples of the Empire and of lots of young people at its heart.

I must have had a great many more real talks with him than I ever had with my own father, who died so young. He was always most forthcoming and at the same time startlingly candid and direct. The first I remember was in the summer preceding the outbreak of the South African War. We were both the guests of Lady St. Helier, who had a pleasant house upon the Thames ; all the afternoon we cruised along the river in a launch. He was most friendly to me, talked to me as if I were a grown-up equal, and afterwards—as Austen used to recount—gave me all kinds of commendation. The negotiations with President Kruger were then in an extremely delicate condition. I was no doubt keen that a strong line should be taken, and I remember his saying, ' It is no use blowing the trumpet for the charge, and then looking around to find nobody following.' Later we passed an old man seated upright in a chair on his lawn at the brink of the river. Lady St. Helier said, ' Look, there is Labouchere.' ' A bundle of old rags ' was Chamberlain's comment as he turned his head away from his venomous political opponent. I was struck by the expression of disdain and dislike which passed swiftly but with intenseness across his face. I realized as by a lightning flash how deadly were the hatreds my agreeable, courteous, vivacious companion had contracted and repaid in his quarrel with the Liberal Party and Mr. Gladstone. Nothing had been left unsaid by his former followers and associates. ' Judas,' ' traitor,' ' ingrate,' ' turncoat '—these were the commonplaces of the Radical vilification by which he was continually assailed.

Six years later, after he had split the Conservative Party and convulsed the country by raising the Protectionist issue, I had my last important conversation with him. I was writing my father's life, and wrote to him asking for copies of letters in his possession. We were at that time in full political battle, and although I was of small consequence I had attacked him with all the ferocity of youth, face to face in Parliament and throughout the country. I was one of those younger Conservatives most prominent in resisting the policy on which he had set his heart and the last efforts of his life. To my surprise he replied to my letter by suggesting that I should come and stay with him for a night at Highbury to see the documents. So I went, not without some trepidation. We dined alone. With the dessert a bottle of '34 port was opened. Only the briefest reference was made to current controversies. ' I think you are quite right,' he said, ' feeling as you do, to join the Liberals. You must expect to have the same sort of abuse flung at you as I have endured. But if a man is sure of himself, it only sharpens him and makes him more effective.' Apart from this our talk lay in the controversies and personalities of twenty years before.

We sat up until two. ' Joe ' produced diaries, letters and memoranda of the 80's, and as each fragment revived memories of those bygone days, he spoke with an animation, sympathy and charm which delighted me. I think it is a pleasing picture of this old Statesman, at the summit of his career and in the hardest of his fights treating with such generous detachment a youthful, active, truculent and, as he well knew, irreconcilable political opponent. I doubt whether the English tradition of not bringing politics into private life has often been carried much farther.

*   *   *   *   *

We have reached the period when Joseph Chamberlain's main effort is triumphant. Great Britain has at last joined the rest of the world as a Protectionist country. No one can suppose that unless there is a world-wide change in fiscal policy, we shall recede from the new system ; and even if there were a great modification in all tariffs and barriers to trade, the idea of preference within the British Empire would still assert its full force. It was indeed an historic and harmonious event which carried his own son as Chancellor of the Exchequer to the fulfilment of his task and mission. The elaborate measures of social reform, the pensions and insurance systems which this century has seen created in our island, the high taxation of wealth enforced in different degrees all over the world but nowhere at such a pitch as in Great Britain—all these are developments of the original impulse towards the material betterment of the masses which in his first prime was so strongly given by ' Radical Joe.' But it was when as an Imperialist he revived in the Tory party the inspiration of Disraeli and made the world-spread peoples of the British Empire realize that they were one, and that their future lay in acting upon this knowledge, that the life-work of Chamberlain entered its widest and loftiest sphere. The conception was not his, nor was he its earliest exponent ; but no man did more to bring it to reality. Here then is the pedestal of what none can doubt is an enduring fame.

SIR
JOHN FRENCH

SIR JOHN FRENCH

SIR JOHN FRENCH

THE life of Lord Ypres, better known as Sir John French, was devoted to a single purpose which was achieved to an extent far beyond his utmost dreams. But, as is often the case, the realization of his ambition brought disillusionment. To command a great British army in a European war was the task for which he had hoped and laboured throughout a long, adventurous career. No day-dream could have seemed more void of reality. Scarcely anything seemed more improbable than that the days of Marlborough and Wellington should repeat themselves, and that the tiny British forces of the nineteenth century should ever again set foot upon a Continent whose hosts, raised under universal service, were counted by many millions ! It was one of those events which are incredible until they happen.

Originally, French was intended for the Navy; but a physical inability to endure heights was fatal to a midshipman's career in the days when sailing ships were still common. He was speedily translated into a regiment of Hussars, and after the lapse of years, on the eve of the South African War, was regarded as the best cavalry leader in the Army. The dispatch of an expeditionary force to the Cape saw him at the head of the cavalry arm at the beginning of a war in which almost everything depended upon horsemen.

It was at this period that I first came in contact with him. Perhaps even the expression ' came in contact ' is too strong; for we were not to meet personally for nearly ten years. Like a good many other Generals at this time, French disapproved of me. I was that hybrid combination of subaltern officer and widely-followed war-correspondent which was not unnaturally obnoxious to the military mind. A young lieutenant hurrying about from one campaign to another, discussing the greatest matters of policy and war with complete assurance and considerable acceptance, distributing praise and blame among veteran commanders, apparently immune from regulation or routine, and gathering war experience and medals all the time—was not a pattern to be encouraged or multiplied.

But to these general prejudices was added a personal antipathy. My old colonel, General Brabazon, had for a time conceived himself to be French's rival in the cavalry world. Although definitely surpassed some years before the South African War began, he had received a brigade, and had served under French in the difficult and anxious operations around Colesberg in the winter of 1899. French was severe and exacting. Brabazon, a much older man, actually his senior in army rank, was self-willed and amazingly outspoken. Friction began; quarrels arose; some, at least, of Brabazon's mordant sayings were mischievously carried to French. Brabazon was deprived of his regular brigade and sent to languish in command of the yeomanry. I was known to sympathize with my former commanding officer, and to be his close friend. I was, therefore, involved in the zone of these larger hostilities.

Although I was with French's column in many a march and skirmish, and although I was intimate with several of his staff, French completely ignored my existence and showed me no sign of courtesy or goodwill. I was sorry for this, because I greatly admired all I had heard of his skilful defence of the Colesberg front, and his dashing gallop through the Boer lines to the relief of Kimberley, and was attracted by this gallant soldierly figure upon whom fell at this moment the gleams of a growing fame. However, I had my own job to do.

The numbness resulting from this South African frost was not relieved until the autumn of 1908. I then attended

some important cavalry manœuvres in Wiltshire, which
French was conducting. He was now recognized as our
leading fighting commander in the event of war. I was
a Cabinet Minister in a Government with a large majority
and an assured tenure. He sent an officer to suggest a
meeting. We came together on more or less equal terms.
There began, almost from our first talk, a friendship which
continued sure and warm through all the violent ups and
downs the next ten years were to bring.

The growing tenseness of the European situation was concealed from the public eye by the bland skies of peace and
platitude. But the steady growth of the German Navy
began to cause profound uneasiness through widening
circles in the British Empire. Ever since the Algeciras
conference of 1905, technical relations—declared non-
committal in policy—had existed between the French and
British General Staffs. Both Sir John French and I were
fully informed upon these secret matters. We therefore
discussed the future and its potent menace in the freedom
of exclusive confidences. After the Agadir crisis of 1911, I
was sent to the Admiralty for the express purpose of raising
our naval precautions to the highest pitch of readiness and
—only less important—to establish effectual co-operation
between the Admiralty and the War Office for the tran-
sporting of the whole Army to France in certain contin-
gencies. When, about a year later, French became Chief
of the Imperial General Staff, our collaboration in grave
matters became the core of an active, happy personal
friendship. We interchanged all the information our
respective appointments afforded. He was repeatedly my
guest on board the Admiralty yacht *Enchantress* at the
manœuvres, exercises and important gunnery practices of
the Fleet. We discussed every aspect, then conceivable,
of a possible war between France and Germany and of
British intervention by sea or land.

I remember the tale he told of his treatment at the German
cavalry manœuvres of 1913. After the formidable display

of scores of squadrons wheeling and whirling in martial exercise was completed, the Kaiser invited him to luncheon. There, taking full advantage of his position as a Sovereign, as a Field Marshal and as a host, William II had thought it right to say, ' You have seen how long my sword is ; you may find it is just as sharp ! ' French, the servant of a Parliamentary government, could only receive this outburst in silence. He was a choleric man, and had great difficulty in mastering himself.

*   *   *   *   *

The Irish question now cut jaggedly across the British political scene. The Liberal Government pursued, amid violent party strife, its Home Rule policy for·Ireland. And Protestant Ulster prepared to resist exclusion from the United Kingdom by armed force. At a certain moment various military posts and magazines in the North were thought to be in danger of seizure by the Orangemen. It was proposed to reinforce the garrison of Ulster by strong Imperial forces from the south of Ireland. There resulted what has been called the Curragh mutiny. The officers, wrongly conceiving that they were ordered to lead their troops against the Ulstermen, with whom all their personal and political sympathies lay, demanded in large numbers to resign their commissions. The men of course stood by their officers. A violent cleavage took place between the Government and the Army. French, dominated by his European preoccupations, had stood staunchly by the Government and by his Secretary of State, Colonel Seely. The crisis subsided as soon as its horrible character was realized upon all sides. But the Secretary of State, entangled in the details of the dispute, resigned, and the Chief of the Imperial General Staff, grievously smitten in the opinion of his military colleagues, felt bound to follow him. This was at the end of May, 1914.

The future now seemed completely closed to French. It is not often that a soldier regains the highest position in time of peace. The vacancy is filled; the lesser gaps are swiftly closed; a new man reigns; new loyalties are created. And in addition, there was a fierce current of military prejudice among the higher military officers against a General who had identified himself so largely with the Liberal administration. It was spread about in all influential quarters that he had no wish for further command; that he was tired out, and that he was out of touch with the sentiment of the Army. He was at this time nearly sixty years of age. This was his *nadir*.

About this time and amid these political eruptions, I was preparing for the test mobilization of the Fleet which had been fixed for the middle of July, 1914. The Fleet had never been fully mobilized before, and I had convinced my advisers at the Admiralty that a practical overhauling of the machinery and procedure would be of more value to the Navy than the usual extensive manœuvres at sea. I had been inspecting the great shipbuilding works of the Tyne, and I asked French to join me. Early in July we cruised down the East Coast, visiting various naval establishments on our way to Portsmouth, where the eight squadrons of the Battle Fleet, sixty-four battleships with their cruisers and flotillas, were already assembling. For a week we were alone, except for a few young officers. The General was in the depths. He was sure his military career was at an end. Full of fire and vigour, he was constrained to face long, empty years of retirement and idleness. If the great war ever came, he would be on the shelf! He was very dignified about it all, and his great personal good temper and simplicity emerged serenely. I remember that we scrambled ashore from a picket-boat before daybreak one morning to watch the first trials of a circular aeroplane upon which a young friend of mine, Sir Archibald Sinclair, had spent a great deal of money. I remember, too, long walks with the general up and down the esplanade at Deal. My impression of French, for all his composure, was that he was a heart-broken man.

Now, observe how swiftly Fortune can change the scene and switch on the lights ! Within a fortnight of this melancholy voyage Sir John French realized his fondest dream. He was Commander-in-Chief of the best and largest army Britain had ever sent abroad, at the beginning of the greatest war men have ever fought ! When next I saw him, it was at the momentous Council of August 5, 1914, when, war having been declared upon Germany, it was decided to send the whole Expeditionary Force to France under his command. And ten days later, this great operation having been achieved by the Admiralty punctually and safely, he came solemn, radiant and with glistening eye to take leave of me before embarking upon the swift vessel which waited at Dover. But the end of war is sour !

* * * * *

French was a natural soldier. Although he had not the intellectual capacity of Haig, nor perhaps his underlying endurance, he had a deeper military insight. He was not equal to Haig in precision of detail ; but he had more imagination, and he would never have run the British Army into the same long drawn-out slaughters.

The first shock of the War was drama at the highest pitch of intensity. Sir John French fell out very early with General Lanrezac, who commanded the Fifth and the left-most of all the French armies. Lanrezac was a remarkable officer, a master of military science on the largest scale. For years he had instructed at the French Staff College. He was one of those Frenchmen who have an almost physical dislike, born of centuries of tradition, for the English. He was contemptuous of the British Headquarters, and seemed to think it a favour that their puny army should be allowed to come to the aid of France. His manners, not only to his Allies, but to his own staff, were odious, and led to his speedy ruin. Nevertheless, Lanrezac, from the very first, realised the folly of Joffre's " Plan XVII." He saw the enormous right-handed movement of the Germans through Belgium, and that it would become dominating. His intelligence maps betrayed day by day the development of this prodigious turning operation. He cried aloud and incessantly to G.Q.G. (Grand-Quartier-Général) from the first week in August, that his Army should be moved to the Sambre and the Meuse, and that he should be reinforced to the utmost possible extent. At length, he was allowed to move his army northwards, and for a week they marched. He arrived in the neighbourhood of Charleroi. Here, he gave his left-hand to the British, and stood with them in the path of the invasion through Belgium against odds of about two to one.

Sir John French, who also reached the area by forced marches, had no thought but to co-operate with him. General Spears, then only a lieutenant, in his brilliant book, " Liaison 1914," has lighted this scene for us. The British Commander-in-Chief went to pay his respects to the High Command of the Fifth Army. French's French was the limit of British effort in that language. In harmony with the eighteenth-century English fashion, he pronounced French words in the most brutal English way. He used to speak of " ' Compiayny ' at the junction of the ' Iny ' and the ' Weeze ' ". At this moment a point of strategic importance was the passage of the Meuse at Huy. Sir John opened the conversation of ceremony by asking whether Lanrezac thought the Germans would try to force the Meuse at Huy. Huy was one of the worst names he could have attempted to pronounce. Spears points out that it can be achieved only by a whistle ! Sir John let it go as " Hoy ". Lanrezac, harassed by his profound knowledge of the general situation, could not contain his scorn at such clumsy ignorance. When Sir John's question was at length translated to him in intelligible terms, he replied insultingly, " Ah no, the Germans are only coming to the Meuse to catch the fishes ! " Sir John, who had seen a great deal of active service, and had five divisions and a cavalry division of professional soldiers in his hand, understood at once that he was being treated with rudeness. On this basis, the extended and severe battles of Charleroi and Mons were fought, side by side, by the two Commanders.

The weight of the German masses in the wooded, broken country, where the French artillery could have so little play, smashed the front of the Fifth Army. Lanrezac, with clairvoyant comprehension, ordered an immediate and continuous retreat. That he saved the situation by his retreat is unquestionable ; but the British Expeditionary Army might well have been rounded up or destroyed. The British, who had held their own in the Battle of Mons, found themselves in peril of being turned on both flanks. Sir John French has naïvely told us in his memoirs that he had a momentary temptation to throw himself into Maubeuge, pending the hoped-for restoration of the Front. There lay the fortress, with its wide encirclements of wire and trenches. Sir John tells us that he was saved from this by remembering Hamley's dictum : " The Commander of a retiring army who throws himself into a fortress, acts like one who, when the ship is foundering, lays hold of the anchor." Of course, he never seriously contemplated so absurd a step. On the contrary, he also made off as fast as he could towards Paris. His orders from home made him independent, and encouraged him, if in doubt, to seek the sea coast. He felt that he commanded the only trained body of troops that the Empire possessed, and that if these were lost, there would be no nucleus on which to build the new armies. However, he conformed as well as he could to the French retreat, and he looked forward amid the confusion to a right-about-turn battle to save Paris. He meant to keep the British Army alive for this last effort.

Arrived in the neighbourhood of Paris, impressed by the imminent fate of the capital, he appealed to Joffre to stand and fight, and promised to do the same. This was also Joffre's intention, but the day and the place were undecided. Sir John received a blankly negative reply, and various towns far to the south of the Seine were mentioned by the French G.Q.G. as points towards which the British Army should retreat. He was not even told ' we are looking for the chance '. Then, when the moment came which Joffre selected, or which Gallieni, Governor of Paris, forced upon him, the British Army was suddenly called upon to turn. Sir John French did not immediately rid himself of the conviction that the French Armies were retreating behind Paris, and did not mean to make a stand in its defence. All we can say is, ' no wonder '. By this time, Lanrezac, who had fought a stiff battle at Guise, and had conducted his own retreat with celerity and skill, was removed from his command, as one might say, by general consent. He went home with his high strategic comprehension, his bad manners, and his grievance.

Then came rather raggedly, but none the less magnificently, the second great effort of France. This was the world-decisive Battle of the Marne, so-called, although it extended from Paris to Verdun, and round the corner to Nancy—a front of over 250 miles. Once he was convinced of Joffre's resolve, Sir John, who had been reinforced from home, wheeled round, and plunged forward. As it happened, the British Army drove right into the gap which had opened between the two German Armies of their swinging right-wing. The advance of the British Army across the Marne and into this gap, decided the immense battle which saved Paris. With comparatively little fighting, the German right-wing was pierced, and the whole line of invading armies recoiled thirty miles to defensive positions. This was one of the greatest military events in all history, and Sir John French is entitled to his share of the glory.

There followed " the race to the sea." We had procured from the French Government the transference of our Army, which, continually fed, now numbered seven or eight divisions and a numerous cavalry, to the sea-flank. I have been told by some of the best French generals (especially General Buat, afterwards Chief of the French General Staff) that a little more audacity in thrusting forward the French left hand, would have swept the Germans out of a great part of their conquests. It was in this sense that the retention of Antwerp became of high importance ; for then, the line might have settled down Antwerp-Ghent-Lille. Certainly, Sir John French bid high and strove hard for this. Detraining in the neighbourhood of Saint-Omer, he pushed on towards Armentières and Ypres. But the Germans had prepared their counter-stroke. Four reserve army corps of youthful, but not untrained volunteers, strongly encadred, were hurled upon the British advance. Sir John, in the truest conception of war, now ran tremendous risks. He spread his front to a desperate extreme. With his right he fought at Armentières ; with his left he struggled towards Menin. A series of cruel, heartrending struggles ensued. We were reduced at times to nothing but a line of rifle pits, held by hard-bitten men, and batteries starved of ammunition. But the line proved impenetrable, and the four young German Army Corps bit the dust. Very high in the annals of the British Army must this grim struggle stand. And no one, if Generals can give anything to modern battles, gave more to it than the British Commander-in-Chief.

Merciful winter descended on the tortured Front, and exhaustion congealed both armies into trench warfare. The supreme episode of French's life was over. The rest of his command was spent in vain attempts to break the steel barrier of wire, machine-guns and artillery, without either the numbers or the apparatus necessary for an offensive. Foch, in March, 1915, lost 100,000 Frenchmen in Artois. Sir John, in April and May, lost 20,000 British at Neuve-Chapelle and Festubert. But his culminating repulse was the Battle of Loos. This was forced upon Sir John French by Joffre. It was to be the companion in the north of the attack by fifty French divisions in Champagne.

I had been very intimate with French all through the year, and always laboured to make things go right between him and Kitchener. I implored him not to agree to this autumn offensive of 1915. His own judgment was the same. I argued against the battle in the Cabinet, till I was suppressed. There never was any means of breaking the German fortified front until we had overwhelming heavy cannon, masses of shells, a far greater superiority of infantry, and, of course, the engine for that particular job—the tank. But nothing availed against the will-power of Joffre and the outlook of the French Staff. Brutal losses, costing perhaps a quarter of a million casualties, were sustained in the last fortnight of September by the French, and, in their proportion, by the British Army. In my small way, I tried my best to stop it. I warned Sir John French that the new battle would be fatal to him. It could not succeed, and he would be made the scapegoat of insane hopes frustrated. So it all fulfilled itself.

*   *   *   *   *

After these disasters in 1915 we were in the trough of the war. The British Government had decided to abandon the Dardanelles. I had resigned my seat at the War Council and set out to join my yeomanry regiment in France. Ministers who resign are always censured ; those who cannot explain their reasons are invariably condemned. I certainly could not attempt any explanation at that juncture. I crossed the Channel on the leave-boat, studying the varied throng in which were men of every regiment in the Army, going back to the trenches, just as they had come out of them— careless figures, jovial figures, haggard figures—a bustling, good-humoured throng of men. I had not heard from French for some time. I had been, as I have mentioned, a severe critic of the battle of Loos. I knew he had been hurt by my strenuous disapproval in Council of this plan to which he had been committed by the French command. I did not worry. When you get to the end of your luck, there is a comfortable feeling you have got to the bottom. However, when the ship arrived at Boulogne quay, and we all filed down the gangway on to the tormented French soil, the Port landing-officer said to me : ' We have orders for

89

you to go to the Commander-in-Chief ; and there is a car here from G.H.Q.'

A few hours later I dined with Sir John French at the Chateau of Blondecq in which, at that time, he resided. Those who have not served in the Great War, or at any rate in the Army, will hardly comprehend the enormous precipices which range upward tier upon tier, from a regimental officer to the Commander-in-Chief of many army corps. French brushed all this aside. He treated me as if I were still First Lord of the Admiralty, and had come again to confer with him upon the future of the war.

After that he told me about his own position. He said, ' I am only riding at single anchor.' He described the various pressures which were being applied to him to induce him to relinquish his command without a row. (In England, considerable efforts are usually made to get things that have been decided on, done without a row.) I had not been aware when in the Cabinet that these processes had gone so far ; but from what he told me I realized the situation.

My closing picture is his final day as Commander-in-Chief. He brought me back from the front, and we drove together during all the daylight hours, from army to army and from corps to corps. He went into the various headquarters and said good-bye to his Generals. I waited, an unofficial personage, in the car. We lunched out of a hamper excellently contrived, in a ruined cottage. His pain in giving up his great command was acute. He would much rather have given up his life. He had, however, a firm belief in the immortality of the soul : if you looked over the parapet, he thought, and got a bullet through your head, all that happened was that you could no longer communicate with your fellows and comrades. There you would be ; knowing (or perhaps it was only *seeing*) all that went on ; forming your ideas and wishes but totally unable to communicate. This would be a worry to you, so long as you were interested in earthly affairs. After a while your centre of interest would shift. He was sure new light would dawn ; better and brighter at last, far off, for all.

If, however, you looked over the parapet on purpose, you would start very ill in the new world.

It poured with rain all day, and this conversation is imprinted in my memory.

JOHN MORLEY

THE AUTHOR WITH JOHN MORLEY

JOHN MORLEY

JOHN MORLEY was a Victorian. He grew and flourished in the long era of peace, prosperity and progress which filled Queen Victoria's famous reign. This was the British Antonine Age. Those who were its children could not understand why it had not begun earlier or why it should ever stop. The French Revolution had subsided into tranquillity; the Napoleonic Wars had ended at Waterloo; the British Navy basked in the steady light of Trafalgar, and all the navies of the world together could not rival its sedate strength. The City of London and its Gold Standard dominated the finance of the world. Steam multiplied the power of man; Cottonopolis was fixed in Lancashire; railroads, inventions, unequalled supplies of superior coal, abounded in the island; the population increased; wealth increased; the cost of living diminished; the conditions of the working classes improved with their expanding numbers.

Englishmen felt sure that they had reached satisfactory solutions upon the material problems of life. Their political principles had stood every test. All that was required was to apply them more fully. Liberty of the Press and of the person, freedom of trade, extension of the franchise, the perfecting of representative Government and of the Parliamentary system, the sweeping away of privileges and abuses —all to be peacefully and constitutionally accomplished— were the tasks before them. Statesmen, writers, philosophers, scientists, poets, all moved forward in hope and buoyancy, in sure confidence that much was well, and that all would be better.

95

The tasks were inspiring and the risks were small. In a land,

> ' Where Freedom slowly broadens down
> From precedent to precedent,'

there was an appointed place for the active Radical reformer. He need not fear the repression of autocratic power, nor the violence of revolutionary success. The world it seemed had escaped from barbarism, superstition, aristocratic tyrannies and dynastic wars. There were plenty of topics to quarrel about, but none that need affect the life or foundations of the State. A varied but select society, observing in outward forms a strict, conventional morality, advanced its own culture, and was anxious to spread its amenities ever more widely through the nation. A sense of safety, a pride in the rapidly-opening avenues of progress, a confidence that boundless blessings would reward political wisdom and civic virtue, was the accepted basis upon which the eminent Victorians lived and moved. Can we wonder? Every forward step was followed by swiftly-reaped advantages : the wider the franchise, the more solid the State ; the fewer the taxes, the more abundant the revenue : the freer the entry of goods into the island, the more numerous and richer were the markets gained abroad. To live soberly then, to walk demurely in the sunshine of fortune, to shun external adventures, to avoid entangling commitments, to enforce frugality upon Governments, to liberate the native genius of the country, to let wealth fructify in the pockets of the people, to open a career broadly and freely to the talents of every class, these were the paths so clearly marked, so smooth, so easy of access, and it was wise and pleasant to tread them.

Morley was the intellectual child of John Stuart Mill. He sat at his feet and fed upon his wisdom. ' In such ideas as I have about political principles,' he said in his Indian Budget Speech of 1907, ' the leader of my Federation was Mr. Mill. There he was, a great and benignant lamp of wisdom and humanity, and I and others kindled our modest rush-lights at that lamp.' To me, when I first saw it, John Morley's ' modest rushlight ' had become a very bright ray. I admired it without seeking to borrow its flame. I approached near enough to read by its light, and to feel its agreeable, genial, companionable warmth. From 1896 onwards I began to meet him and to delight in his company. Rosebery was often more impressive in conversation ; Arthur Balfour always more easy and encouraging ; Chamberlain more commanding and forceful ; but there was a rich and positive quality about Morley's contributions, and a sparkle of phrase and drama which placed him second to none among the four most pleasing and brilliant men to whom I have ever listened. His manner and aspect were captivating. His art in private was to understand the opposite point of view, and to treat it with so much sympathy and good humour, while adhering to his own, that the hearers were often led to believe themselves in agreement with him, or at any rate that the remaining differences were small and not final. This sometimes led to disappointment ; for Morley, though in conversation he paraded and manœuvred nimbly and elegantly around his own convictions, offering his salutations and the gay compliments of old-time war to the other side, always returned to his fortified camp to sleep.

*   *   *   *   *

As a speaker, both in Parliament and on the platform, Morley stood in the front rank of his time. There was a quality about his rhetoric which arrested attention. He loved the pageantry as well as the distinction of words, and many passages in his speeches dwell in my memory. As may be guessed, he was better on a set occasion than in the movement of debate. He pleaded unpopular causes with a courage and sincerity which commanded the respect of the House. His gifts of intellect and character were admired on all sides. Sometimes in my day, when he was already ageing, his vitality flagged under the strain of a long speech, and he was then in danger of losing the House.

But I remember well the fierce, moving phrases of his indictment of the Boer War in 1901. ' Blood has been shed. Thousands of our women have been made widows ; thousands of children are fatherless. Millions of wealth, accumulated by the toil and skill of men, have been flung down the abyss. . . . The expenditure of £150,000,000 has brought material havoc and ruin unspeakable, unquenched and for long unquenchable racial animosity, a task of political reconstruction of incomparable difficulty, and all the other consequences which I need not dwell upon of this war, which I think a hateful war, a war insensate and infatuated, a war of uncompensated mischief and of irreparable wrong.'

However we were destined to find a better outcome than he foresaw, and to work together for it.

When Sir Henry Campbell-Bannerman's Government was formed in December, 1905, he would, I daresay, have liked to become Foreign Secretary. Before the Election, which did not take place till the New Year, I went to see him in the small but highly ornamented circular room at the India Office. I found him despondent. ' Here I am,' he said, ' in a gilded pagoda.' He was gloomy about the forth-coming election. He had had too long experience of defeat to nourish a sanguine hope. He spoke of the innate strength of the Conservative hold upon England. I talked to him encouragingly. ' It will be a great majority—one of the greatest ever known.' And so indeed it proved.

At the India Office he was an autocrat and almost a martinet. After several years, he shaped the first modest proposals for Indian representative government, now known as the ' Morley-Minto Reforms.' He, the ardent apostle of Irish self-government, felt no sense of contradiction in declaring his hostility to anything like ' Home Rule for India.' He went out of his way to challenge Radical opinion on this issue, and in an impressive speech, he warned his own supporters of the perils of applying to the vast Indian scene the principles which he applauded in Ireland and in South Africa. ' There is I know a school of thought who say that we might wisely walk out of India, and that the Indians can manage their own affairs better than we can. Anyone, who pictures to himself the anarchy, the bloody chaos that would follow, might shrink from that sinister decision.'   And again : ' When across the dark distances, you hear the sullen roar and scream of carnage and confusion, your hearts will reproach you with what you have done.'   All his thought and outlook made a strong impression upon me.   But times have changed, and I have lived to see the chiefs of the Conservative party rush in where Radical Morley feared to tread.   Only time can show whether his fears were groundless.

His literary output was very large.   He earned his living by his pen.   His celebrated essay on ' Compromise ' was for many years a guide to Liberal youth, and its insistence on the duty of independent individual judgment in every sphere of life and in respect of every creed and institution, is a healthy tonic in these days of totalitarian heresy.   He was a formidable critic and reviewer.   He edited the series of ' Twelve English Statesmen,' of which Rosebery's ' Pitt ' was one.   Amid the general chorus of praise which acclaimed this work, Morley's comment strikes a different note :—

Nothing can be more agreeable to read, or more brightly written, in spite of a certain heaviness, due partly to excess of substantives, and partly to too great a desire to impress not only the author's meaning, but his opinion.'   Tart !

Another and larger series was ' English Men of Letters,' to which he himself contributed ' Burke.'   His friendship for my father, in whose company he had delighted, induced him to turn a kindly eye upon the proof-sheets of my ' Life of Lord Randolph Churchill.'   Like Lord Rosebery, he took a keen interest in this record, and I have a file of long and deeply-instructive letters of comment and suggestion from him upon it, all written in his magnificent handwriting.   His own works fill a good shelf in any well-chosen modern library.   His ' Life of Mr. Gladstone ' is not only a splendid biography, but also the most authoritative contemporary account of the struggle for Irish Home Rule. As such, it will hold a permanent place in our annals as well as in our literature. His ' Cromwell,' ' Cobden ' and ' Walpole ' are contributions of the highest quality. He had dived deeply into the history of modern France from the days of the Encyclopædists and the Revolution which they heralded. ' Diderot,' ' Voltaire ' and ' Rousseau ' ' are, and will probably remain,' says General Morgan in his agreeable tribute,* ' the most penetrative, the most sympathetic, and the best-informed studies in the English language.' ' His style,' says the same writer, ' is austere. It has more grace than charm ; it diffuses light but it never generates heat. . . . He is the most impersonal of all our great writers of prose.' It is indeed true that the colour which he allowed himself in rhetoric was only sparingly used in his writings.

He shared my father's trust in the English people. When I, one day, reminded him of Lord Randolph's words ' I have never feared the English democracy ' and ' Trust the people,' and said I had been brought up on this, he said ' Ah, that is quite right. The English working man is no logician, like the French " Red," whom I also know. He is not thinking of new systems, but of having fairer treatment in this one.' I have found this true.

From 1908 onwards my seat in the Cabinet was next to his. Six years of constant, friendly, and to me stimulating propinquity ! Week after week, often several times a week, we had faced side by side the national, party, and personal troubles and business of a period of hard political strife. Cabinet neighbours, if they are friends, have a natural tendency to share confidences, especially about their colleagues and their colleagues' performances. Whispered and scribbled comments pass to and fro. Physically they survey the council scene from the same point of view. Personally they become much engaged to one another. And to me John Morley was always a fascinating companion, a man

* ' John, Viscount Morley,' by J. H. Morgan. Murray.

linked with the past, the friend and contemporary of my father, the representative of great doctrines, an actor in historic controversies, a master of English prose, a practical scholar, a statesman-author, a repository of vast knowledge on almost every subject of practical interest. It was an honour and privilege to consult and concert with him on equal terms, across the gulf of thirty-five years of seniority, in the swift succession of formidable and perplexing events.

Such men are not found to-day. Certainly they are not found in British politics. The tidal wave of democracy and the volcanic explosion of the War have swept the shores bare. I cannot see any figure which resembles or recalls the Liberal statesmen of the Victorian epoch. To make head against the aristocratic predominance of those times, a Lancashire lad, the son of a Blackburn doctor without favour or fortune, had need of every intellectual weapon, of the highest personal address, and of all that learning, courtesy, dignity and consistency could bestow. Nowadays when ' one man is as good as another—or better,' as Morley once ironically observed, anything will do. The leadership of the privileged has passed away ; but it has not been succeeded by that of the eminent. We have entered the region of mass effects. The pedestals which had for some years been vacant have now been demolished. Nevertheless, the world is moving on ; and moving so fast that few have time to ask—whither. And to these few only a babel responds.

But in John Morley's prime the course was clear and conscious, and the issues not so large as to escape from human control.

*   *   *   *   *

In 1910, my friend began to feel the weight of years. He was then over seventy, and the India Office became a burden he could not easily bear. He intimated this to Mr. Asquith. No doubt Asquith was conscious of the divergence on foreign policy which existed between Morley and Grey. At any rate he acquiesced. When I heard about this I was distressed. So I wrote as follows to the Prime Minister :

HOME OFFICE,
Oct. 22, 1910.

It is with some diffidence that I write to you on a matter which you may consider outside my province.

I had a talk with Morley yesterday and found a distinct undercurrent of feeling in his mind that he had been somewhat easily let go. He would of course be very much vexed with me for coming to such a conclusion, still more for repeating it to you. But I do so because I am strongly of opinion that Morley's complete detachment from the Government at this stage might prove very disadvantageous to us, and secondly because I have a deep personal affection for him, and am proud to sit in Council by his side.

From what he said yesterday I am convinced that you could even now retain his services in some great office without administrative duties. Such an office is vacant at the present time ; for Crewe is not only Colonial Secretary but Privy Seal. I would therefore venture respectfully and earnestly to suggest to you to invite Morley to stay with us in a post which would relieve him from the administrative burden he has found so heavy, and would at the same time associate him with your Government in an effective and distinguished manner. The Cabinet will be spared a very heavy loss in counsel and distinction, if you find yourself able to make this offer.

I may add that the Chancellor of the Exchequer whom I saw this morning authorized me to say on his behalf to you that ' he saw great danger in Morley's being separated from us entirely at the present time.'

Please do not be offended by my addressing you on such a subject. Only its importance and my wish to see your administration successful has prompted me. In no case let Morley know I have written.

I was delighted a few weeks later when this transition

was actually accomplished, though by a somewhat different method, and my honoured companion continued by me in his accustomed seat as Lord President of the Council.

* * * * *

Morley's political life was ended by the War. The Memorandum on Resignation which his literary executors gave to the public five years after his death, and fifteen years after the outbreak of War, is a document of absorbing and permanent historical interest. It is marked by much vagueness about the dates and sequence of events. It is, of course, a partial and personal record. Yet it is, none the less, as true and living a presentment of the War crisis within the British Cabinet as has ever been, or probably will ever be given. All is there, and these fragments so shrewdly selected, so gracefully marshalled, are a better guide to the true facts than the meticulously exact, voluminously complete accounts which have appeared from numerous quarters. In a style which arrests eyes jaded with the commonplace, Morley has revealed, partly consciously but for the most part unconsciously, both the sundering from the past which Armageddon meant, and his own inability to comprehend the new scale and violence of the modern world.

It was from my close and intimate proximity and friendship that I witnessed the horrible impact of the Great War upon the statesman who above all others then alive represented the Victorian Age and the Gladstonian tradition. I found that my neighbour was dwelling in a world which was far removed from the awful reality. At such a juncture his historic sense was no guide ; it was indeed an impediment. It was vain to look back to the Crimean War, to the wars of 1866 and 1870, and to suppose that any of the political reactions which had attended their declaration or course would repeat themselves now. We were in the presence of events without their equal or forerunner in the whole experience of mankind. This frightful, monstrous thing, that had been so long whispered, was now actually upon us. All the greatest armies were mobilizing. Twelve or fourteen millions of men were getting into harness, raising deadly weapons, and rolling forward by every road and railway towards long-appointed destinations.

Morley, resolute for neutrality, not indeed at all costs, but—as it seemed to me—at fatal cost in days, was absorbed by ideas of parley, of the fate of Liberalism, of the party situation. He had spent his life building up barriers against war in Parliament, in the constituencies, and in the national mind. Surely all these ramparts of public opinion would not collapse together. He was old; he was frail; but outside this Cabinet room, were there not forces of Radical democracy strong and fierce enough to make head against the madness that was sweeping across Europe, and even, alas! infecting the Liberal Administration, originally formed by Sir Henry Campbell-Bannerman himself. My responsibility on the other hand was to make sure that whatever else happened or did not happen, the British Fleet was ready and in its proper station in good time This involved the demanding of certain measures from the Cabinet one after another as they fell due. So there we sat side by side, hour after hour, through this flaming week.

The majority of the Cabinet was for leaving France and Germany and the other Powers great and small to fight it out as they pleased, and Morley found himself looked to as leader by a gathering band. But the issues were clouded and tangled. There was Belgium and the faith of Treaties. There were the undefended coasts of France, and the possibility of the German fleet ' on our very doorstep ' cannonading Calais, while the French battleships as the result of tacit agreement with us were stationed in the Mediterranean. Morley was no doctrinaire or fanatic. The ' doorstep ' argument weighed with him. It persuaded the Cabinet. John Burns alone resisting and resigning, they agreed unitedly that the Germans should be told we could not allow them in the Channel. This was a far-reaching decision. From that moment Morley, too, was on the slippery slope. The week wore on. The Fleet went silently to its Northern base. The ' Precautionary Period ' measures were authorized by the Cabinet.

' One of these days,' writes Morley, ' I tapped Winston on the shoulder, as he took his seat next me. " Winston, we have beaten you after all." He smiled cheerfully. Well he might. *O pectora caeca !* '

But it was not me he had to beat. It was the avalanche, the whirlwind, the earthquake, roaring forth in triple alliance. So when later on he told me he must resign, I said in effect that if he would wait for two or three days more, everything would be clear, and we should be in full agreement. The Germans would make everyone easy in his conscience. They would accept all responsibilities and sweep away all doubts. Already their vanguards pouring through Luxembourg approached the Belgian frontier. Nothing could recall or deflect them. They were launched ; and the catastrophe now imminent and certain would convince and unite the British Empire as it had never been convinced and united before. ' They cannot stop now. If they tried, they would be thrown into utter confusion. They must go on in spite of frontiers, treaties, threats, appeals, through cruelties and horrors, trampling on until they meet the main French Armies and the largest battles of history are fought. Remember all the others are marching too.'

I offered to illustrate the position on the map. But he took another line. ' You may be right—perhaps you are —but I should be no use in a War Cabinet. I should only hamper you. If we have to fight, we must fight with single-hearted conviction. There is no place for me in such affairs.' To this I could find no answer, except to repeat that all would speedily be made plain, and that in forty-eight hours what was going to happen in Belgium, and perhaps in the North Sea, would make him feel quite differently about things. But he persisted. Gently, gaily

almost, he withdrew from among us, never by word or sign
to hinder old friends or add to the nation's burden.

I can only surmise his action had he taken my counsel.
What would have been the effect upon his strong, courageous
and authoritarian spirit of the German invasion of Belgium,
of the resistance of the Belgian King and people, of the
struggle at Liège, of the horrors of Louvain ? Personally,
I believe he would have marched heart and soul at the
head of his fellow-countrymen, if he had waited only for
forty-eight hours. But looking back I am glad I did not
prevail upon him. It was better for him, for his repute
and for the great period and conceptions he embodied, that
he should ' testify ' however impotently, and raise unavailing
hands of protest and censure against the advancing deluge.
The old world of culture and quality, of hierarchies and
traditions, of values and decorum deserved its champions.
It was doomed : but it did not lack its standard-bearer.

In the end Morley was left to go alone. The pressure of
events of which I had tried to warn him soon afforded
reasons, opportunity, excuses enough to the colleagues who
had proffered him their support. They stayed—with
various fortunes and different explanations : and Lloyd
George so successfully adapted himself to the new conditions as to become the prime relentless war leader, the
apostle of the knock-out blow,' the undisputed master of
the triumph. It is for these backsliding colleagues that the
sharpest censures of Morley's memorandum are reserved.
' Winston, at whom I looked with paternal benignity,' was
never the object of his reproach. I rejoice in this. To have
had an intense antagonism with an honoured friend on a
supreme issue, without losing either his friendship or comprehension, has in it some enduring elements of comfort as
one looks back along the lengthening, fading track of life.

Morley had risen to eminence and to old age in a brilliant,
hopeful world. He lived to see that fair world shattered,
its hopes broken, its wealth squandered. He lived to see
the fearful Armageddon, ' the angry vision of this hideous

war,' the nations hurled against each other in the largest, the most devastating, and nearly the most ferocious of all human quarrels. He lived to see almost everything he toiled for and believed in dashed to pieces. He endured the cataclysm of fire and sword ; but he also survived to see the island he loved so well emerge once again victorious in the supreme ordeal. He lived even to recognize the immense, fascinating, yet mysterious and unmeasured new growths which everywhere are bursting forth amid the ruins of the structures he had known.

HINDENBURG

Graphic Photo Union

HINDENBURG WITH HITLER

HINDENBURG

HINDENBURG! The name itself is massive. It harmonizes with the tall, thick-set personage with beetling brows, strong features, and heavy jowl, familiar to the modern world. It is a face that you could magnify tenfold, a hundredfold, a thousandfold, and it would gain in dignity, nay, even in majesty ; a face most impressive when gigantic. In 1916 the Germans made a wooden image of him, colossal, towering above mankind ; and faithful admirers, by scores of thousands, paid their coins to the War Loan for the privilege of hammering a nail into the giant who stood for Germany against the world. In the agony of defeat the image was broken up for firewood. But the effect remained—a giant : slow-thinking, slow-moving, but sure, steady, faithful, warlike yet benignant, larger than the ordinary run of men.

His life was that of a soldier and his youth a preparation for arms. He fought as a subaltern in all the battles through which Bismarck founded the indestructible might of the German people, at last after centuries of petty feud formidably united. He fought against Austria at Königgrätz in 1866. He fought against France in 1870. On the bloody slopes of St. Privat, the tomb of the Prussian Guard, Hindenburg marched with dauntless tread. Half the regiment of the Guard to which he belonged fell. He fought at Sedan. Observing the immense circle of Prussian batteries firing upon the doomed French, he remarked with gusto, ' Napoleon, too, is stewing in that cauldron.'

He loved the old world of Prussia. He lived in the famous tradition of Frederick the Great. *' Toujours en vedette,*' as the German military saying goes—'Always on the look-out.' He revelled in the 'good old Prussian spirit of Potsdam'; the officer class, poor, frugal, but pursuing honour with feudal fidelity, their whole existence devoted to King and country; a class most respectful to the aristocracy and the lawfully-constituted authorities; a class, the enemy of change. Hindenburg had nothing to learn from modern science and civilization except its weapons; no rule of life but duty; no ambition but the greatness of the Fatherland.

The years rolled by. The subaltern rose in the military hierarchy. He held a succession of important commands. He was one of the leading generals of the German army. Always he waited for the day when he would be leading into battle not a mere company but whole army corps against the accursed Frenchmen. Still the years rolled on. A younger generation came knocking at the door. Deep peace lapped the nations. At the top of the ladder of promotion Hindenburg found only the shelf of retirement. So, then, the great day would be for others. He retired in modest circumstances to his home. From 1911 he dwelt like Cincinnatus on his farm. If he did not forget the world, it seemed that the world had forgotten him. Then came the explosion. From all her frontiers the pent-up might of Germany surged upon the foe. The wonderful military machine Hindenburg had shared in perfecting was launched simultaneously upon France and Russia. But he was out of it. He sat in his home. The greatest battles in the world were fought without him. The Russian armies poured into East Prussia, the land he loved so well, every inch of which he knew. Would the call never come to him? Was there no room, then, in this supreme struggle for him? And was 'Old Hindenburg' relegated to the past?

The call came. The Russian masses wended on victoriously in the East. The advance in the West approached its climax. Suddenly there is a telegram—3 p.m., August 22,

1914. It is from Main Headquarters: 'Are you prepared for immediate employment?' Answer: 'I am ready.' Within a few hours he was speeding eastwards to command the German armies against Russia, against odds of between three or four to one. In the train he met his chief of staff, who was already managing everything and issuing all the orders with the underlying, over-riding authority of the German General Staff. Nothing is more becoming than the relations which Hindenburg preserved with Ludendorff. Certainly it was a marvellous partnership. His lieutenant was a prodigy of mental energy, cast in a military form. Hindenburg was not jealous; he was not petty; he was not fussy. He took the responsibility for all that his brilliant, much younger, subordinate conceived and did. There were moments when the nerve of Ludendorff flickered, and in these moments the solid, simple strength of Hindenburg sustained him. The awful battle of Tannenberg destroyed the Russian armies in the north; the invaders were swept from German soil by little more than one-third of their number. Their losses exceeded twice over the total numbers of their conquerors.

The dazzling victories in the East came just at the moment when the German people became aware of the fact that they had been repulsed from Paris and that the mighty onrush which was to have ended the War in the first six weeks had failed. They nursed and warmed themselves with the good tidings that Hindenburg had smashed the Russians. Thenceforward Hindenburg with his astounding Chief Staff Officer, Ludendorff, became the main pillar of German hope. The English military historians have used the cabalistic symbol HL to represent this famous combination which during the War and to the outer world at least presented itself as a pendant to the comradeship of Lee and Jackson and farther back to the brotherhood of Marlborough and Eugene. HL swiftly became the rival of Main Headquarters. Moltke had disappeared with the failure at the Marne, and a new chief, perhaps the ablest of

German commanders, Falkenhayn, directed the German armies. He still looked to the West as the scene upon which the decision would be obtained. Here were the greatest forces, here were the hated French, here above all in his own words was ' our most dangerous enemy . . . England, with whom the conspiracy against Germany stands and falls.'

But the eastern war lords thought differently. They believed that with six or eight additional army corps they could destroy quite swiftly the military power of Russia. Let them have this force or even less ; let it be used in a great left-handed turning movement from the north, and they would scoop up more than a million Russian troops in the Warsaw salient and bring about the immediate retreat of all the southern Russian armies at grips with Austria. After that everybody could return to the West and finish with the French. Such was the difference in strategic thought. There was also a difference of interests and of honourable rivalries in the common cause.

These divergences, although veiled under the strict forms of military discipline, rapidly became acute. Falkenhayn in the West disposed of seven times the forces of Hindenburg. He was the German generalissimo ; he had the Emperor's ear ; he had control of the general staff. H. lived on what they could get from him ; they were only the junior partners. But they had one great advantage. They had only to fight against Russians. All the German generals who fought the Russians soon had victories to their credit. So did the Russian generals who fought the Austrians. But just as the Russian commanders who fought the Germans had only frightful disasters to report, so the Germans on the Western front found themselves faced by the armies of civilizations at least the equal of their own. Falkenhayn delivered his tremendous thrust at the Channel ports. He sent against the gasping British lines from Armentières to the sea the Army Corps which would have decided matters in the East. Among these were the four new Army Corps, improvised as has been described from the valiant volunteer youth of Germany, who perished before the thin but impenetrable lines of the British professional divisions and their French reinforcements. Meanwhile in the East, Hindenburg and Ludendorff, with just not quite enough strength, twice failed in audacious attempts against enormous odds to capture Warsaw. 1914 closed amid cold, stern, mutual recriminations, all strictly confined to the highly-instructed circles of the German general staff.

But all through 1915 Falkenhayn retained the control. Not only did he differ from H⌐ about the emphasis between West and East, but he had his own view on the Eastern strategy. He did not agree with the Hindenburg left-handed northern scoop. On the contrary, Austria must be succoured and kept in the field. If additional efforts must be made in the East their direction should be to the southward, carrying forward the Austrian army behind a right-handed German punch. And here the British enterprise against the Dardanelles fortified Falkenhayn's view. To win Bulgaria and strike down Serbia, to establish through-communications with Turkey—these objects seemed to claim unquestionable priority. Great and victorious operations of this kind were executed by Falkenhayn's orders. In the summer the German eastern punch was delivered on the Austrian front at Gorlice-Tarnow under the command of Mackensen. There were great successes. Under their pressure Russia recoiled with appalling losses, and for other reasons the British assault upon Turkey collapsed. Meanwhile H⌐, although co-operating actively and conducting war on an immense scale, were nevertheless marooned in the north. 1915 was Falkenhayn's year. He, too, had gathered a crop of the easier victories which grew in the East for the German sickle.

The differences of strategic opinion, emphasized by simpler causes of friction, tended to separate H⌐ from Main Headquarters. Hindenburg and his ambitious lieutenant continued to propose great movements in the north.

They were always restricted to a minor rôle. Falkenhayn in the full tide of success laid his plans for 1916, and now he made his fatal error. He decided to launch his main offensive in the West. He selected Verdun as the crucial point. Here upon this great bastion of the French front, almost its strongest point, the vital point for which the French must conquer or perish, he would use all the reserves of the German military machine and the bulk of its terrific artillery.

It should have been fairly obvious at the time that this was a most unpromising undertaking; for the armies of France and Britain in the West were capable of defending themselves, if not in one position then in another, against any margin of superiority which Germany could marshal. But Falkenhayn had his way and he had his chance. All through the spring of 1916 his cannon blasted Verdun, and the soul of the French nation met him there. In the upshot he wore himself out as much as he wore the French, and by June the great Verdun offensive already had the aspect of a stalemate. It was soon to present itself to the world in the guise of recognizable defeat.

And now in July began the great allied counter-offensive of the Somme. The new British armies crashed into battle in conjunction with the French left. They suffered terrible losses, but such was the weight of the impact and so unceasing week after week and month after month were their assaults that Falkenhayn had to close down his Verdun battles and only held his own on the Somme by ceding ground steadily and at the cost of the flower of the German troops. At the critical moment the Russians in the south, who were thought to be all beaten or dead, advanced against the Austrians and under Brusilov annihilated large portions of the Austrian front. On this, Roumania, long hesitating, declared herself upon the Allies' side. This was the second supreme crisis of the war for Germany.

These events have been recounted because without knowledge of them it is impossible to understand the rise of

Hindenburg and Ludendorff. They had had a long time to wait. They represented the unfashionable minority school in the German General Staff. But their criticisms were pointed by terrific lessons in the West. Now it seemed they were entirely justified. All the gains of 1915 had been thrown away. France and Britain were found inexpugnable, and Russia was still alive. A new power long affiliated to Germany had joined the ranks of her still-gathering foes.

Hindenburg was at Brest-Litovsk on the morning of August 28, when he received orders to repair forthwith to the Emperor's headquarters. ' The only reason the Chief of the Military Cabinet gave me was this, " The position is serious." I put down the receiver and thought of Verdun, Italy, Brusilov and the Austrian Eastern Front ; then of the news " Roumania has declared war on us." Strong nerves would be required ! '

Hindenburg's account of what followed is characteristic.

' In front of the castle at Pless I found my All-Highest War Lord awaiting the arrival of Her Majesty the Empress. . . . . The Emperor immediately greeted me as Chief of the General Staff of the Field Army and General Ludendorff as my First Quartermaster General. The Imperial Chancellor too had appeared from Berlin, and apparently was as much surprised as I myself at the change in the office of Chief of the General Staff, a change which His Majesty announced to him in my presence.'

Henceforward the entire direction of the German war machine fell into the hands of the redoubtable pair. Not only this, but they increasingly absorbed to themselves the main political authority in Germany. They stabilized the Austrian front against Russia. They destroyed Roumania. They preserved their lines unbroken against the British until the longed-for winter days came. With the new year they made a prudent withdrawal in the West which completely disconcerted the Allied plans. Suddenly, swiftly and silently the Germans withdrew to the new immense fortifications of the Hindenburg Line, and gained a four months' breathing-space. The stakes were raised on both sides and the fury of the War intensified. Russia disintegrated into revolution and ruin. The Peace of Brest-Litovsk was signed. H. could now look forward to a last supreme opportunity in 1918. Their plans were not interrupted by the murderous struggles with the British at Passchendaele. They knew themselves in a position to bring a reinforcement of a million men and five thousand guns from the Russian front, and to have in 1918 for the first time since the very beginning of the War a large and substantial superiority in the West.

But these great measures of generalship were accompanied by a fatal error. H. were led to believe that a submarine campaign on a gigantic scale would starve England and force the British Empire to make peace. Against the wish of the Kaiser, against the appeals of the German Chancellor and the Foreign Office, they insisted on unlimited submarine warfare, and on April 6th, 1917, the United States declared war upon Germany. Here Hindenburg was acting outside the military sphere in which he and his colleagues were expert. They staked too much upon a purely mechanical device. They looked too little to the tremendous psychological reactions upon the Allies, upon the whole world, above all upon their own people, which must follow the apparition of a fresh, mighty antagonist among the forces against Germany. They utterly underrated the power of the United States. Moreover they had miscalculated the mechanical aspect. The British Navy was not unequal to the extraordinary strain of the submarine attack. By no great margin, but quite decisively, they reached beneath the surface of the seas, groped for, found and strangled the German submarines. By the summer of 1917 it was certain that the seas would remain open, that Britain would be fed, and that American troops in millions could be carried to France.

The only question remaining was whether the German

armies reinforced from Russia could beat the British and the French, as they had beaten the Italians, before over-whelming hostile forces gradually developed in the West. This was the great issue fought out in 1918, and there is no need to recall the prodigious battles which from the 21st of March to the beginning of July tore the Anglo-French front. But the effort overtaxed the German strength; the two great nations with whom they were locked in des-perate grip had greater reserves of strength and virtue than Germany could muster. The American weight grew unceas-ingly. In the end, under the pressure of superior cannon and superior numbers, the armies of the Kaiser bent and bowed, and behind them the civil population, long pinched by the British blockade, broke into turbulent confusion. It was indeed now the world that was coming against them in an irresistible tide. Millions of men, scores of thousands of cannon, thousands of tanks; the heroic constancy of France and the unrelenting will-power, which they always recog-nized, of England. And behind, the measureless, now rapidly-gathering forces of the United States. Too much! The German front was broken, and the homeland behind the front crumpled beneath the strain. The proud armies recoiled; Ludendorff was dismissed. Hindenburg bided with his Sovereign to the end. We must suppose that he approved, and perhaps enjoined, the Kaiser's departure to Holland. For himself he went home with the troops. What was Revolution compared to Defeat?

' I was at the side of my All-Highest War Lord during these fateful hours. He entrusted me with the task of bringing the Army back home. When I left my Emperor in the afternoon of November 9, I was never to see him again! He went, to spare his Fatherland further sacrifices and enable it to secure more favourable terms of peace.'

A pause of years; and then out of the confusion and miseries of vanquished Germany Hindenburg was suddenly raised to the summit of power. The German people in their despair saw in him a rock to which they might cling.

President of the German Republic! Will he accept the office? First the Kaiser must release him from his oath of allegiance. The Kaiser consented. Nearly a decade has passed since then.* Hindenburg's eighty-fourth birthday was celebrated by a nation which felt its recovering strength and was resuming its position in the world. It would be well if we could end the story at this point. We cannot here unravel the part he played in the melancholy and terrible convulsions into which Germany has since been thrown, but it must certainly have been at intervals decisive. It makes no addition to his fame.

One incident must, however, be mentioned. The greatest blot on Hindenburg's career is his treatment of his Chancellor Brüning, and not only of Brüning but of the millions of Germans, a large majority of the nation, who upon Brüning's appeal placed their faith in Hindenburg to save themselves from Hitler and all that Hitler meant. No sooner was the Presidential election over, no sooner had Hindenburg defeated Hitler by Brüning's aid, than the old Field-Marshal turned upon his colleague and comrade, and repudiated the trust of his supporters. He dismissed Brüning with a few short words across the table. Some official grimaces, a bow and a scrape, and the Chancellor, who was leading Germany swiftly back to a high and honoured position in Europe, was brushed out of power. The lank, obscure, glass-eyed, stiff-collared official, hitherto known only to the world by his mishandling of German affairs in the United States, von Papen, was to universal surprise arbitrarily placed at the summit of power. It is said, but it is not necessary to pursue the point, that quite small sordid questions about compensation money payments in respect of Junker estates in East Prussia in which President Hindenburg's son was personally involved were not without their influence upon this shattering decision.

Events now rolled forward with gathering momentum. The transition from Papen to Schleicher (now murdered)

* Written in 1934.

and from Schleicher to Hitler were but an affair of months. In the last phase we see the aged President, having betrayed all the Germans who had re-elected him to power, joining reluctant and indeed contemptuous hands with the Nazi leader. There is a defence for all this, and it must be made on behalf of President von Hindenburg. He had become senile. He did not understand what he was doing. He could not be held physically, mentally or morally responsible for opening the floodgates of evil upon German, and perhaps upon European, civilization. We may be sure that the renowned veteran had no motive but love of his country, and that he did his best with declining mental strength to cope with problems never before presented to a ruler.

* * * * *

Dusk deepens into dark. It is time to sleep. Nightmares, hideous choices, unanswerable riddles, pistol-shots disturb an old man's torpor. Where is the path ? Always uphill ! Worse to come ? *Vorwärts*—always *vorwärts*— then silence.

BORIS
SAVINKOV

Keystone View Company

SAVINKOV BEFORE THE SOVIET TRIBUNAL

BORIS SAVINKOV

'HOW do you get on with Savinkov ? ' I asked M. de Sazonov when we met in Paris in the summer of 1919.

The Czar's former Foreign Minister made a deprecating gesture with his hands.

' He is an assassin. I am astonished to be working with him. But what is one to do ? He is a man most competent, full of resource and resolution. No one is so good.'

The old gentleman, grey with years, stricken with grief for his country, a war-broken exile striving amid the celebrations of victory to represent the ghost of Imperial Russia, shook his head sadly and gazed upon the apartment with eyes of inexpressible weariness.

' Savinkov. Ah, I did not expect we should work together.'

* * * * *

Later on it was my duty to see this strange and sinister man myself. The ' Big Five ' had just decided to support Koltchak, and Boris Savinkov was his accredited agent. I had never seen a Russian Nihilist except on the stage, and my first impression was that he was singularly well cast for the part. Small in stature ; moving as little as possible, and that noiselessly and with deliberation ; remarkable grey-green eyes in a face of almost deathly pallor ; speaking in a calm, low, even voice, almost a monotone ; innumerable cigarettes. His manner was at once confidential and dignified ; a ready and ceremonious address, with a frozen, but not a freezing, composure ; and through all the sense of an unusual personality, of veiled power in strong restraint. As one looked more closely into this countenance and watched its movement and expression, its force and attraction became evident. His features were agreeable ; but though still only in the forties, his face was so lined and crow's-footed that the skin looked in places—and particularly round the eyes—as if it were crinkled parchment. From these impenetrable eyes there flowed a steady regard. The quality of this regard was detached and impersonal, and it seemed to me laden with doom and fate. But then I knew who he was, and what his life had been.

Boris Savinkov's whole life had been spent in conspiracy. Without religion as the Churches teach it ; without morals as men prescribe them ; without home or country ; without wife or child, or kith or kin ; without friend ; without fear ; hunter and hunted ; implacable, unconquerable, alone. Yet he had found his consolation. His being was organized upon a theme. His life was devoted to a cause. That cause was the freedom of the Russian people. In that cause there was nothing he would not dare or endure. He had not even the stimulus of fanaticism. He was that extraordinary product—a Terrorist for moderate aims. A reasonable and enlightened policy—the Parliamentary system of England, the land tenure of France, freedom, toleration and goodwill—to be achieved whenever necessary by dynamite at the risk of death. No disguise could baffle his clear-cut perceptions. The forms of government might be revolutionized ; the top might become the bottom and the bottom the top ; the meaning of words, the association of ideas, the rôles of individuals, the semblance of things might be changed out of all recognition without deceiving him. His instinct was sure ; his course was unchanging. However winds might veer or currents shift, he always knew the port for which he was making ; he always steered by the same star, and that star was red.

During the first part of his life he waged war, often single-handed, against the Russian Imperial Crown. During the latter part of his life, also often single-handed, he fought the Bolshevik Revolution. The Czar and Lenin seemed to him the same thing expressed in different terms, the same tyranny in different trappings, the same barrier in the path of Russian freedom. Against that barrier of bayonets, police, spies, gaolers and executioners he strove unceasingly. A hard fate, an inescapable destiny, a fearful doom ! All would have been spared him had he been born in Britain, in France, in the United States, in Scandinavia, in Switzerland. A hundred happy careers lay open. But born in Russia with such a mind and such a will, his life was a torment rising in crescendo to a death in torture. Amid these miseries, perils and crimes he displayed the wisdom of a statesman, the qualities of a commander, the courage of a hero, and the endurance of a martyr.

*   *   *   *   *

In his novel, *The Pale Horse*, written under an assumed name, Savinkov has described with brutal candour the part he played in the murders of M. de Plehve and the Grand Duke Serge. He depicts with an accuracy that cannot be doubted the methods, the daily life, the psychological state and the hair-raising adventures of a small group of men and women, of whom he was the leader, working together for half a year in mortal pursuit of a High Personage. From the moment when, posing as a British subject with a passport signed by Lord Lansdowne in his pocket and ' three kilograms of dynamite under the table ', he arrives in the town of N., till the murder of ' the Governor ' who is blown to pieces in the street, and the death, execution or suicide of three out of his four companions, all is laid bare. Most instructive of all is the account given by implication of the relations of the actual Terrorists with the Nihilist Central Committee who lay deep and secure in the underworld of the great cities of Europe and the United States.

'M. le Ministre,' he said to me, ' I know them well, Lenin

and Trotsky. For years we worked hand in hand for the liberation of Russia. Now they have enslaved her worse than ever.'

Between Savinkov's first forlorn war against the Czar and his second against Lenin there was a brief but remarkable interlude. The outbreak of the Great War struck Savinkov and his fellow revolutionary, Bourtzev, in exactly the same way. They saw in the cause of the Allies a movement towards freedom and democracy. Savinkov's heart beat in sympathy with the liberal nations of the West, and his ardent Russian patriotism, put to the test, sundered him from the cold Semitic internationalists with whom he had been so long associated. Even under the Czar, Bourtzev was invited back to Russia, and threw himself into the task of national defence. Savinkov returned with the Revolution. In June, 1917, he was appointed by Kerensky, then Minister for War, to the post of Political Commissar of the 7th Army on the Galician front. The troops were in mutiny. The death penalty had been abolished. German and Austrian agents had spread the poison of Bolshevism through the whole Command. Several regiments had murdered their officers. Discipline and organization were gone. Equipment and munitions had long been lacking. Meanwhile the enemy battered ceaselessly on the crumbling front.

Here was the opportunity for his qualities. No sincere revolutionary could impugn his blood-dyed credentials of Nihilism. No loyal officer could doubt his passion for victory. And when it came to political philosophy and the interminable arguments with which the Russians beguiled the road to ruin, there lived no more accomplished student or devastating critic of Karl Marx than the newly-appointed Commissar. Alone, though not unarmed, he visited regiments who had just killed their officers, and brought them back to their duty. On one occasion he is reported to have shot with his own hand the delegates from a Bolshevik Soldiers' Council who were seducing a hitherto loyal unit.

Meanwhile his organizing gifts amid a thousand difficulties repaired the administrative structure. In a month he had put a new heart into the discouraged Army Commander and his staff, and had so far redisciplined the Army as to enable it to take the offensive and win a notable action at Brzezany early in July.

Kerensky, becoming aware of Savinkov's good work, having himself seen evidence of it on a visit to the 7th Army front, appointed him forthwith Chief Commissar for the Army Group of the South Western front, then commanded by General Gutor. Savinkov had no sooner reached the scene than the front was broken by the Germans at Tarnopol (July 16–19, 1917). The military disaster was followed by wholesale desertions to the enemy, mutinies, massacres of officers and widespread revolt among the civil population. At the instance of Savinkov, Gutor was replaced on the 20th July by General Kornilov. We now approach one of the great mischances of Russian history. In Kornilov Savinkov believed that he had found the man who was to be the complement to his own character, a simple, obstinate soldier, popular among officers and men, with rigid views upon discipline, with no class prejudices, a sincere love of Russia and a knowledge of how to carry through schemes propounded by others. The time had come for a strong and ruthless hand, preferably corporate, if the Army was to be steadied and the country saved. Together with Kornilov, who in all Army matters shared his views, Savinkov demanded the reimposition of the death penalty for cowardice, desertion or espionage, both behind the line and among the fighting troops. Kerensky thus had at his disposal at this most fateful moment in Russian destinies both the political and the military man of action whom the crisis demanded ; and both these men were heart and soul together. Here already at the summit of power was the triumvirate that could even at the eleventh hour have saved Russia from the awful fate which impended, which could have gained at a stroke both Russian victory and Russian freedom. Those who united could have retrieved all were in the event destroyed separately.

* * * * *

Space does not allow me to unravel the melancholy tangle of ill luck and cunning devices by which Kornilov was separated from Kerensky, and Savinkov rendered powerless to prevent the breach. For a time all marched in the right direction. Kornilov became Commander-in-Chief of all the Russian Armies, and Savinkov Deputy Minister of War. Here with one hand upon the vain, doctrinaire, but none the less forceful and well-meaning head of the Government, and the other on the loyal bull-dog soldier, Savinkov seemed to be the appointed agent of Russian salvation. A little more time, a little more help, a little more confidence, a few more honest men, the blessing of Providence and a rather better telephone service—all would have been well! But the tides of chaos mounted swiftly, the German artillery thundered on the front, and the Bolshevik infection spread behind the lines. Profound and adroit intrigues divided the doubting Kerensky from the headstrong Kornilov. On September 9 the General claimed by a *coup d'état* dictatorial powers and was arrested at Kerensky's orders. Savinkov, although exonerated after an inquiry of all complicity in the attempt and placed in full command of Petrograd during the crisis, became the target of the extremist element and was driven to resign. Loyal to Kerensky, loyal to Kornilov, loyal above all to Russia, he lost the control of affairs at the very moment when his was the only hand that could have averted the impending ruin.

The Bolshevik revolution of October followed. Kerensky and his supine Government vanished from the scene. Savinkov, eluding his foes, joined General Alexiev on the Don and drew the sword against the new tyranny. This desperate and ultimately vain struggle occupied the rest of his life. He became the official representative of the Russian cause in Europe, first to Alexiev, then to Koltchak, and lastly to

Denikin.   Responsible for all the relations with the Allies
and with the not less important Baltic and Border States
which formed at that time the ' Sanitary Cordon ' of the
west, the ex-Nihilist displayed every capacity whether for
command or intrigue.   Finally, when in 1919 resistance on
the soil of Russia was beaten down and the new armies
raised in her defence shattered or destroyed, Savinkov on
Polish territory formed armies of his own.   This last feat
was little short of miraculous.   Without funds, staff or
equipment, with only his old friend Pilsudski as protector,
with an authority among the anti-Bolshevik Russians
always doubtful and disputed, he nevertheless had by
September, 1920, collected 30,000 officers and men and
formed them into two organized corps.   This last effort,
prodigious as it had been, was also doomed to failure.   The
consolidation of the Bolshevik power, the increasing inclination of the Great Powers to make arrangements with
the successful despotism, the pressure of events upon the
small Border States, the internal dissensions of his poverty-
stricken army, dissipated the last vestiges of strength.
Forced to quit Poland, Savinkov continued the fight from
Prague.   All hopes of invading Russia with an armed power
having vanished, he organized the widespread guerrilla of
the Green Guards—a sort of Robin Hood warfare—throughout broad areas of Soviet territory.   Gradually, with every
circumstance of ruthless terrorism and butchery, all resistance to the Bolsheviks in Russia was stamped out, and the
vast populations from the Pacific to Poland and from
Archangel to Afghanistan congealed into the long night of
another glacial period.

It was a little before the final failure that I saw him for
the last time.   Mr. Lloyd George sought information on
the Russian situation, and I was authorized to bring Savinkov to Chequers.*   We motored there together.   The scene
upon arrival must have been a novel experience for Savinkov.
It was Sunday.   The Prime Minister was entertaining

* The new country home of British Prime Ministers.

several leading Free Church divines, and was himself surrounded by a band of Welsh singers who had travelled from their native Principality to do him choral honours. For several hours they sang Welsh hymns in the most beautiful manner. Afterwards we had our talk. I recall only one of its episodes. The Prime Minister argued that revolutions like diseases run a regular course, that the worst was already over in Russia, that the Bolshevik leaders confronted with the responsibilities of actual government would quit their Communistic theories or that they would quarrel among themselves and fall like Robespierre and St. Just, that others weaker or more moderate would succeed them, and that by successive convulsions a more tolerable regime would be established.

' Mr. Prime Minister,' said Savinkov in his formal way, ' you will permit me the honour of observing that after the fall of the Roman Empire there ensued The Dark Ages.'

* * * * *

In the end the Bolshevik revenge was complete. After two years of subterranean negotiations they lured him back to Russia. Krassin was at one time the intermediary, but there were others. The trap was carefully baited. All resistance by arms, it was said, was now impossible. But within the Bolshevik Government itself the elements of sanity needed only the aid of such a man as Savinkov. The Government could be reconstructed not on a Bolshevik but on a Social-Revolutionary basis. Names and formulas might be kept for a time in order to mask a profound shifting of the balances. ' Why not help us to save ourselves ? ' whispered seductive voices. In June, 1924, Kamenev and Trotsky definitely invited him to return. The past would be condoned, a mock trial would be staged followed by an acquittal and high employment. ' Then we shall all be together as in the old days, and break the Communist tyranny as we have broken the Czar.' It seems incredible that with his knowledge of these men and of what he had done against them, Savinkov should have entered the trap. Perhaps it was this very knowledge that betrayed him. He thought he knew their mentality, and trusted to the perverted code of honour of conspirators. It is even possible that truth was mingled with falsehood in their snares. Anyhow they got him.

Physical torture was not applied. For their arch-enemy they had reserved more ingenious and refined cruelties. Later events have made us familiar with these, and their effect in extorting confessions. Tormented in his prison cell with false hopes and shifting promises, squeezed by the most subtle pressures, he was at length induced to write his notorious letter of recantation and to proclaim the Bolshevik Government as the liberator of the world. Thus shamed before history, branded by his friends as a Judas, he could feel each week the rigours of his confinement sensibly increasing ; and his final appeal to Djerjinski was answered only by mockery. Whether he was quietly shot in prison or committed suicide in his despair, is uncertain and unimportant. They had destroyed him body and soul. They had reduced his life's efforts to meaningless grimace, had made him insult his cause, and had fouled his memory for ever. Yet when all is said and done, and with all the stains and tarnishes there be, few men tried more, gave more, dared more and suffered more for the Russian people.

HERBERT
HENRY ASQUITH

Keystone View Company

HERBERT HENRY ASQUITH AFTER THE WAR

HERBERT HENRY ASQUITH

A SQUITH was a man who knew where he stood on every question of life and affairs in an altogether unusual degree. Scholarship, politics, philosophy, law, religion, were all spheres in which at the time when I knew him best he seemed to have arrived at definite opinions. On all, when the need required it, his mind opened and shut smoothly and exactly, like the breech of a gun. He always gave me the impression—perhaps natural for a younger man in a subordinate station—of measuring all the changing, baffling situations of public and Parliamentary life according to settled standards and sure convictions : and there was also the sense of a scorn, lightly and not always completely veiled, for arguments, for personalities and even for events which did not conform to the pattern he had with so much profound knowledge and reflection decidedly adopted.

In some respects this was a limitation. The world, nature, human beings do not move like machines. The edges are never clear-cut, but always frayed. Nature never draws a line without smudging it. Conditions are so variable, episodes so unexpected, experiences so conflicting, that flexibility of judgment and a willingness to assume a somewhat humbler attitude towards external phenomena may well play their part in the equipment of a modern Prime Minister. But Asquith's opinions in the prime of his life were cut in bronze. Vast knowledge, faithful industry, deep thought were imbedded in his nature ; and if, as was inevitable in the rough and tumble of life, he was forced to submit and bow to the opinions of others, to the force of events, to the passions of the hour, it was often with barely concealed repugnance and disdain. If one is to select his greatest characteristic, this massive finality stands forth, for good or ill, above and beyond all others.

He had the power to convey a remarkable proportion of the treasures of his intellect and the valour of his blood to the children of both his marriages. His second surviving son rose in the War from Sub-Lieutenant to Brigadier-General, gaining with repeated wounds amid the worst fighting the Distinguished Service Order with two clasps, and the Military Cross. To Raymond, his eldest son, the inheritance passed in extraordinary perfection. Everything seemed easy to Raymond. He repeated without apparent effort all his father's triumphs at Oxford. The son, like the father, was without question the finest scholar of his year and the most accomplished speaker in the University debates. Verse or prose; Greek, Latin or English; law, history or philosophy, came easily to Raymond as they had come thirty years before to Henry Asquith. The brilliant epigram, the pungent satire, the sharp and not always painless rejoinder, a certain courtly but rather formal manner, distinguished in youth the son, as they had his father before him. Address and charm in conversation, the nice taste in words, the ready pen and readier tongue, the unmistakable air of probity and independence, and the unconscious sense of superiority that sprang from these, belonged as of native right to both. And now we have seen in the third generation Raymond's son, the present Earl of Oxford and Asquith, pursuing at the university the same triumphant academic career.

It seemed quite easy for Raymond Asquith, when the time came, to face death and to die. When I saw him at the Front in November and December of 1915, he seemed to move through the cold, squalor and peril of the winter trenches as if he were above and immune from the common ills of the flesh, a being clad in polished armour, entirely undisturbed, presumably invulnerable. The War which found the measure of so many never got to the bottom of him, and when the Grenadiers strode into the crash and thunder of the Somme, he went to his fate cool, poised, resolute, matter-of-fact, debonair. And well we know that his father, then bearing the supreme burden of the State, would proudly have marched at his side.

The political activities of Henry Asquith's daughter, Lady Violet Bonham-Carter, are of course well-known. Her father —old, supplanted in power, his Party broken up, his authority flouted, even his long-faithful constituency estranged —found in his daughter a champion redoubtable even in the first rank of Party orators. The Liberal masses in the weakness and disarray of the Coalition period saw with enthusiasm a gleaming figure, capable of dealing with the gravest questions and the largest issues with passion, eloquence and mordant wit. In the two or three years when her father's need required it, she displayed force and talent equalled by no woman in British politics. One wildfire sentence from a speech in 1922 will suffice. Lloyd George's Government, accused of disturbing and warlike tendencies, had fallen. Bonar Law appealed for a mandate of ' Tranquillity.' ' We have to choose,' said the young lady to an immense audience, ' between one man suffering from St. Vitus's Dance and another from Sleeping Sickness.' It must have been the greatest of human joys for Henry Asquith in his dusk to find this wonderful being he had called into the world, armed, vigilant and active at his side. His children are his best memorial, and their lives recount and revive his qualities.

* * * * *

At the time when I knew him best he was at the height of his power. Great majorities supported him in Parliament and the country. Against him were ranged all the stolid Conservative forces of England. Conflict unceasing grew year by year to a more dangerous intensity at home, while abroad there gathered sullenly the hurricane that was to wreck our generation. Our days were spent in the furious party battles which arose upon Home Rule and the Veto of the House of Lords, whilst always upon the horizon deadly shapes grew or faded, and even while the sun shone there was a curious whisper in the air.

He was always very kind to me and thought well of my mental processes ; was obviously moved to agreement by many of the State papers which I wrote. A carefully-marshalled argument, cleanly printed, read by him at leisure, often won his approval and thereafter commanded his decisive support. His orderly, disciplined mind delighted in reason and design. It was always worth while spending many hours to state a case in the most concise and effective manner for the eye of the Prime Minister. In fact I believe I owed the repeated advancement to great offices which he accorded me, more to my secret writings on Government business than to any impressions produced by conversation or by speeches on the platform or in Parliament. One felt that the case was submitted to a high tribunal, and that repetition, verbiage, rhetoric, false argument, would be impassively but inexorably put aside.

In Cabinet he was markedly silent. Indeed he never spoke a word in Council if he could get his way without it. He sat, like the great Judge he was, hearing with trained patience the case deployed on every side, now and then interjecting a question or brief comment, searching or pregnant, which gave matters a turn towards the goal he wished to reach ; and when at the end, amid all the perplexities and cross-currents of ably and vehemently expressed opinion, he summed up, it was very rarely that the silence he had observed till then, did not fall on all.

He disliked talking ' shop ' out of business hours, and would never encourage or join in desultory conversation on public matters. Most of the great Parliamentarians I have known were always ready to talk politics and let their fancy play over the swiftly-moving scene—Balfour, Chamberlain, Morley, Lloyd George, threw themselves with zest into the discussion of current events. With Asquith, either the

Court was open or it was shut. If it was open, his whole attention was focussed on the case ; if it was shut, there was no use knocking at the door. This also may have been in some respects a limitation. Many things are learnt by those who live their whole lives with their main work ; and although it is a great gift at once to have an absorbing interest and to be able to throw it off in lighter hours, it seemed at times that Asquith threw it off too easily, too completely. He drew so strict a line between Work and Play that one might almost think work had ceased to attract him. The habit, formed in the life of a busy lawyer, persisted. The case was settled and put aside ; judgment was formed, was delivered, and did not require review. The next case would be called in its turn and at the proper hour. Of course he must have communed deeply with himself, but less I believe than most men at the summit of a nation's affairs. His mind was so alert, so lucid, so well stored, so thoroughly trained that once he had heard the whole matter thrashed out, the conclusion came with a snap ; and each conclusion, so far as lay with him, was final.

In affairs he had that ruthless side without which great matters cannot be handled. When offering me Cabinet office in his Government in 1908, he repeated to me Mr. Gladstone's saying : ' The first essential for a Prime Minister is to be a good butcher,' and he added ' there are several who must be pole-axed now.' They were. Loyal as he was to his colleagues, he never shrank, when the time came and public need required it, from putting them aside —once and for all. Personal friendship might survive if it would. Political association was finished. But how else can States be governed ?

His letters to colleagues were like his conduct of Government business. They were the counterpart of his speeches. Innately conservative and old-fashioned, he disliked and disdained telephones and typewriters. He who spoke so easily in public had never learnt to dictate. All must be penned by him. A handwriting at once beautiful and

Secret

8 Ap. 08

My dear Winston

With the King's
approval, I have the
great pleasure of offering you
the post of President of the
Board of Trade in the
new administration.

It is my intention to
seek the consent of Parliament
to placing the office on the
same level, as regards salary

of states, while retaining its present title, with the Secretaryships of State. But I am afraid that the change cannot come into effect during the current year.

I shall hail with much gratification your accession to the Cabinet, both on public & on personal grounds.

I return to England to-morrow

Yours always

H H Asquith

serviceable, rapid, correct and clear, the fewest possible words and no possibility of misunderstanding ; and if argument or epigram or humour found their place, it was because they slipped from the pen before they could be bridled. He wrote other letters in which no such compression was practised. They were addressed to brighter eyes than peer through politicians' spectacles.

When work was done, he played. He enjoyed life ardently ; he delighted in feminine society ; he was always interested to meet a new and charming personality. Women of every age were eager to be taken in to dinner by him. They were fascinated by his gaiety and wit, and by his evident interest in all their doings. He would play bridge for modest stakes for hours every evening, no matter what lightnings were flashing around the house or what ordeals the morrow would swiftly be thrusting upon him.

*   *   *   *   *

I saw him most intimately in the most agreeable circumstances. He and his wife and elder daughter were our guests on the Admiralty yacht for a month at a time in the three summers before the War. Blue skies and shining seas, the Mediterranean, the Adriatic, the Ægean ; Venice, Syracuse, Malta, Athens, the Dalmatian coast ; great fleets and dockyards ; the superb setting of the King's Navy ; serious work and a pleasure cruise filled these very happy breathing-spaces. In one whole month, with continuous agitation at home and growing apprehension abroad, he maintained towards me, who stood so near him in responsibility, a reserve on all serious matters which was unbreakable. Once and once only did he invite discussion. Important changes impended in the Government. He asked my opinion about men and offices, expressed agreement or difference in the most confiding manner. He weighed the persons concerned in nicely-balanced scales, then closed and locked the subject, put the invisible key in his pocket, and resumed a careful study of a treatise on the monuments and inscriptions of

Spalato before which the yacht had just dropped anchor. But some weeks later the appointments were made in the exact sense of the discussion.

For the rest, you would not have supposed he had a care in the world. He was the most painstaking tourist. He mastered Baedeker, examined the ladies upon it, explained and illuminated much, and evidently enjoyed every hour. He frequently set the whole party competing who could write down in five minutes the most Generals beginning with L, or Poets beginning with T, or Historians with some other initial. He had innumerable varieties of these games and always excelled in them. He talked a great deal to the Captain and the navigators about the ship and the course and the weather. His retort in Parliament, ' The Right Honourable Gentleman must wait and see,' was then current. There was a cartoon in *Punch* in which he was depicted asking the young officer on the bridge, ' Why is she pitching so much this morning ? ' To which the response was alleged to have been, ' Well, you see, sir, it is all a question of Weight and Sea.' Although only an apocryphal pun, this deserves to survive.

For the rest he basked in the sunshine and read Greek. He fashioned with deep thought impeccable verses in complicated metre, and recast in terser form classical inscriptions which displeased him. I could not help much in this. But I followed with attention the cipher telegrams which we received each day, and of course we were always on the new wireless of the Fleet.

One afternoon we drove along a lovely road near Cattaro —a harbour in those days of peculiar interest, not merely for its scenery. We suddenly met endless strings of mules and farm horses. We asked where they were going and what for ? We were told ' They are dispersing. The manœuvres are cancelled.' The Balkan and European crisis of 1913 was over !

*   *   *   *   *

I cannot deem Mr. Spender's agreeable, competent

biography * a complete or final memorial of one of the most important, solid, and square-cut figures of our time. The author's judicial habit of mind and sweet reasonableness (apart from preconceived opinions) are well known. The picture which he has drawn upon this extensive canvas is so subdued in tone and so stinted in colour that it does not revive the image or personality of a stern, ambitious, intellectually proud man fighting his way with all necessary ruthlessness through some of the most rugged and terrible years our history has known. The day will be awaited when some far more vigorous and vital representation of this great statesman, jurist, and tribune will be given to his fellow-countrymen. The course of Asquith's life was not all so smooth and cool, so easy and unruffled as Mr. Spender's pages suggest. He should have drawn the picture of Asquith and his times with stronger strokes, with higher lights and darker shadows. It would have accorded more with reality, and his hero would have lost nothing in the process. The two main episodes of Asquith's public career—the struggle with the House of Lords about Home Rule, and the declaration and the waging of the war upon Germany —comprise many important pros and cons which have been either omitted from the narrative or so much softened as to become unnoticeable.

In all great controversies much depends on where the tale begins. Mr. Asquith and the Liberal Party were sincerely faithful to the cause of Home Rule ; but it must not be forgotten that their dependence for office upon eighty Irish votes was the spur which alone extorted action, and that in 1906, when an independent Liberal majority was hoped for, Home Rule was rigidly excluded from the platform and the programme. It was this sinister influence of eighty Irish votes—now happily for ever withdrawn from the House of Commons—making and unmaking Governments, swaying the fortunes of both great British political

* *The Life of Lord Oxford and Asquith,* by J. A. Spender and Cyril Asquith. 1934.

parties, which poisoned nearly forty years of our public life. The unconstitutional resistance of Ulster will be judged by history in relation to the fact that the Ulster Protestants believed that the Home Rule Bills were driven forward not as a result of British convictions, but by the leverage of this Irish voting power. That the lawless demonstrations in Ulster were the parent of many grievous ills cannot be doubted ; but if Ulster had confined herself simply to constitutional agitation, it is extremely improbable that she would have escaped forcible inclusion in a Dublin Parliament.

These were hard facts. Mr. Asquith fought for the Irish cause and the Liberal Party in the years before the War with dignity and resolution ; but he could not himself have been unconscious that he fought for them upon a basis which was to some extent vitiated, first, by his dependence upon the Irish vote, and, secondly, by the refusal of his followers to extend the same measure of freedom to Ulster as they proffered to Southern Ireland. When this is remembered, it will be seen that his career as leader in this bitter campaign was not such an example of long-suffering injured innocence as Mr. Spender's pages would imply. There was hardihood and wrong-doing on both sides. The conflict with the House of Lords which ended in the passage of the Parliament Act cannot be judged apart from the Irish quarrel with which it was interwoven. I shall certainly not cease to accuse the intolerable partisanship by which the House of Lords broke the credit of the great Liberal majority returned in 1906. But matters would have never come to the pass they did, and brother Englishmen would never have been brought—in appearance at least—to the verge of civil war, but for the baleful, extraneous influence of the Irish feud. It was in this very rough battle, with all its fierce and unfair fighting on both sides, that Asquith held by force and art the foremost place.

The vigour of his conduct at the outbreak of the Great War is not usually realized. That Asquith meant to carry the British Empire unitedly into the war against German aggression not only upon Belgium *but also upon France* is undoubted. Never for one moment did he waver in his support of Sir Edward Grey, and no one had in the eight preceding years more consistently guarded that naval supremacy which ensured alike our safety and our power of intervention. As a war-leader he showed on several notable occasions capacity for calculated or violent action. To him alone I confided the intention of moving the Fleet to its war station on July 30. He looked at me with a hard stare and gave a sort of grunt. I did not require anything else. He overruled Lord Fisher's misgivings about the Dardanelles almost with a gesture. For nearly a month before the naval attempt to force the Straits on March 18, 1915, he did not call the Cabinet together. This was certainly not through forgetfulness. He meant to have the matter put to the proof. After the first repulse he was resolute to continue. Unhappily for himself and all others, he did not thrust to the full length of his convictions. When Lord Fisher resigned in May and the Opposition threatened controversial debate, Asquith did not hesitate to break his Cabinet up, demand the resignations of all Ministers, end the political lives of half his colleagues, throw Haldane to the wolves, leave me to bear the burden of the Dardanelles, and sail on victoriously at the head of a Coalition Government. Not ' all done by kindness ' ! Not all by rosewater ! These were the convulsive struggles of a man of action and of ambition at death-grips with events.

One would imagine from Mr. Spender's description of the break-up of the Coalition in December, 1916, that Mr. Asquith was a kind of Saint Sebastian standing unresisting with a beatific smile, pierced by the arrows of his persecutors. As a matter of fact, he defended his authority by every resource in his powerful arsenal. The Prime Minister's position of eminence and authority and the air of detachment arising therefrom enabled him to use the potent instrument of Time with frequent advantage in domestic affairs. Repeatedly he prevented the break-up of his Government or the resignation of important Ministers by refusing to allow a decision to be taken. ' What we have heard to-day leaves much food for thought ; let us all reflect before we meet again how we can bring ourselves together.' In times of Peace, dealing with frothy, superficial party and personal bickerings, this was often successful. War, untamable, remorseless, soon snapped this tackle. The phrase ' Wait and see,' which he had used in Peace, not indeed in a dilatory but in a minatory sense, reflected with injustice, but with just enough truth to be dangerous, upon his name and policy. Although he took every critical decision without hesitation at the moment when he judged it ripe, the agonized nation was not content. It demanded a frenzied energy at the summit ; an effort to compel events rather than to adjudicate wisely and deliberately upon them. ' The Generals and Admirals have given their expert advice, and on that evidence the following conclusions must be drawn '—not his words but his mode—proved a policy inadequate to the supreme convulsion. More was demanded. The impossible was demanded. Speedy victory was demanded, and the statesman was judged by the merciless test of results. The vehement, contriving, resourceful, nimble-leaping Lloyd George seemed to offer a brighter hope, or at any rate a more savage effort.

The fullest and most authoritative account of the fall of Asquith's Government is found in Lord Beaverbrook's revealing pages.* This is one of the most valuable historical documents of our day, and in the main its assertions remain unchallenged. Here we see Mr. Lloyd George advancing to his goal, now with smooth and dexterous artifice, now with headlong charge. We see Mr. Asquith at bay. A new light is thrown upon his conduct at this juncture. He was certainly not the helpless victim which his enemies have believed and his biographer has depicted. Misunderstanding

* *Politicians and the War*, 1914–1916, Vol. 2.

the account given to him by Mr. Bonar Law of the attitude of the Conservative Ministers, he committed a fatal blunder, and made a virtual accommodation with Mr. Lloyd George. Reassured the next morning that he had overwhelming Liberal and Conservative support in the Cabinet, he set out to try conclusions with him in good earnest. When he found himself weak, he temporized and retreated ; when he felt himself strong, he struck back with all his might ; and at the end, when he resolved to put his rival to the test, of forming a Government or being utterly discredited, he was at once adamant and jocular. He played the tremendous stake with iron composure. He bore defeat with fortitude and patriotism.

* * * * *

I shall never cease to wonder why Mr. Asquith, with a large Liberal majority at his back, did not in the crisis of the 1916 winter invoke the expedient of a Secret Session, and seek the succour of the House of Commons. There, is the final citadel of a Prime Minister in distress. No one can deny him his right in peace or war to appeal from the intrigues of Cabinets, caucuses, clubs, and newspapers to that great assembly, and take his dismissal only at their hands. Yet the Liberal Government which fell in 1915, the Asquith Coalition which fell in 1916, the Lloyd George Coalition which fell in 1922—all were overthrown by secret, obscure, internal processes of which the public only now know the main story. I am of opinion that in every one of these cases the result of confident resort to Parliament would have been the victory of the Prime Minister of the day.

It was not to be. Parliament listened bewildered to the muffled sounds of conflict proceeding behind closed doors, and dutifully acclaimed the victor who emerged. Thus did Lloyd George gain the truncheon of State. High Constable of the British Empire, he set out upon his march.

* * * * *

Mr. Asquith was probably one of the greatest peace-time

Prime Ministers we have ever had. His intellect, his sagacity, his broad outlook and civic courage maintained him at the highest eminence in public life. But in war he had not those qualities of resource and energy, of prevision and assiduous management, which ought to reside in the executive. Mr. Lloyd George had all the qualities which he lacked. The nation, by some instinctive, almost occult process, had found this out. Mr. Bonar Law was the instrument which put Mr. Asquith aside and set another in his stead. Asquith fell when the enormous task was but half completed. He fell with dignity. He bore adversity with composure. In or out of power, disinterested patriotism and inflexible integrity were his only guides. Let it never be forgotten that he was always on his country's side in all her perils, and that he never hesitated to sacrifice his personal or political interests to the national cause. In the Boer War, in the Great War, whether as Prime Minister or Leader of the Opposition, in the constitutional outrage of the General Strike—in every one of these great crises he stood firm and unflinching for King and Country. The glittering honours, his Earldom and his Garter, which the Sovereign conferred upon him in his closing years, were but the fitting recognition of his life's work, and the lustre and respect with which the whole nation lighted his evening path were a measure of the services he had rendered, and still more of the character he had borne.

LAWRENCE OF
ARABIA

The Daily Mirror

LAWRENCE OF ARABIA

LAWRENCE OF ARABIA*

I DID not meet Lawrence till after the War was over. It was the spring of 1919, when the Peace-makers, or at any rate the Treaty-makers, were gathered in Paris and all England was in the ferment of the aftermath. So great had been the pressure in the War, so vast its scale, so dominating the great battles in France, that I had only been dimly conscious of the part played in Allenby's campaigns by the Arab revolt in the desert. But now someone said to me: 'You ought to meet this wonderful young man. His exploits are an epic.' So Lawrence came to luncheon. Usually at this time in London or Paris he wore his Arab dress in order to identify himself with the interests of the Emir Feisal and with the Arabian claims then under harsh debate. On this occasion, however, he wore plain clothes, and looked at first sight like one of the many clean-cut young officers who had gained high rank and distinction in the struggle. We were men only and the conversation was general, but presently someone rather mischievously told the story of his behaviour at an Investiture·some weeks before.

The impression I received was that he had refused to accept the decorations which the King was about to confer on him at an official ceremony. I was Secretary of State for War, so I said at once that his conduct was most wrong, not fair to the King as a gentleman and grossly disrespectful

* Most of this essay has already been published in ' T. E. Lawrence, by his Friends, 1937,' and is also drawn from my address at the unveiling of his memorial at his Oxford school. It is reprinted here for the sake of completeness.—W. S. C.

to him as a sovereign. Any man might refuse a title or a decoration, any man might in refusing state the reasons of principle which led to his action, but to choose the occasion when His Majesty in pursuance of his constitutional duty was actually about to perform the gracious act of personally investing him, as the occasion for making a political demonstration, was monstrous. As he was my guest I could not say more, but in my official position I could not say less.

It is only recently that I have learned the true facts. The refusal did in fact take place, but not at the public ceremonial. The King received Lawrence on October 30 in order to have a talk with him. At the same time His Majesty thought it would be convenient to give him the Commandership of the Bath and the Distinguished Service Order to which he had already been gazetted. When the King was about to bestow the Insignia, Lawrence begged that he might be allowed to refuse them. The King and Lawrence were alone at the time.

Whether or not Lawrence saw I had misunderstood the incident, he made no effort to minimize it or to excuse himself. He accepted the rebuke with good humour. This was the only way in his power, he said, of rousing the highest authorities in the State to a realization of the fact that the honour of Great Britain was at stake in the faithful treatment of the Arabs and that their betrayal to the Syrian demands of France would be an indelible blot on our history. The King himself should be made aware of what was being done in his name, and he knew no other way. I said that this was no defence at all for the method adopted, and then turned the conversation into other and more agreeable channels.

But I must admit that this episode made me anxious to learn more about what had actually happened in the desert war, and opened my eyes to the passions which were seething in Arab bosoms. I called for reports and pondered them. I talked to the Prime Minister about it. He said that the

French meant to have Syria and rule it from Damascus, and that nothing would turn them from it. The Sykes-Picot agreement which we had made during the War had greatly confused the issue of principle, and only the Peace Conference could decide conflicting claims and pledges. This was unanswerable.

I did not see Lawrence again for some weeks. It was, if my memory serves me right, in Paris. He wore his Arab robes, and the full magnificence of his countenance revealed itself. The gravity of his demeanour; the precision of his opinions; the range and quality of his conversation; all seemed enhanced to a remarkable degree by the splendid Arab head-dress and garb. From amid the flowing draperies his noble features, his perfectly-chiselled lips and flashing eyes loaded with fire and comprehension shone forth. He looked what he was, one of Nature's greatest princes. We got on much better this time, and I began to form that impression of his strength and quality which since has never left me. Whether he wore the prosaic clothes of English daily life or afterwards in the uniform of an Air Force mechanic, I always saw him henceforward as he appears in Augustus John's brilliant pencil sketch.

I began to hear much more about him from friends who had fought under his command, and indeed there was endless talk about him in every circle, military, diplomatic and academic. It appeared that he was a savant as well as a soldier : an archæologist as well as a man of action : a brilliant scholar as well as an Arab partisan.

It soon became evident that his cause was not going well in Paris. He accompanied Feisal everywhere as friend and interpreter. Well did he interpret him. He scorned his English connections and all question of his own career compared to what he regarded as his duty to the Arabs. He clashed with the French. He faced Clemenceau in long and repeated controversies. Here was a foeman worthy of his steel. The old Tiger had a face as fierce as Lawrence's, an eye as unquailing and a will-power well matched. Clemenceau had a deep feeling for the East; he loved a paladin, admired Lawrence's exploits and recognized his genius. But the French sentiment about Syria was a hundred years old. The idea that France, bled white in the trenches of Flanders, should emerge from the Great War without her share of conquered territories was insupportable to him, and would never have been tolerated by his countrymen.

Everyone knows what followed. After long and bitter controversies both in Paris and in the East, the Peace Conference assigned the mandate for Syria to France. When the Arabs resisted this by force, the French troops threw the Emir Feisal out of Damascus after a fight in which some of the bravest of the Arab chiefs were killed. They settled down in the occupation of this splendid province, repressed the subsequent revolts with the utmost sternness, and rule there to this day by the aid of a very large army.*

I did not see Lawrence while all this was going on, and indeed when so many things were crashing in the post-War world the treatment of the Arabs did not seem exceptional. But when from time to time my mind turned to the subject I realized how intense his emotions must be. He simply did not know what to do. He turned this way and that in desperation, and in disgust of life. In his published writings he has declared that all personal ambition had died within him before he entered Damascus in triumph in the closing phase of the War. But I am sure that the ordeal of watching the helplessness of his Arab friends to whom he had pledged his word, and as he conceived it the word of Britain, maltreated in this manner, must have been the main cause which decided his eventual renunciation of all power in great affairs. His highly-wrought nature had been subjected to the most extraordinary strains during the War, but then his spirit had sustained it. Now it was the spirit that was injured.

In the spring of 1921 I was sent to the Colonial Office to take over our business in the Middle East and bring matters into some kind of order. At that time we had recently

* Written in 1935.

suppressed a most dangerous and bloody rebellion in Iraq, and upwards of forty thousand troops at a cost of thirty million pounds a year were required to preserve order. This could not go on. In Palestine the strife between the Arabs and the Jews threatened at any moment to take the form of actual violence. The Arab chieftains, driven out of Syria with many of their followers—all of them our late allies—lurked furious in the deserts beyond the Jordan. Egypt was in ferment. Thus the whole of the Middle East presented a most melancholy and alarming picture. I formed a new department of the Colonial Office to discharge these new responsibilities. Half a dozen very able men from the India Office and from those who had served in Iraq and Palestine during the war formed the nucleus. I resolved to add Lawrence to their number, if he could be persuaded. They all knew him well, and several had served with or under him in the field. When I broached this project to them, they were frankly aghast—' What ! wilt thou bridle the wild ass of the desert ? ' Such was the attitude, dictated by no small jealousy or undervaluing of Lawrence's qualities, but from a sincere conviction that in his mood and with his temperament he could never work at the routine of a public office.

However, I persisted. An important post was offered to Lawrence, and to the surprise of most people, though not altogether to mine, he accepted at once. This is not the place to enter upon the details of the tangled and thorny problems we had to settle. The barest outline will suffice. It was necessary to handle the matter on the spot. I therefore convened a conference at Cairo to which practically all the experts and authorities of the Middle East were summoned. Accompanied by Lawrence, Hubert Young, and Trenchard from the Air Ministry, I set out for Cairo. We stayed there and in Palestine for about a month. We submitted the following main proposals to the Cabinet. First, we would repair the injury done to the Arabs and to the House of the Sherifs of Mecca by placing the Emir Feisal upon the throne of Iraq as King, and by entrusting the Emir Abdulla with the government of Trans-Jordania. Secondly, we would remove practically all the troops from Iraq and entrust its defence to the Royal Air Force. Thirdly, we suggested an adjustment of the immediate difficulties between the Jews and Arabs in Palestine which would serve as a foundation for the future.

Tremendous opposition was aroused against the first two proposals. The French Government deeply resented the favour shown to the Emir Feisal, whom they regarded as a defeated rebel. The British War Office was shocked at the removal of the troops, and predicted carnage and ruin. I had, however, already noticed that when Trenchard undertook to do anything particular, he usually carried it through. Our proposals were accepted, but it required a year of most difficult and anxious administration to give effect to what had been so speedily decided.

Lawrence's term as a Civil Servant was a unique phase in his life. Everyone was astonished by his calm and tactful demeanour. His patience and readiness to work with others amazed those who knew him best. Tremendous confabulations must have taken place among these experts, and tension at times must have been extreme. But so far as I was concerned, I received always united advice from two or three of the very best men it has ever been my fortune to work with. It would not be just to assign the whole credit for the great success which the new policy secured to Lawrence alone. The wonder was that he was able to sink his personality, to bend his imperious will and pool his knowledge in the common stock. Here is one of the proofs of the greatness of his character and the versatility of his genius. He saw the hope of redeeming in a large measure the promises he had made to the Arab chiefs and of re-establishing a tolerable measure of peace in those wide regions. In that cause he was capable of becoming—I hazard the word—a humdrum official. The effort was not in vain. His purposes prevailed.

Towards the end of the year things began to go better. All our measures were implemented one by one. The Army left Iraq, the Air Force was installed in a loop of the Euphrates, Baghdad acclaimed Feisal as king, Abdulla settled down loyally and comfortably in Trans-Jordania. One day I said to Lawrence : ' What would you like to do when all this is smoothed out ? The greatest employments are open to you if you care to pursue your new career in the Colonial Service.' He smiled his bland, beaming, cryptic smile, and said : ' In a very few months my work here will be finished. The job is done, and it will last.'—' But what about you ? '—' All you will see of me is a small cloud of dust on the horizon.'

He kept his word. At that time he was, I believe, almost without resources. His salary was £1,200 a year, and governorships and great commands were then at my disposal. Nothing availed. As a last resort I sent him out to Trans-Jordania where sudden difficulties had arisen. He had plenary powers. He wielded them with his old vigour. He removed officers. He used force. He restored complete tranquillity. Everyone was delighted with the success of his mission, but nothing would persuade him to continue. It was with sadness that I saw ' the small cloud of dust ' vanishing on the horizon. It was several years before we met again. I dwell upon this part of his activities because in a letter recently published he assigns to it an importance greater than his deeds in war. But this is not true judgment.

The next episode was the writing, the printing, the binding and the publication of his book ' The Seven Pillars.' This is perhaps the point at which to deal with this treasure of English literature. As a narrative of war and adventure, as a portrayal of all that the Arabs mean to the world, it is unsurpassed. It ranks with the greatest books ever written in the English language. If Lawrence had never done anything except write this book as a mere work of the imagination his fame would last—to quote Macaulay's hackneyed phrase—' as long as the English language is spoken in any quarter of the globe.' ' The Pilgrim's Progress,' ' Robinson Crusoe,' ' Gulliver's Travels ' are dear to British homes. Here is a tale originally their equal in interest and charm. But it is fact, not fiction. The author was also the commander. Cæsar's Commentaries deal with larger numbers, but in Lawrence's story nothing that has ever happened in the sphere of war and empire is lacking. When most of the vast literature of the Great War has been sifted and superseded by the epitomes, commentaries and histories of future generations, when the complicated and infinitely costly operations of its ponderous armies are the concern only of the military student, when our struggles are viewed in a fading perspective and a truer proportion, Lawrence's tale of the revolt in the desert will gleam with immortal fire.

We heard that he was engaged upon this work and that a certain number of those whom he regarded as worthy of the honour were invited to subscribe £30 for a copy. I gladly did so. In the copy which eventually reached me he wrote at an interval of eleven years two inscriptions which I greatly value, though much has changed since then, and they went far beyond the truth at the time. He refused to allow me to pay for the book. I had deserved it, he said.

In principle the structure of the story is simple. The Turkish armies operating against Egypt depended upon the desert railway. This slender steel track ran through hundreds of miles of blistering desert. If it were permanently cut the Turkish armies must perish : the ruin of Turkey must follow, and with it the downfall of the mighty Teutonic power which hurled its hate from ten thousand cannons on the plains of Flanders. Here was the Achilles' heel, and it was upon this that this man in his twenties directed his audacious, desperate, romantic assaults. We read of them in numerous succession. Grim camel-rides through sun-scorched, blasted lands, where the extreme desolation of nature appals the traveller. With a motor-car or aeroplane we may now inspect these forbidding solitudes,

Winston Churchill
who made a happy
ending to this show.
1.12.26.   TES.

W.S.C.
And eleven years after we set our hands to making our honest
settlement, all our work still stands: the countries having
gone forward, our interests having been saved, and nobody
killed, either on our side or the other. To have planned
for eleven years is statesmanship. I ought to have given
you two copies of this work!

TES.

their endless sands, the hot savage wind-whipped rocks, the mountain gorges of a red-hot moon. Through these with infinite privation men on camels with shattering toil carried dynamite to destroy railway bridges and win the war, and, as we then hoped, free the world.

Here we see Lawrence the soldier. Not only the soldier but the statesman ; rousing the fierce peoples of the desert, penetrating the mysteries of their thought, leading them to the selected points of action and as often as not firing the mine himself. Detailed accounts are given of ferocious battles with thousands of men and little quarter fought under his command on these lava landscapes of hell. There are no mass-effects. All is intense, individual, sentient—and yet cast in conditions which seemed to forbid human existence. Through all, one mind, one soul, one will-power. An epic, a prodigy, a tale of torment, and in the heart of it—a Man.

*   *   *   *   *

The impression of the personality of Lawrence remains living and vivid upon the minds of his friends, and the sense of his loss is in no way dimmed among his countrymen. All feel the poorer that he has gone from us. In these days dangers and difficulties gather upon Britain and her Empire, and we are also conscious of a lack of outstanding figures with which to overcome them. Here was a man in whom there existed not only an immense capacity for service, but that touch of genius which everyone recognizes and no one can define. Alike in his great period of adventure and command or in these later years of self-suppression and self-imposed eclipse, he always reigned over those with whom he came in contact. They felt themselves in the presence of an extraordinary being. They felt that his latent reserves of force and will-power were beyond measurement. If he roused himself to action, who should say what crisis he could not surmount or quell ? If things were going very badly, how glad one would be to see him come round the corner.

Part of the secret of this stimulating ascendancy lay of course in his disdain for most of the prizes, the pleasures and comforts of life. The world naturally looks with some awe upon a man who appears unconcernedly indifferent to home, money, comfort, rank or even power and fame. The world feels, not without a certain apprehension, that here is someone outside its jurisdiction; someone before whom its allurements may be spread in vain; someone strangely enfranchised, untamed, untrammelled by convention, moving independently of the ordinary currents of human action; a being readily capable of violent revolt or supreme sacrifice, a man, solitary, austere, to whom existence is no more than a duty, yet a duty to be faithfully discharged. He was indeed a dweller upon the mountain tops where the air is cold, crisp and rarefied, and where the view on clear days commands all the Kingdoms of the world and the glory of them.

Lawrence was one of those beings whose pace of life was faster and more intense than the ordinary. Just as an aeroplane only flies by its speed and pressure against the air, so he flew best and easiest in the hurricane. He was not in complete harmony with the normal. The fury of the Great War raised the pitch of life to the Lawrence standard. The multitudes were swept forward till their pace was the same as his. In this heroic period he found himself in perfect relation both to men and events.

I have often wondered what would have happened to Lawrence if the Great War had continued for several more years. His fame was spreading fast and with the momentum of the fabulous throughout Asia. The earth trembled with the wrath of the warring nations. All the metals were molten. Everything was in motion. No one could say what was impossible. Lawrence might have realized Napoleon's young dream of conquering the East; he might have arrived at Constantinople in 1919 or 1920 with many of the tribes and races of Asia Minor and Arabia at his back. But the storm wind ceased as suddenly as it had arisen. The skies became clear ; the bells of Armistice rang out. Mankind returned with indescribable relief to its long-interrupted, fondly-cherished ordinary life, and Lawrence was left once more moving alone on a different plane and at a different speed.

When his literary masterpiece was written, lost and written again ; when every illustration had been profoundly considered and every incident of typography and paragraphing settled with meticulous care ; when Lawrence on his bicycle had carried the precious volumes to the few—the very few he deemed worthy to read them—happily he found another task to his hands which cheered and comforted his soul. He saw as clearly as anyone the vision of Air power and all that it would mean in traffic and war. He found in the life of an aircraftsman that balm of peace and equipoise which no great station or command could have bestowed upon him. He felt that in living the life of a private in the Royal Air Force he would dignify that honourable calling and help to attract all that is keenest in our youthful manhood to the sphere where it is most urgently needed. For this service and example, to which he devoted the last twelve years of his life, we owe him a separate debt. It was in itself a princely gift.

Lawrence had a full measure of the versatility of genius. He held one of those master keys which unlock the doors of many kinds of treasure-houses. He was a savant as well as a soldier. He was an archæologist as well as a man of action. He was an accomplished scholar as well as an Arab partisan. He was a mechanic as well as a philosopher. His background of sombre experience and reflection only seemed to set forth more brightly the charm and gaiety of his companionship, and the generous majesty of his nature. Those who knew him best miss him most ; but our country misses him most of all ; and misses him most of all now. For this is a time when the great problems upon which his thought and work had so long centred, problems of aerial defence, problems of our relations with the Arab peoples, fill an ever larger space in our affairs. For all his reiterated renunciations I always felt that he was a man who held himself ready for a new call. While Lawrence lived one always felt—I certainly felt it strongly—that some overpowering need would draw him from the modest path he chose to tread and set him once again in full action at the centre of memorable events.

It was not to be. The summons which reached him, and for which he was equally prepared, was of a different order. It came as he would have wished it, swift and sudden on the wings of Speed. He had reached the last leap in his gallant course through life.

> All is over! Fleet career,
>   Dash of greyhound slipping thongs,
> Flight of falcon, bound of deer,
> Mad hoof-thunder in our rear,
>   Cold air rushing up our lungs,
>   Din of many tongues.

King George the Fifth wrote to Lawrence's brother, ' His name will live in history.' That is true. It will live in English letters; it will live in the traditions of the Royal Air Force; it will live in the annals of war and in the legends of Arabia.

'F. E.' FIRST
EARL OF BIRKENHEAD

'F.E.'

'F. E.'

FIRST EARL OF BIRKENHEAD

A HUNDRED years ago, Thomas Smith was the best runner and the most redoubtable knuckle-fighter in the West Riding of Yorkshire. He earned his living as a miner. In those days the miners were a class apart. They were 'bound' to their employers by engagements whose terms recalled the serfdom of the Middle Ages; they lived, for the most part, in self-contained communities, lives of hard privation, and were regarded by more fortunate workers as little better than savages. It was a fierce world. According to routine the pit, its darkness, its thousand lurking dangers, and its warlike comradeships, swallowed up the son of a mining family.

But Thomas Smith resolved that his boy, for one, should have a different life. With great pains he had him educated, and the youth, seizing his opportunities, obtained a post as schoolmaster, first at Wakefield, and afterwards at Birkenhead. A devout and uncompromising Nonconformist of the harshest and narrowest school, this Thomas Smith had brought home as bride a strange, wild creature of swift, fierce moods and a will that matched his own. It is said she was of gipsy stock; she certainly possessed the dark but vivid beauty that sometimes goes with Romany blood. A curious match, but a happy one; nay, with remarkable consequences; for students of heredity may note that the grandchild of Thomas and Bathsheba Smith became Lord Chancellor of England. He was Frederick Edwin Smith, first Earl of Birkenhead.

Our country draws its strength from many sources. And in the last century and a half she has discovered fresh reserves of leadership in the men of the new middle classes, created by the expansion of enterprise and wealth which followed the Industrial Revolution. Without name or influence to help them, often with no money save what they won by their own efforts, these sons of merchants and manufacturers, of doctors, lawyers, and clergymen, of authors, teachers, and shopkeepers, have made their way to the front rank in public life and to the headship of almost every great business by native worth alone. Their contribution to government has been rich and varied. It is impossible, looking back, to imagine what we should have been without them. Blot them from the pages, and how much is left of the political history of the nineteenth and twentieth centuries·? Peel, Gladstone, and Disraeli; Bright, Cobden, and the Chamberlains; Asquith, Bonar Law, and Baldwin are all swept from the scene.

Frederick Edwin Smith was one of these types, though he sprang from a more rugged strain. His father, Thomas's son, as his filial biographer tells us in an agreeable and entertaining book,* left home hurriedly at the age of seventeen after an argument on the subject of Sunday skating. He joined the Army, served on the North-West Frontier, and was a sergeant-major at twenty-one. When he returned to England, he devoted himself for a time to the family business; then studied law and was called to the Bar. He entered politics, and seemed on the threshold of a distinguished legal and Parliamentary career when he died suddenly at the age of forty-three. This meant that Frederick Edwin had his own way to make in the world. He was sixteen.

An uncle was prepared to help him through Oxford, but only on condition that he won an open scholarship. He won it. After much pleasant idleness and whole-hearted enjoyment of university life, he found himself in debt and

* 'Frederick Edwin, Earl of Birkenhead.' Birkenhead.

with no prospect of extricating himself from his difficulties unless he took a First Class in Schools. He shut himself up in his lodgings, and for six months worked fourteen hours a day. He got his First Class, and next year became Vinerian Law Scholar and a Fellow of Merton College. He was called to the Bar in 1899. By 1904 he was earning £6,000 a year, and in 1908 he took silk. His Parliamentary repu-tation was by then already firmly established. He had become a national figure with his maiden speech.

That speech was a daring gamble. He knew it to be so. As he drove to Westminster with his wife on the evening that he expected to catch the Speaker's eye, he told her of his resolve to stake all upon this single throw, and that he had counted the cost of failure.

'If I fail,' he said, ' there will be nothing for me but to remain silent for three years until my disgrace is forgotten.'

'Must you risk so much?' she asked.

The speech was a triumph. I only heard the latter part. But I could feel from the moment I came in that the crowded House was listening to a new figure of the first rank. Tim Healy, the Irish Nationalist, a master of invective and one of the most brilliant debaters in the House, scribbled a note as the young member sat down amid a storm of cheering. It was passed along the benches. ' I am old, and you are young,' it said, ' but you have beaten me at my own game.'

I did not come to know him till he was thirty-four. An ardent Conservative, he was angry with me for leaving that party on the Protection issue. His own father had been in the 'eighties a keen admirer of Lord Randolph Churchill, and had taught him to embrace not only the conceptions of Tory Democracy, but to think kindly of one who had done much to make it a living force in modern politics. ' F. E.,' to use his famous soubriquet, felt a strong antag-onism to me for breaking a continuity. He did not wish to meet me. It was only after the Parliament of 1906 had run some months of its course that we were introduced to one another by a common friend as we stood at the bar of the House of Commons before an important division. But from that hour our friendship was perfect. It was one of my most precious possessions. It was never disturbed by the fiercest party fighting. It was never marred by the slightest personal difference or misunderstanding. It grew stronger as nearly a quarter of a century slipped by, and it lasted till his untimely death. The pleasure and instruction of his companionship were of the highest order. The world of affairs and the general public saw in F. E. Smith a robust, pugnacious personality, trampling his way across the battlefields of life, seizing its prizes as they fell, and exulting in his prowess. They saw his rollicking air. Acquaintances and opponents alike felt the sting of his taunts or retorts in the House of Commons and at the Bar. Many were prone to regard him as a mere demagogue whose wits had been sharpened upon the legal grindstone. It is a judgment which those who practise the popular arts before working-class audiences in times of faction are likely to incur. The qualities which lay behind were not understood by his fellow-countrymen till the last ten years of his life.

But his close friends, and certainly I, acclaimed him for what he was—a sincere patriot ; a wise, grave, sober-minded statesman ; a truly great jurist ; a scholar of high attainments ; and a gay, brilliant, loyal, lovable being. We made several considerable journeys together. We both served for many years in the Oxfordshire Hussars. We were repeatedly together at Blenheim. We met and talked on innumerable occasions : never did I separate from him without having learnt something, and enjoyed myself besides. He was always great fun ; but more than that he had a massive common sense and a sagacious comprehension which made his counsel invaluable, whether in public broil or private embarrassment. He had all the canine virtues in a remarkable degree—courage, fidelity, vigilance, love of the chase. He had reached settled and somewhat sombre conclusions upon a large number of questions, about which

many people are content to remain in placid suspense.
Man of the world; man of affairs; master of the law;
adept at the written or spoken word; athlete; sportsman;
book-lover—there were few topics in which he was not
interested, and whatever attracted him, he could expound
and embellish.

But with all his versatility, he was one of the most consistent men I ever knew. His political action through all
the convulsions of our time was of a piece. It lay upon the
same plane and advanced through the same processes of
thought to the same end. He was always one of those
Tories who united pride in the glories of England to an
earnest sympathy with the wage-earning masses and cottage
homes. He dwelt with pride upon his humble origin, he
exaggerated it, and boasted of it. He exulted in the free
and civilized society which opened the most spacious opportunities to talent, however poor in gear or favour. He was
never so rigid a party man as was inferred from the uncompromising vigour and partisanship of his pre-war speeches.
The idea of a national party or government always appealed
to him. Indeed it excited him. His unswerving friendship
and admiration for Mr. Lloyd George dated from our attempt
in 1910 to form a national coalition to settle the Irish and
constitutional issues then at stake, and to prepare against
the European perils then already visible to many eyes. His
mind was never really sealed against a Home Rule policy,
provided that the rights of Ulster were effectively defended.
The latter part of his life saw many things accomplished
with his assistance which his heart had desired, or at least
which his mind had never rejected.

Twenty-two years ago when the first coalition was formed,
and I began again to work with the Tories in everything
but Protection, we found ourselves colleagues first in war
and afterwards in peace. For nearly ten years we sat together in Cabinet; and I can hardly recall any question,
certainly none of first importance, upon which we were not
in hearty and natural agreement. Most of all did I deplore

his absence during those years when it seemed to me that the future of India was at stake. With his aid, I believe different and superior solutions might have been reached.

* * * * *

For all the purposes of discussion, argument, exposition, appeal or altercation, F. E. had a complete armoury. The bludgeon for the platform ; the rapier for a personal dispute ; the entangling net and unexpected trident for the Courts of Law ; and a jug of clear spring water for an anxious per-plexed conclave. Many examples are given by his son of his use of these various methods. There can scarcely ever have been a more sustained, merciless interchange than took place between him and Judge Willis in the Southwark County Court.

A boy who had been run over was suing a tramway com-pany for damages. F. E. appeared for the company. The case for the lad was that the accident had led to blindness. The judge, a kindly if somewhat garrulous soul, allowed sympathy to outrun discretion.

' Poor boy, poor boy ! ' he exclaimed. ' Blind ! Put him on a chair so that the jury can see him.'

This was weighting the scale of justice, and F. E. was moved to protest.

' Perhaps your honour would like to have the boy passed round the jury box,' he suggested.

' That is a most improper remark,' exclaimed the judge.

' It was provoked by a most improper suggestion,' was the startling reply.

Judge Willis tried to think of a decisive retort. At last it arrived.

' Mr. Smith, have you ever heard of a saying by Bacon—the great Bacon—that youth and discretion are ill-wedded companions ? '

' Yes, I have,' came the instant repartee. ' And have you ever heard of a saying of Bacon—the great Bacon—that a much-talking judge is like an ill-tuned cymbal ? '

' You are extremely offensive, young man,' exclaimed the judge.

' As a matter of fact,' said Smith, ' we both are ; but I am trying to be, and you can't help it.'

Such a dialogue would be held brilliant in a carefully-written play, but that these successive rejoinders, each one more smashing than the former, should have leapt into being upon the spur of the moment is astounding.

Scarcely less striking, perhaps, is the fact that Judge Willis went on giving openings for F. E.'s merciless wit.

' What do you suppose I am on the Bench for, Mr. Smith ? '

' It is not for me, your honour, to attempt to fathom the inscrutable workings of Providence.'

The same lightnings flashed from him on the public platform—and sometimes in homely guise. At one election meeting, a heckler was being rude to the candidate for whom F. E. had been speaking. He listened with growing impatience, and finally intervened to suggest that the man should remove his cap when putting a question.

' I'll take off my boots if you like,' came a raucous shout.

' Ah, I knew you'd come here to be unpleasant,' remarked F. E.

On another occasion, in the crowning period of his life, he was addressing a meeting in his old constituency. He said at one point : ' And now I shall tell you exactly what the Government has done for all of you.'

' Nothing ! ' shouted a woman in the gallery.

' My dear lady,' said Lord Birkenhead, ' the light in this hall is so dim as to prevent a clear sight of your undoubted charms, so that I am unable to say with certainty whether you are a virgin, a widow, or a matron, but in any case I will guarantee to prove that you are wrong. If you are a virgin flapper, we have given you the vote ; if you are a wife, we have increased employment and reduced the cost of living ; if you are a widow, we have given you a pension— and if you are none of these, but are foolish enough to be a tea drinker, we have reduced the tax on sugar.'

The spontaneity is the marvel. I should like to go on quoting such hammer-strokes. Many of them are preserved in the excellent ' Life ' which his son has written. F. E. was able, in any setting, as I can testify, to give an answer which turned the laugh, if it did not turn the company, against his assailant. People were afraid of him and of what he would say. Even I, who knew him so well, refrained from pushing ding-dong talk too far when others were present lest friendship should be endangered.

I cannot speak at first hand of his forensic success, for I only once heard him address a Court of Law. I did not think him so good in the House of Commons as upon the platform or at a public dinner. He was only a comparatively short time—ten or twelve years—in the House, and his character and style were formed upon other moulds. Still, no one can contest his many remarkable Parliamentary feats. He seemed to me more at home in the House of Lords, and more dominating upon that assembly than ever in the Lower Chamber. To hear him wind up a debate from the Woolsack, speaking for an hour at a time without a note, without a gesture, with hardly an alteration of tone, dealing with point after point, weaving them all into an ordered texture of argument, darting aside, now here, now there, upon some retaliatory foray, but returning always surely and easily to his main theme, and reaching his conclusion without the slightest appearance of effort ; all this constituted an impressive and enviable gift. For this gift he was grateful. He rejoiced in using it. ' I always feel best,' he said to me, ' when I am on the unpinioned wing.'

He was good upon the platform because he understood thoroughly the outlook, feelings and prejudices of the ordinary patriotic Tory man-in-the-street. This same quality helped him with a jury. He could strike with faultless accuracy the simple major keynotes to which the full-blooded English father or husband or eager youngster would respond ; and he spoke with the greatest sureness and freedom upon all the most delicate questions of life and morals, sportsmanship and fair play.

But most of all I liked to hear him in the Cabinet. He was a singularly silent member. He had acquired in the legal profession the habit of listening mute and motionless hour after hour, and he rarely spoke until his counsel was sought. Then his manner was so quiet, so reasonable, so matter-of-fact and sensible, that you could feel opinion being changed ; and promptly, as he warmed to his subject, there grew that glow of conviction and appeal, instinctive and priceless, which constitutes true eloquence. Often I have thought of Mr. Pitt's famous translation of some Latin epigram, which if he were here F. E. would tell me—' Eloquence is like the flame. It requires fuel to feed it, motion to excite it, and it brightens as it burns.' In my experience he and Mr. Lloyd George were both at their best in gatherings of ten or a dozen men, every one of whom was well informed upon the question at issue, and upon whom the effect of claptrap in any of its innumerable varieties would only be disastrous.

I have said he was remarkably consistent in opinion. He was more ; he was persistent. In every affair, public or personal, if he was with you on the Monday, you would find him the same on the Wednesday, and on the Friday when things looked blue, he would still be marching forward with strong reinforcements. The opposite type of comrade or ally is so very common that I single this out as a magnificent characteristic. He loved pleasure ; he was grateful for the gift of existence ; he loved every day of his life. But no one could work harder. From his youth he worked and played with might and main. He had a singular power of concentration, and five or six hours sustained thought upon a particular matter was always within his compass. He possessed what Napoleon praised, the mental power ' *de fixer les objets longtemps sans être fatigué.*' No doubt he presumed often in his legal work upon his great quickness in mastering a difficult field and getting to the roots. He was never entangled in the briars of detail. I remember after he had taken silk and was in the front rank at the Bar, how it was the fashion in the Liberal Government circles of those days to say that he had no real grasp of the fundamentals of the law. I lived to see him take his place among the great Lord Chancellors who have interpreted that marvellous structure of English good sense and right feeling.

His son tells us of his becoming a Privy Councillor at the Coronation in 1910. I think I had something to do with that. I knew Mr. Asquith thought highly of him, and liked his mind with refined professional appreciation. I urged his inclusion as a Privy Councillor in the non-party honours list. The author tells us of the curious reaction which this proposal when made by the Prime Minister produced upon Mr. Balfour, then leader of the Opposition. I do not think it was jealousy or fear of subsequent complications. Mr. Balfour had his long-built-up ideas about how patronage and promotion should be distributed among members of the party over which he and his uncle had reigned for a generation. At any rate he opposed it, and in order to carry the proposal it was found necessary to confer another Privy Councillorship upon Mr. Bonar Law. This probably turned the scale in favour of Mr. Bonar Law's leadership, and may traceably have altered the course of history. However, it is always being altered by something or other.

Looking back, I think that the post-war years of the Coalition must be regarded as the great period of F.E.'s life. And there was nothing in it that became him more than the part he played in the final settlement of the difficult and dangerous Irish controversy that had distorted English politics for over thirty years. The general public, and particularly that section of it which supported Conservative principles, still remembered him as ' Galloper Smith,' and one of the most bitter and able opponents of Home Rule in pre-war years. The efforts he had made to secure a solution of the Irish question on the basis of the exclusion of Ulster were either not known or had been forgotten. Since then, the Easter Rebellion had revealed the Irish Sinn Feiners as striking at the British Empire in extremity ; and after came assassination and terrorism.

F. E. felt that it was his duty to aid a final effort to end the long, deadly, and obsolete quarrel. He took a leading part in the negotiations with the Sinn Fein delegates. He was one of the signatories of the Irish Treaty.

' I may have signed my political death-warrant to-night,' he remarked, as he laid down his pen.

' I may have signed my actual death-warrant,' said Michael Collins.

The statesman and the generous, warm-hearted man were again revealed in Birkenhead's speech in the Upper Chamber on the Matrimonial Causes Bill. His son regards it as ' the finest speech of his life,' and others have expressed a similar judgment. Its sustained eloquence, depth of feeling and vigour of thought and argument recall the great days of Parliamentary oratory and the giants of debate.

' I, my Lords,' he said, ' can only express my amazement that men of saintly lives, men of affairs, men whose opinions and experience we respect, should have concentrated upon adultery as the one circumstance which ought to afford relief from the marriage tie. Adultery is a breach of the carnal obligations of marriage. Insistence upon the duties of continence and chastity is important ; it is vital to society. But I have always taken the view that that aspect of marriage was exaggerated and somewhat crudely exaggerated in the Marriage Service. I am concerned to-day to make this point by which I will stand or fall, that the moral and spiritual sides of marriage are incomparably more important than the physical side . . . If you think of all that marriage means to most of us—the memories of the world's adventure faced together in youth so heedlessly and yet so confidently, the tender comradeship, the sweet association of parenthood, how much more these count than the bond which nature in its ingenious telepathy has contrived to secure and render agreeable the perpetuation of the species.'

'What,' he asked, 'is the remedy open to a poor woman who, when she married, gave up the pitiful pursuit by which she had made her living until her marriage and, relying on the marriage, is left penniless, and is left for the whole of her life unable to identify her husband, unable to obtain the slightest relief from the law ? She is neither wife nor widow ; she has a cold hearthstone ; she has fatherless children for the rest of her life . . .

'We are told that such a woman as I have described is to remain chaste. I have only to observe that for two thousand years human nature has resisted in the warmth of youth these cold admonitions of the cloisters, and I do not believe that the Supreme Being has set a standard which two thousand years of Christian experience has shown that human nature in its exuberant prime cannot support.'

'Those who have spoken in opposition to the present proposal say with the best motives, but with malignant results : " We deny you any hope in this world. Though an honest man loves you, sin shall be the price of your union, and bastardy shall be the fate of your children." I cannot and do not believe that society, as it is at present constituted, will for long acquiesce in a conclusion so merciless.'

Thus he convinced the House of Lords. But the House of Commons, under organized pressures, had other views. To-day, after eighteen years, this question, with all its consequences to public morality and private happiness, has reached a solution on the lines he boldly traced.

*   *   *   *   *

F. E. was the only one of my contemporaries from conversation with whom I have derived the same pleasure and profit as I got from Balfour, Morley, Asquith, Rosebery and Lloyd George. One did feel after a talk with these men that things were simpler and easier, and that Britain would be strong enough to come through all her troubles. He has gone, and gone when sorely needed. His record remains. It is not in every aspect a model for all to copy. Whose is? He seemed to have a double dose of human nature. He burned all his candles at both ends. His physique and constitution seemed to be capable of supporting indefinitely every form of mental and physical exertion. When they broke the end was swift. Between the setting of the sun and night there was only the briefest twilight. It was better so. Prolonged ill-health and deprivation of all the activities upon which his life was built would have pressed very hard upon him.

It must surely be an inspiration to youth to learn in the career of the first Earl of Birkenhead, as from other figures in these pages, that there is no bar of class, privilege or riches in our island to prevent the full fruition of outstanding capacity.

Some men when they die after busy, toilsome, successful lives leave a great stock of scrip and securities, of acres or factories or the goodwill of large undertakings. F. E. banked his treasure in the hearts of his friends, and they will cherish his memory till their time is come.

MARSHAL FOCH

À M. Winston Churchill
en souvenir de la grande guerre

F. Foch
28.10.19.

MARSHAL FOCH

A SINGULAR degree of integrity and harmony pervades the life of Marshal Foch. The drama of the conflict between France and Germany has fascinated the attention of the whole world, and ruined the prosperity of a large part of it. The life of Marshal Foch lay in the centre of this drama. He felt its passions and its pangs perhaps more intensely than any other human being; and he wielded the supreme executive power in its climax and decision. He was just old enough to serve as a volunteer lieutenant in the Franco-German War of 1870 ; but he was employed with troops so young and raw that they were never exposed to the fire of the enemy. He saw, he suffered, he comprehended. He could do nothing. The ardent youth in whose veins flowed Gascon and warrior blood, whose keen intelligence revealed the high issues, whose well-nerved sensitiveness responded to every touch, was forced to be the helpless witness of his country's downfall. He was fitted in an extraordinary degree to feel alike her agony and his own impotence.

But he was also fitted to nourish within himself those deep and in some respects mystic forces which were the resultants of his pain. Fortified by a simple, practical but intense religious conviction, animated by natural love of his country and focused by the highest forms of professional military intellectualism, Foch from the year 1870 onward embodied within the brain and frame of a mortal the spirit which the French call ' La Revanche ' and which is ill-translated by the word Revenge. Ill-translated, because in this revenge there was no zest of spite or cruelty, no greed of material gains or personal splendours, no desire however deeply concealed to humiliate or maltreat the German enemy —only a life-long wish and aim and toil to see the France which had been levelled in the dust of 1870 some day restored to her honourable seat. He began his career a little cub brushed aside by the triumphant march of the German armies to Paris and victory ; he lived to see all the might of valiant Germany prostrate and suppliant at his pencil tip. In the weakest position he endured the worst with his country ; at the summit of power he directed its absolute triumph.

Let us first dwell upon the most lovable traits of this remarkable and, it may well be argued, predestined being. His personal charm and deft address made its persistent appeal to all with whom he came in contact. His fidelity to his country, whatever its government or form of government and to his religion, no matter what obstacle it imposed upon his military career, constituted for him an abiding element of strength. His undaunted and ever-flowing combative energy, as a man in contact with other personalities and harrying remorseless detail, as a Commander with a front crumbling under the German flail, was proved inexhaustible even by the Great War. His power of cold endurance was the equal of his energy. He preserved a strict respect for the Constitution of his country, and for the position of the Ministerial Chiefs of a system which was certainly not his. He nourished an understanding, impartial and detached we must admit, of the feelings of the allied armies and countries gathered under his command, and lastly a chivalry—all a soldier's—to the ancient and terrible foe beneath whose heel he had writhed and over whose head he was in turn to triumph. When, after the hard terms of the Armistice had been accepted by the Germans, prudent and vigilant civilian counsel urged the immediate disarmament of the German fighting troops, Foch exclaimed—' They have fought well, let them keep their weapons.'

*   *   *   *   *

It is too soon altogether to measure the military stature

of Foch. We are too near to the event, and the event was so utterly different from all previous experience of war. The conditions under which the highest command was exercised in Armageddon bore no relation to those under which Alexander, Hannibal, Caesar, Gustavus of Sweden, Marlborough and Napoleon proved their fortunes. All the pressures and all the strains were present in this modern age, they were in fact so protracted as to become obscured, but they did not approach the intense epitome of action which was achieved in the great battles of the past. Compared with Cannae, Blenheim or Austerlitz, the vast world-battle of 1918 is a slow-motion picture. We sit in calm, airy, silent rooms opening upon sunlit and embowered lawns, not a sound except of summer and of husbandry disturbs the peace ; but seven million men, any ten thousand of whom could have annihilated the ancient armies, are in ceaseless battle from the Alps to the Ocean. And this does not last for an hour, or for two or three hours ; it lasts nearly a year. Evidently the tests are of a different kind ; it is certainly too soon to say that they are of a higher order.

I had made the acquaintance of Foch at manœuvres before the war ; and during the struggle I came in contact with him on three occasions which illustrated not inaptly his chequered fortunes. The first was in 1917 when, though myself out of office, I made a considerable tour of the French front upon the courteous invitation of M. Painlevé. This was for Foch a period of eclipse. The reaction and re-crimination which followed the awful slaughters of the Somme and its disappointment had been finally fatal to Joffre, and Foch as his fighting lieutenant had followed him into disfavour. The brilliant part he had played in the battles on the Marne and the Yser in 1914 had been overlaid by the ghastly losses sustained by the French army in his obstinate and ill-starred offensive in Artois in the spring of 1915. France shuddered at her dwindling manhood, and turned to other leaders and new methods. Foch was assigned a high advisory post in Paris, and it was here in a modest office near the Invalides that he received me. Certainly no one ever appeared less downcast or conscious of being at a discount. He discussed with the utmost frankness and vigour the whole scene of the war, and particularly those Eastern spheres in which I had been so much interested. His postures, his captivating manner, his vigorous and often pantomimic gestures—comical, if they had not been fully expressive— the energy of his ideas when his interest was aroused, made a vivid impression upon me. He was fighting all the time, whether he had armies to launch or only thoughts.

I have elsewhere described my second meeting with him. It was at Beauvais on April 3, 1918. Now he was Commander-in-Chief of all the Allied armies. The disaster of March 21 and the bitter wisdom of the Doullens Conference had forced Haig to propose and Pétain, the French Commander-in-Chief, to accept, his over-lordship. He had succeeded to a fearsome inheritance. A wide gap had been torn in the Allied front; the British Fifth Army was broken and largely destroyed; the French relief had not yet arrived; only a thin and ragged line of dismounted cavalry, of improvised detachments from the schools of instruction and of exhausted survivors from the disaster, stood between the German advance and Amiens with its almost vital railway lines. Farther to the south in the French zone Montdidier had just fallen. Foch, with a handful of Staff Officers, his ' military family,' and with an authority none too clearly defined, had to demand further sacrifices from the British and draw from Pétain northwards the reserves which that General always thought should be kept to cover the capital. Certainly a terrible hour. I can see him now, as for the benefit of Clemenceau and me, he described the situation and explained with map and pencil, like a schoolmaster teaching a class with a blackboard, the reasons for his confidence. He showed how each succeeding day the wave of invasion was smaller and how the tremendous initial impulse was dying away. Calm he certainly was not. He was vehement, passionate, persuasive, but clairvoyant and, above all, indomitable.

I did not see him again until the early autumn when the German offensive had been decisively mastered, when the tide had finally turned, when all was well and would undoubtedly be better. Now he was at the summit of power. His word was law. French, British, American and Belgian armies conformed with dutiful precision to the directions of a victorious leader, and the German line rolled ever backward before them.

But how grim was the ordeal he had passed through between April and September! He had had to put a strain upon the British Army during the prolonged crisis of the Battle of the North which the British High Command deemed unfair, and which certainly was hazardous in the last degree. When confronted with the fierce demands of war-hardened Generals for a reasonable measure of French assistance, he had uttered a series of his characteristic phrases—'Cramponnez partout' (Cling on everywhere), 'Jamais la relève pendant la bataille' (No relief for tired troops during the battle). As to his own contribution—'On fait ce qu'on peut' (One does what one can). This was scanty fare for the British Army, 'Back to the wall,' being battered to pieces by vastly superior German forces. He doled his reinforcements with a grudging hand. He drew every ounce of life energy out of Haig's struggling army. That army, cruelly tried, did not fail. It won, but only by an inch. By the most horrible sacrifices and exertions it held its own. In consequence, the awful question of choosing between the Channel Ports, and keeping the union of the British and French armies did not arise, and Foch's boast 'I will give up neither' (Ni l'un, ni l'autre) was in fact made good by British blood. He rode a gallant horse nearly to death; nearly, but not quite. It lived, and that particular race was won. And who can ever say he was wrong? On the contrary, although we suffered so frightfully, we must now proclaim that he was right. But the tension at the time between the British Command and the Generalissimo was extreme. After the Battle of the North had died down a bitter sediment remained. The French, it was thought in the highest circles of the British Army and Government, were using the unified command to throw a disproportionate strain upon their chief ally. Terrible thought, arising from knowledge, from intense suffering and cold experience!

While the British Chiefs were in this mood an even worse blow had fallen. The French centre was surprised at the Chemin des Dames on May 27, and an enormous incursion of the enemy followed. Four or five British divisions, all of which had lost more than half their numbers in the northern battle, had been asked for by Foch to fill a quiet sector of the French front where they could rest and recuperate. These mutilated, tortured units found themselves in the brunt of the new onslaught and were almost destroyed. The disaster of May 25, while it aggravated the stresses between the British High Command and Foch, woefully undermined his prestige in Paris. There always remained on his moral flank Pétain, a skilful, frigid, scientific soldier with the whole of the wonderful machine of the French staff at his disposal. It was known that Pétain's views differed on important points from those of Foch.

The six-weeks period from the first of June to the middle of July, 1918, must be recorded as the climax of Foch's ordeal. So far he had nothing to show but a first-class French disaster and a deep British sensation of ill-usage. His claim to enduring military greatness must be founded largely upon his conduct in this test. He could never have survived if behind him there had not been a being of a different order, of equal courage and of even greater personal force. Clemenceau, the faithful and dreaded Tiger, prowled the French capital and guarded from all subversion the authority of the commanding Chief. It was in this situation, depressed, precarious, disputed, half undermined, that Marshal Foch, faced by the new German offensive of July 12, did not hesitate to overrule Pétain, to withdraw the reserves which stood between Paris and the enemy, and hurl them under Mangin at the German flank. This decision, judged in its circumstances and in its results, must ever be regarded as one of the greatest deeds of war and examples of fortitude of soul which history has recorded.

But all this was over now. The Allies were united, the enemy were beaten, Foch was supreme and victory certain. I find myself at his chateau on a lovely autumn afternoon trying to win his enthusiasm for a vast tank programme for the campaign of 1919 with a grave, quiet and courteous gentleman who knew he had nothing before him but measureless success and immortal fame.

I had another meeting with him. It was in the War Office, in 1920, after the war was over. The allies were holding the line of the Rhine and occupying the Rhineland. The British army, now reduced to small dimensions, sat in Cologne. The French, for reasons which I cannot fathom, and which may have been connected with some design for an autonomy of the Rhineland, wished to garrison Cologne themselves, and move the British to a less important sector of the front. They sent Foch to suggest this change tentatively in the first instance to me. The illustrious marshal unfolded his case with some hesitation. He confined himself to considerations of military convenience ; but as he proceeded I became to some extent aware of what lay behind, and I found myself hostile. The idea of the British headquarters on the Rhine being shifted from the famous city of Cologne, after the part we had played in getting there, did not seem at all right to me. So I said when the case was fully deployed, ' Don't you think you could let us all come home ? '

I remember noticing how the shade fell in successive veils over the Marshal's noble, expressive and always kindly countenance. Not another word was ever said upon the subject. Our conversation continued agreeably. This was the last time I saw him.

＊　　＊　　＊　　＊　　＊

The magnitude of the events which Marshal Foch directed is of course beyond compare in the annals of war. But it will be found, I believe, as time passes, that the valour of his spirit and the shrewd sagacity of his judgment were of the highest order. Fortune lighted his crest. His peculiar gift of obstinate combativeness which had gained his laurels at the Marne and the Yser, when the only hope was not to despair, led him to serious disasters in the offensive battles of Artois and the Somme. In 1914 he had saved the day by refusing to recognize defeat. In 1915 and in 1916 he broke his teeth upon the Impossible. But 1918 was created for him. In the first phase of the Ludendorff offensive no one knew so well as he how to use every ounce of strength to defend every inch of ground, and so to hoard reserves. In the second phase, when the initiative passed to the Allies, they had for the first time in the war not only the superior numbers, but the cannon, the shells, the tanks and the aeroplanes—in short the apparatus indispensable for a successful advance. Then it was that the characteristic genius of Foch attained its full and decisive expression, and with cries of ' *Allez à la bataille,*' ' *Tout le monde à la bataille,*' he heaved the mighty wave of allied armies, French, British, American and Belgian, forward in vast, united, irresistible attack.

LEON TROTSKY,
ALIAS BRONSTEIN

Keystone View Company

LEON TROTSKY

LEON TROTSKY, *ALIAS* BRONSTEIN

WHEN the usurper and tyrant is reduced to literary controversy, when the Communist instead of bombs produces effusions for the capitalist Press, when the refugee War Lord fights his battles over again, and the discharged executioner becomes chatty and garrulous at his fireside, we may rejoice in the signs that better days are come. I have before me an article that Leon Trotsky *alias* Bronstein has recently contributed to *John o' London's Weekly* in which he deals with my descriptions of Lenin, with the Allied Intervention in Russia, with Lord Birkenhead and other suggestive topics. He has written this article from his exile in Turkey while supplicating England, France and Germany to admit him to the civilizations it has been —and still is—the object of his life to destroy. Russia— his own Red Russia—the Russia he had framed and fashioned to his heart's desire regardless of suffering to others or hazard to himself—has cast him out. All his scheming, all his daring, all his writing, all his harangues, all his atrocities, all his achievements, have led only to this—that another ' comrade,' his subordinate in revolutionary rank, his inferior in wit, though not perhaps in crime, rules in his stead, while he, the once triumphant Trotsky whose frown meted death to thousands, sits disconsolate—a skin of malice stranded for a time on the shores of the Black Sea and now washed up in the Gulf of Mexico.

But he must have been a difficult man to please. He did not like the Czar, so he murdered him and his family. He did not like the Imperial Government, so he blew it up.

He did not like the Liberalism of Guchkov and Miliukov, so he overthrew them. He could not endure the Social Revolutionary moderation of Kerensky and Savinkov, so he seized their places. And when at last the Communist regime for which he had striven with might and main was established throughout the whole of Russia, when the Dictatorship of the Proletariat was supreme, when the New Order of Society had passed from visions into reality, when the hateful culture and traditions of the individualist period had been eradicated, when the Secret Police had become the servants of the Third International, when in a word his Utopia had been achieved, he was still discontented. He still fumed, growled, snarled, bit and plotted. He had raised the poor against the rich. He had raised the penniless against the poor. He had raised the criminal against the penniless. All had fallen out as he had willed. But nevertheless the vices of human society required, it seemed, new scourgings. In the deepest depth he sought with desperate energy for a deeper. But —poor wretch—he had reached rock-bottom. Nothing lower than the Communist criminal class could be found. In vain he turned his gaze upon the wild beasts. The apes could not appreciate his eloquence. He could not mobilize the wolves, whose numbers had so notably increased during his administration. So the criminals he had installed stood together, and put him outside.

Hence these chatty newspaper articles. Hence these ululations from the Bosphorus. Hence these entreaties to be allowed to visit the British Museum and study its documents, or to drink the waters of Malvern for his rheumatism, or of Nauheim for his heart, or of Homburg for his gout, or of some other place for some other complaint. Hence these broodings in Turkish shades pierced by the searching eye of Mustafa Kemal. Hence these exits from France, from Scandinavia. Hence this last refuge in Mexico.

It is astonishing that a man of Trotsky's intelligence should not be able to understand the well-marked dislike of civilized governments for the leading exponents of Communism. He writes as if it were due to mere narrow-minded prejudice against new ideas and rival political theories. But Communism is not only a creed. It is a plan of campaign. A Communist is not only the holder of certain opinions ; he is the pledged adept of a well-thought-out means of enforcing them. The anatomy of discontent and revolution has been studied in every phase and aspect, and a veritable drill book prepared in a scientific spirit for subverting all existing institutions. The method of enforcement is as much a part of the Communist faith as the doctrine itself. At first the time-honoured principles of Liberalism and Democracy are invoked to shelter the infant organism. Free speech, the right of public meeting, every form of lawful political agitation and constitutional right are paraded and asserted. Alliance is sought with every popular movement towards the left.

The creation of a mild Liberal or Socialist regime in some period of convulsion is the first milestone. But no sooner has this been created than it is to be overthrown. Woes and scarcity resulting from confusion must be exploited. Collisions, if possible attended with bloodshed, are to be arranged between the agents of the New Government and the working people. Martyrs are to be manufactured. An apologetic attitude in the rulers should be turned to profit. Pacific propaganda may be made the mask of hatreds never before manifested among men. No faith need be, indeed may be, kept with non-communists. Every act of goodwill, of tolerance, of conciliation, of mercy, of magnanimity on the part of Governments or Statesmen is to be utilized for their ruin. Then when the time is ripe and the moment opportune, every form of lethal violence from mob revolt to private assassination must be used without stint or compunction. The citadel will be stormed under the banners of Liberty and Democracy ; and once the apparatus of power is in the hands of the Brotherhood, all opposition, all contrary opinions must be extinguished by death. Democracy is but a tool to be used and afterwards broken ; Liberty but a sentimental folly unworthy of the logician. The absolute rule of a self-chosen priesthood according to the dogmas it has learned by rote is to be imposed upon mankind without mitigation progressively for ever. All this, set out in prosy text-books, written also in blood in the history of several powerful nations, is the Communist's faith and purpose. To be forewarned should be to be forearmed !

I wrote this passage nearly seven years ago : but is it not an exact account of the Communist plot which has plunged Spain into the present hideous welter against the desires of the overwhelming majority of Spaniards on both sides ?

It is probable that Trotsky never comprehended the Marxian creed : but of its drill-book he was the incomparable master. He possessed in his nature all the qualities requisite for the art of civic destruction—the organizing command of a Carnot, the cold detached intelligence of a Machiavelli, the mob oratory of a Cleon, the ferocity of Jack the Ripper, the toughness of Titus Oates. No trace of compassion, no sense of human kinship, no apprehension of the spiritual, weakened his high and tireless capacity for action. Like the cancer bacillus he grew, he fed, he tortured, he slew in fulfilment of his nature. He found a wife who shared the Communist faith. She worked and plotted at his side. She shared his first exile to Siberia in the days of the Czar. She bore him children. She aided his escape. He deserted her. He found another kindred mind in a girl of good family who had been expelled from a school at Kharkov for persuading the pupils to refuse to attend prayers and to read Communist literature instead of the Bible. By her he had another family. As one of his biographers (Max Eastman) puts it : ' If you have a perfectly legal mind, she is not Trotsky's wife, for Trotsky never divorced Alexandra Ivovna Sokolovski, who still uses the name of Bronstein.' Of his mother he writes in cold and chilling terms. His father—old Bronstein—died of typhus in 1920 at the age of 83. The triumphs of his son brought no comfort to this honest hard-working and believing Jew. Persecuted by the Reds because he was a bourgeois ; by the Whites because he was Trotsky's father, and deserted by his son, he was left to sink or swim in the Russian deluge, and swam on steadfastly to the end. What else was there for him to do ?

Yet in Trotsky, in this being so removed from the ordinary affections and sentiments of human nature, so uplifted, shall we say, above the common herd, so superbly fitted to his task, there was an element of weakness especially serious from the Communist point of view. Trotsky was ambitious, and ambitious in quite a common worldly way. All the collectivism in the world could not rid him of an egoism which amounted to a disease, and to a fatal disease. He must not only ruin the State, he must rule the ruins thereafter. Every system of government of which he was not the head or almost the head was odious to him. The Dictatorship of the Proletariat to him meant that he was to be obeyed without question. He was to do the dictating on behalf of the proletariat. ' The toiling masses,' the ' Councils of Workmen, Peasants and Soldiers,' the gospel and revelation of Karl Marx, the Federal Union of Socialist Soviet Republics, etc., to him were all spelt in one word : Trotsky. This led to trouble. Comrades became jealous. They became suspicious. At the head of the Russian Army which he reconstructed amid indescribable difficulties and perils, Trotsky stood very near the vacant Throne of the Romanovs.

The Communist formulas he had used with devastating effect upon others, were now no impediment to him. He discarded them as readily as he had discarded his wife, or his father, or his name. The Army must be remade ; victory must be won ; and Trotsky must do it and Trotsky profit from it. To what other purpose should revolutions be made ? He used his exceptional prowess to the full.

The officers and soldiers of the new model army were fed, clothed and treated better than anyone else in Russia. Officers of the old Czarist regime were wheedled back in thousands. ' To the devil with politics—let us save Russia.' The salute was reintroduced. The badges of rank and privilege were restored. The authority of commanders was re-established. The higher command found themselves treated by this Communist upstart with a deference they had never experienced from the Ministers of the Czar. The abandonment by the Allies of the Russian Loyalist cause crowned these measures with a victory easy but complete. In 1922 so great was the appreciation among the military for Trotsky's personal attitude and system that he might well have been made Dictator of Russia by the armed forces, but for one fatal obstacle.

He was a Jew. He was still a Jew. Nothing could get over that. Hard fortune when you have deserted your family, repudiated your race, spat upon the religion of your fathers, and lapped Jew and Gentile in a common malignity, to be baulked of so great a prize for so narrow-minded a reason ! Such intolerance, such pettiness, such bigotry were hard indeed to bear. And this disaster carried in its train a greater. In the wake of disappointment loomed catastrophe.

For meanwhile the comrades had not been idle. They too had heard the talk of the officers. They too saw the possibilities of a Russian army reconstituted from its old elements. While Lenin lived the danger seemed remote. Lenin indeed regarded Trotsky as his political heir. He sought to protect him. But in 1924 Lenin died : and Trotsky, still busy with his army, still enjoying the day-to-day work of administering his department, still hailed with the acclamations which had last resounded for Nicholas II, turned to find a hard and toughly-wrought opposition organized against him.

Stalin the Georgian was a kind of General Secretary to the governing instrument. He managed the caucus and manipulated the innumerable committees. He gathered the wires together with patience and pulled them in accordance with a clearly-perceived design. When Trotsky advanced hopefully, confidently indeed, to accept the succession to Lenin, the party machine was found to be working in a different direction. In the purely political arena of Communist activities Trotsky was speedily outmanœuvred. He was accused on the strength of some of his voluminous writings of ' Anti-Leninism.' He does not seem to have understood that Lenin had replaced God in the Communist mind. He remained for some time under the impression that any such desirable substitution had been effected by Trotsky. He admitted his heresy and eagerly explained to the soldiers and workers the very cogent reasons which had led him to it. His declarations were received with blank dismay. The Ogpu was set in motion. Officers known to be under an obligation to Trotsky were removed from their appointments. After a period of silent tension he was advised to take a holiday. This holiday after some interruptions still continues.

Stalin used his success to build a greater. The Politbureau, without the spell of Lenin, or the force of Trotsky, was in its turn purged of its remaining elements of strength. The politicians who had made the Revolution were dismissed and chastened and reduced to impotence by the party manager. The caucus swallowed the Cabinet, and with Stalin at its head became the present Government of Russia. Trotsky was marooned by the very mutineers he had led so hardily to seize the ship.

What will be his place in history ? For all its horrors, a glittering light plays over the scenes and actors of the French Revolution. The careers and personalities of Robespierre, of Danton, even of Marat, gleam luridly across a century. But the dull, squalid figures of the Russian Bolsheviks are not redeemed in interest even by the magnitude of their crimes. All form and emphasis is lost in a vast process of Asiatic liquefaction. Even the slaughter of millions and the misery of scores of millions will not attract future generations to their uncouth lineaments and outlandish names. And now most of them have paid the penalty of their crimes. They have emerged from the prison-cells of the Cheka, to make their strange unnatural confessions to the world. They have met the death in secret to which they had consigned so many better and braver men.

But Trotsky survives. He lingers on the stage. He has forgotten his efforts, which Lenin restrained, to continue the War against Germany rather than submit to the conditions of Brest-Litovsk. He has forgotten his own career as a War Lord and the opportunist remaker of the Russian Army. In misfortune he has returned to Bolshevik Orthodoxy. Once again he has become the exponent of the purest sect of Communism. Around his name gather the new extremists and doctrinaires of world-revolution. Upon him is turned the full blast of Soviet malignity. The same vile propaganda which he used with so much ruthlessness upon the old regime, is now concentrated upon himself by his sole-surviving former comrade. All Russia from Poland to China, from the North Pole to the Himalayas, is taught to regard him as the supreme miscreant seeking in some way or other to add new chains to the workers, and bring the Nazi invader into their midst. The name of Lenin, the doctrine of Karl Marx, are invoked against him at the moment when he frantically endeavours to exploit them. Russia is regaining strength as the virulence of communism abates in her blood. The process may be cruel, but it is not morbid. It is a need of self-preservation which impels the Soviet Government to extrude Trotsky and his fresh-distilled poisons. In vain he screams his protests against a hurricane of lies ; in vain he denounces the bureaucratic tyranny of which he would so blithely be the head ; in vain he strives to rally the underworld of Europe to the overthrow of the Russian Army he was once proud to animate. Russia has done with him, and done with him forever.

He will perhaps have leisure to contemplate his handiwork. No one could wish him a better punishment than that his life should be prolonged, and that his keen intelligence and restless spirit should corrode each other in impotence and stultification. Indeed we may foresee a day when his theories, exploded by their application, will have ceased even to be irritating to the active, hopeful world outside, and when the wide tolerance which follows from a sense of security, will allow him to creep back, discredited and extinct, to the European and American haunts, where so many of his early years were spent. It may be that in these future years, he will find as little comfort in the work which he has done, as his father found in the son he had begotten.

ALFONSO XIII

ALFONSO XIII

Keystone View Company

ALFONSO XIII

TO be born a king; never to have been anything else
but a king; to have reigned for forty-six years, and
then to be dethroned! To begin life again in middle age
under novel and contracted conditions with a status and
in a state of mind never before experienced, barred from
the one calling to which a lifetime has been devoted!
Surely a harsh destiny! To have given his best, to have
faced every peril and anxiety, to have accomplished great
things, to have presided over his country during all the
perils of the twentieth century; to have seen it grow in
prosperity and reputation; and then to be violently rejected
by the nation of which he was so proud, of whose tradition
and history he was the embodiment; the nation he had
sought to represent in all the finest actions of his life—
surely this was enough to try the soul of mortal man.

The vicissitudes of politicians bear no relation to such a
trial. Politicians rise by toils and struggles; they expect
to fall; they hope to rise again. Nearly always, in or out
of office, they are surrounded and sustained by great parties.
They have many companions in misfortune. Their work
with all its interest and variety continues. Politicians know
they are but the creatures of the day. They hold no golden
casket enshrining the treasure of centuries to be shattered
irretrievably in their hands. They are ready to take the
rough with the smooth along the path of life they have
chosen for themselves. Yet even politicians suffer some
pangs. Mr. Birrell, wit and sage, was thrown out of office
in 1916 by the events of the Dublin rebellion, and later in
the same year his chief, Mr. Asquith, fell beneath the pres-

sures of the Great War. Said Birrell, as he contemplated this latter event, ' It must be very painful to him. Even I, who only fell off a donkey (i.e. the Irish Chief Secretary-ship), did not like it at all ; but Asquith has fallen off an elephant in the face of the whole British Empire.' But to be a king and then to be deposed—that is an experience incomparably more poignant.

Alfonso XIII was a posthumous child. His cradle was a throne. For a while during his mother's regency phila-telists delighted in Spanish stamps which bore the image of a baby. Later came the cherubic lineaments of a child, later still the profile of a youth, and finally the head of a man. A severe upbringing : governesses, tutors and a queen-mother drilled him in the kingly profession. The education of princes is very exacting. Scholastic, religi-ous and military discipline converge to grip the boy. Teachers, bishops and generals stand over every hour and every path of the youthful life. All inculcate the sense of majesty ; all emphasize the idea of duty ; all ingeminate decorum. Real kings have a unique point of view. Not even the most eminent of their subjects has the same association with the life of the whole people. Lifted far above party and faction, they personify the spirit of the State. But that anyone so reared and trained, so surfeited with honour, should grow to be a practical, genial man of the world, with a noble air, but without a scrap of conceit or humbug, proves that he was endowed at birth with an attractive nature.

A delicate princeling brought up without the roughening of public-school training, Alfonso steeled his character and his physique by a life in the open air. His childhood of conscious regality would have spoiled most children ; but he sought to be a swimmer, a horseman and a climber. He first practised mountaineering by climbing up the side of the palace at Miramar. Alert, wiry, and keyed to con-stant alacrity, his mind and his body corresponded to each other. He has never been soft or luxurious ; his pleasures have been those of a man, and his bearing always the bearing of a king. His devotion to polo certainly changed the Spanish cavalry officer. It is difficult to imagine the Spanish army without his eager and courageous leadership.

Alfonso had scarcely reached manhood when a teacher called Danger added his lessons to the royal curriculum. In the dark underworld of Spanish politics there are many secret societies to which the bomb and the pistol present themselves with a hideous melodramatic attraction. Everyone remembers the tragedy that marred and nearly obliterated the royal wedding day. The long, splendid procession, the joyous crowds ; in their coach of state the young king and the beautiful English princess who had become his bride, the dark furtive figure peering from the upper window, the small packet of monstrous power, the shattering explosion, the street a shambles, scores of men and women writhing in their blood, or smitten into death ; the consternation and panic around the grisly scene ; the king, calm and cold as steel, helping his bride to descend from the shattered vehicle, hiding from her eyes the awful spectacle around ; the bright scarlet uniforms of the detachment of the 16th Lancers sent from England in her honour as they thrust themselves forward to be of aid— the whole scene is stamped on the memory of the generation in which it occurred,

But that was not to be the end of the day. The head of the procession had already reached the palace. What had happened to delay the king and queen ? Presently the truth was known ; and soon after, the royal couple arrived, stained with blood but uninjured, and proceeded inflexibly with the appointed ceremonial. It was not enough to appear at the palace windows to reassure the anxious crowd. The king must take an open motor-car and drive out unguarded and almost alone among the multitude of his subjects, to receive their tributes of loyalty and thankfulness that he had been delivered from an appalling peril.

This was the spirit which was to animate his bearing in all times of danger.

I first had the honour of meeting him when I visited Madrid in the spring of 1914. He invited me to luncheon, and afterwards he talked with great freedom and intimacy in a small room near by. I had come to Madrid to play polo, and in this way we met several times. One day he asked me to go for a drive with him in his motor-car, and we made a long excursion towards the Escorial. Here the conversation turned on the anxious state of Europe. Presently the king said, abruptly :

' Mr. Churchill, do you believe in the European War ? '

I replied, ' Sir, sometimes I do ; sometimes I don't.'

' That is exactly how I feel,' he said. We discussed the various possibilities with which the future seemed loaded. His deep regard for England was evident in everything he said. Although nearly twenty years had passed since I had accompanied the Spanish forces in Cuba, he presented me with the war medal for that campaign before I left Madrid.

No one could be surprised that Spain preserved a strict neutrality in the great struggle of Armageddon. The historical barriers between Spain and the Allied and Associated Powers were not to be surmounted. The deepest bitter memory of the Spaniard is the Napoleonic invasion and the agony of the Peninsular War. Even after a hundred years there could be no unity of sentiment between France and Spain. Gibraltar, though a faded cause of irritation, still plays a part in Spanish thought. But the real hatred was for the United States, and the final loss of the last remnants of the Spanish colonial empire left an aching void in the breasts of a proud race. The aristocracy were pro-German, the middle classes anti-French. As the king said, ' Only I and the mob are for the Allies.' The best that could be hoped for was that Spain should be neutral in the struggle ; and certainly she prospered by her abstention from it.

The king told me of the other attempts upon his life.

One in particular I remember. He was riding back from a parade when an assassin suddenly sprang in front of his horse and presented a revolver at barely a yard's distance. 'Polo comes in very handy,' said the king, 'on these occasions. I set my horse's head straight at him and rode into him as he fired.' Thus he escaped. In all there were five actual attempts and many abortive plots. The acquaintance I made with him in 1914 has been renewed on his many visits to England, and always he has made me feel a sense of his vigilant care for the interest of his country, and his earnest desire for the material welfare and progress of its people. The autograph of King Alfonso is a truly remarkable symbol. Experts in handwriting profess to find in it deep resources of firmness and design; it certainly possesses style. Yet few sovereigns can ever have been less pompous. The gloomy, solemn etiquette of the Spanish court has in its late master produced a modern, democratic man of the world, moving easily and naturally in every kind of society. To separate the king from the man, and public functions from the pleasures of private life, was always Alfonso's wish and habit. It has been observed that this prince, the head of all the grandees in Spain, was himself most often photographed in polo kit, flannels or unconventional garb. The man and the scene were rich in contrasts.

Nothing could rob the king of his natural gaiety and high spirits. The long years of ceremonial, the cares of state, the perils which beset him, have left untouched that fountain of almost boyish merriment and jollity. When I met him on one of his recent visits to London he had come straight from almost the gravest political crisis of his reign. He spoke of this with simple modesty and a kind of imperturbable selflessness. But what seemed to fill his mind was the St. George's by-election then at its height. The placards on the houses and motor-cars; the political excitement of his many friends in Mayfair; the exertions of the Press lords: the society canvassers and orators of both sexes—all the hubbub and chatter aroused his genuine interest. It seemed great fun, and a game in which he would like to participate. He enjoyed prowling about incognito and seeing and hearing for himself.

His conversation, grave or gay, is pervaded by a natural charm and lighted by a twinkling eye. King or no king, no one could wish for a more agreeable companion, and sure I am that his popularity in the United States, were he to pay them a visit, would be immediate and lasting. He has a great liking for England and English ways, and this would translate itself very readily into an appreciation of American life and society. Certainly no figure could be less tragic, more seemingly care-free than the astute statesman, harassed monarch and hunted man. There recurred to my memory, as I watched him, the officers home on leave from the trenches of Flanders, happy in the family circle, dancing joyously at ball or cabaret, laughing at the comedies of the music halls, without apparently a trace upon them of the toils and perils from which they had come but yesterday, and to which they would return to-morrow.

The troubles which led to the fall of the Monarchy in Spain came slowly to a head. Their origin lay in the breakdown of the parliamentary system through its lack of contact with realities and with the public will. Parties artificially disciplined and divided produced a long succession of weak governments containing few, if any, statesmen capable of bearing a real responsibility or wielding power adequate to the occasion. The long, desultory warfare in Morocco—the legacy of centuries—gnawed away at Spanish contentment like an ulcer, with stabbing pains of disaster from time to time. There was not among Spanish politicians that strict convention, which is a bond of honour in all parties in Great Britain, to shield the Crown from all unpopularity or blame. Cabinets and ministers fell like houses of cards, and gladly left the king to bear their burdens. He did so without demur. Meanwhile, the war with the Moors dawdled on and the public grievance grew. It grew even in spite of the riches and prosperity which neutrality in the great struggle had brought to Spain. The obstinate, strong and intractable forces of the Church and Army, and the almost independent institution of the artillery corps, confronted Alfonso with another series of problems of the most perplexing character, which acted and were reacted upon by the sterile confusion of the parliamentary machine.

Only very great patience, skill, and knowledge of the Spanish character and of the factors at work, enabled him to tread his way through the kind of situation which Mr. Bernard Shaw has illuminated for modern eyes in the witty scenes and dialogue of *The Apple Cart*. Our Fabian dramatist and philosopher has rendered a service to monarchy which never perhaps could have been rendered from any other quarter. With his unsparing derision he has held up before the Socialists of every land the weaknesses, the meannesses, the vanities and the follies of the trumpery figures who float upwards and are borne forward upon the swirls and eddies of so-called democratic politics. The sympathies of the modern world, including many of its advanced thinkers, are powerfully attracted by the gay and sparkling presentation of a king, ill-used, let-down, manipulated for personal and party ends, yet sure of his value to the mass of his subjects, and striving not unsuccessfully to preserve their permanent interests, and to discharge his duty.

How does Alfonso XIII stand as a king, and how does he stand as a man ? These are the questions which we must ask when a reign of thirty years of conscious power has come to its close. The end was bitter. Almost friendless, almost alone in the old palace of Madrid, surrounded by hostile multitudes, King Alfonso knew he had to go. An epoch had closed. Are we to judge him as a despotic statesman, or as a limited constitutional sovereign ? Was he in fact for nearly thirty years the real ruler of one of the oldest branches of the European family of nations ? Or was he merely an engaging polo-playing sportsman, who happened to be a king, wore his royal dignities with easy grace, and looked for ministers, parliamentary or extra-parliamentary, to carry him pleasantly forward from year to year? Did he think for Spain, or did he think for himself; or did he merely enjoy the pleasures of life without thinking too much about anything at all? Did he govern or reign? Are we dealing with the annals of a nation or with the biography of an individual?

History alone can give decisive answers to these questions. But I shall not shrink from pronouncing now that Alfonso XIII was a cool, determined politician who used continuously and in full the whole influence of his kingly office to control the policies and fortunes of his country. He deemed himself superior, not alone in rank, but in capacity and experience, to the ministers he employed. He felt himself to be the one strong, unmoving pivot around which the life of Spain revolved. His sole object was the strength and fame of his realm. Alfonso could not conceive the dawn of a day when he would cease to be in his own person identified with Spain. He took at every stage all the necessary and possible steps that were within his ken to secure and preserve his control of the destiny of his country, and used his powers and discharged this trust with much worldly wisdom and with dauntless courage. It is therefore as a statesman and as a ruler, and not as a constitutional monarch acting usually upon the advice of ministers, that he would wish to be judged, and that history will judge him. He need not shrink from the trial. He has, as he has said, a good conscience.

The municipal elections were a revelation to the king. All his life he had been pursued by conspirators and assassins; but all his life he had freely trusted himself to the good will of his people. He had never hesitated to mingle in crowds or to travel alone, unguarded, where he listed. He had found many friends in every walk of life and always, when recognized, ovations and respect. He therefore felt sure that he had behind him the steady loyalty of the nation;

and having laboured continually and faithfully in its service, he felt he had deserved its affection. A lightning flash lit up the darkened scene. He saw around him on every side widespread, inveterate and, it seemed, almost universal hostility, and especially, hostility personal to himself. He gave vent to one of those arresting utterances, wrung from him in this memorable period, which show the force and quality of his comprehension of life, ' I feel as if I had gone to call upon an old friend and found that he was dead.' It was indeed a withering episode. Explain it as you will —the hard times all over the world, the political incapacity of the monarchist party, the drift of the times, the propaganda of Moscow—it was without disguise a gesture of repulsion from the Spanish nation, piercing to the heart.

Everyone has been struck by the contrast between the fierce, sullen aversion of the Spaniards for their king and his remarkable popularity at the moment of his fall among the democracies of France and England. At home all scowls, abroad all cheers. Sovereigns accused of despotism and driven from their thrones have been wont to receive asylum in foreign lands ; but never before have they been welcomed in Paris and London with widespread, spontaneous demonstrations of regard and approval. How shall we explain it ? The Spaniards, to whom democratic institutions carry with them the hope of some great new advance and amelioration, regarded Alfonso as an obstacle to their progress. The British and French democracies, who already enjoy all these advantages, know more about it. They regarded the king as a sportsman ; the Spaniards knew him as a ruler. The articulate forces in France, Britain and, we doubt not, in the United States, were more attracted by the character and personality of King Alfonso than by the character and personality of the Spanish people. They were surprised that the nation had not liked such a sovereign. The Spanish people had a view of their own ; and that is the view that must prevail. Alfonso would not wish it otherwise himself.

Men and kings must be judged in the testing moments of their lives. Courage is rightly esteemed the first of human qualities, because, as has been said, it is the quality which guarantees all others. Courage, physical and moral, King Alfonso has proved on every occasion of personal danger or political stress. Many years ago in the face of a difficult situation Alfonso made the proud declaration, no easy boast in Spain, ' I was born on the throne, I shall die on it.' That this was an intense self-prompted resolve and rule of conduct cannot be doubted. He has been forced to abandon it, and to-day in his prime he is an exile. But it should not be supposed that this decision, the most painful of his life, was taken only at the last moment, or under immediate duress. For more than a year before he had let it be known that as king he would not oppose the settled will of the Spanish people, constitutionally expressed, upon the question of republic or monarchy. After all, would any modern king wish to reign over a people who did not want him ? If the General Election throughout Spain by a large majority had produced a strongly republican Cortes, it was understood on all sides that a Constituent Assembly would have come into being. Then in the most formal manner the king would have laid down his powers and placed himself at the disposal of the government desired by his former subjects.

It was not to be. The actual crisis came suddenly, unexpectedly, upon a false issue, as the result of mere municipal elections into which the fundamental questions ought never to have entered—elections, moreover, at which the forces favourable to the monarchy had made no preparation for effectual political action. Even so there was a large monarchical majority ; but no one waited for the final result. The crisis came attended by every circumstance of violence and affront. By his bearing throughout this odious ordeal, King Alfonso proved that he rated the welfare of his country far above his personal sentiments or pride, and even more above his interests. The issue was unfair, the procedure injurious. The means of armed resistance were not lacking; but the king felt that the cause had become too particular to himself to justify the shedding of Spanish blood by Spanish hands. He was himself the first to raise in the palace the cry of ' Long live Spain ! ' He has since achieved another remarkable pronouncement : ' I hope I shall not go back ; for that will only mean that the Spanish people are not prosperous and happy.' Such declarations provide us with the means of judging the spirit of his reign. He made mistakes, he made perhaps as many mistakes as the royal or parliamentary rulers of other great countries ; he was as unsuccessful as most of these have been in satisfying the vague urges of this modern age. But we see that the spirit which has animated him through all these long years of difficulty has been one of faithful service to his country, and that he has been governed always by love and respect for his people.

*   *   *   *   *

And what lay beyond ? What has Spain achieved in the meantime ? How many Generals who deserted their Sovereign lived to face the firing squads of the Republic ? How many of the ' advanced politicians ' and high-browed writers, who hounded down the Monarchy are now exiles and fugitives from their native land ? How many great Spanish newspapers, whose leading articles proclaimed the dawn of freedom, are now ruined or gagged. How many of the unthinking crowds who cheered the new dispensation are now in the graves of untimely and violent death, or mourn in cold privation the slaughter of their dear ones ? Nor is the end of the Spanish torment in sight. The Spaniards are tearing each other to pieces. There seems to be no reason why they should stop, and every day less likelihood that anyone will try to stop them. Many scores of thousands of men and women of every class, rank, and calling have fallen—not in the bold ranks of battle, but by murderous execution or primordial butchery in the streets and fields of the peninsula. But it is all going on, and with added fury month by month. Hatreds and blood feuds multiply ceaselessly. Each part of the nation feels that it can only live by the extermination of the other. And whoever wins may wreak a vengeance and impose a subjugation on the conquered which in its turn would breed a new pestilence.

When all this has run its course, when the tally of human misery and infernal crime has been cast up, may there not be many Spaniards who will wonder whether after all a limited monarchy and a Parliamentary Constitution mutually protecting each other were not worth some patient trouble to preserve or to restore. May they not soon regard the reign of Alfonso XIII as a happy age—now gone, if not forever, at least for a generation ? Should that mood come, then the work done by the King and the peace he kept at home amid difficulties now obvious to the world will win a more just judgment than has yet been accorded.

DOUGLAS HAIG

In memory of the Great War.
Douglas Haig

DOUGLAS HAIG

EARLY in 1919 Lord Haig walked ashore at Dover after the total defeat of Germany and disappeared into private life. There was an interlude of pageantry, of martial celebrations, of the Freedom of Cities, of banquets and the like; but in fact the Commander-in-Chief of the British Armies in France passed, as he left the gangway and set foot on the pier, from a position of almost supreme responsibility and glorious power to the ordinary life of a country gentleman. Titles, grants, honours of every kind, all the symbols of public gratitude were showered upon him; but he was given no work. He did not join in the counsels of the nation; he was not invited to reorganize its army; he was not consulted upon the Treaties; no sphere of public activity was opened to him.

It would be affectation to pretend that he did not feel this. He was fifty-eight—an age at which Marlborough still had four great campaigns to fight; he was in the fullest enjoyment of his gifts and faculties; he had been accustomed all his life to work from morning till night; he was full of energy and experience, and apparently at the moment when he was most successful, there was nothing for him to do; he was not wanted any more. He must just go home and sit by the fire and fight his battles over again. He became one of the permanent unemployed.

So he looked around from his small house at Bemersyde beyond the Border and saw that a great many of his soldiers and brother officers were in the same plight so far as work was concerned, and that in addition many were stricken with wounds, and many more were hard put to it to keep their homes together. To their cause and fortunes then he devoted himself. They accepted him as their Leader in the disappointments of Peace as in the bitter trials of War. He acquired great influence over this immense and powerful body of men. Alike by example and guidance he led them away from all courses prejudicial or dangerous to the State, and did his best to improve their material conditions. He collected money on their behalf, he gave personal attention to grievous cases, he trapesed about the Empire weaving the soldiers of so many distant lands into the comradeship of a victorious army. Thus he occupied himself, and the world went on its way ; and politicians dealt with all the interesting topics as they arose, and settled matters generally—or thought they did ; and everybody seemed quite satisfied.

But we must understand that the great masses of ordinary work-a-day people, when in their busy lives they had time to think about things, wondered why it was that the Commander whose name was linked with hard-won but unlimited victory had no place in the hierarchy of the State. However, they did not know what to do about it, and he said nothing : he just went on with his work for the ex-service men. This, though it cheered his heart, by no means—once the organization was set up—occupied his time or gave scope to his abilities. So the years passed.

People began to criticize his campaigns. As soon as the war-censorship, actual and moral, was lifted, pens ran freely. There was no lack of material. There was deep resentment against slaughters on a gigantic scale alleged upon notable occasions to have been needless and fruitless. All this will long continue to be debated. However, Haig said nothing. He neither wrote nor spoke in his own defence. Some of his Staff Officers without his knowledge published a controversial rejoinder. The volume was extremely ill received by the Press and the public. But neither the serious criticism nor the unsatisfying defence extorted any public utterance from Haig.

The next thing heard about the Field Marshal was that he had fallen down dead like a soldier shot on the battle-field, and probably from causes that had originated there. Then occurred manifestations of sorrow and regard which rose from the very heart of the people and throughout the Empire. Then everybody saw how admirable had been his demeanour since the peace. There was a majesty about it which proved an exceptional greatness of character. It showed a man capable of resisting unusual strains, internal and external, even when prolonged over years ; it showed a man cast in a classic mould.

The qualities revealed by his life and conduct after the War cast a new light upon his contribution to the victory. One can see from a different angle and in a different medium the strength of will and character which enabled him to withstand the various intense stresses to which he was subjected. With his front crumbling under the greatest of German assaults, or with his own army collapsing in the mud and blood of Paschendaele, with an Ally always exacting and frequently irregular, with the Government at home searching high and low for someone to replace him, he preserved at all times a majestic calm. He lived each day without departing from his convictions, or seeking sensational effects, or courting popularity, or losing heart. He was equally sure of his professional qualifications and of his constitutional duty ; and he acted at all times in strict accordance with these definite conceptions. When the news of frightful slaughters, often barren, and the ruin of operations in which he had trusted, and for which he bore the awful responsibility, were reported to him, he was fortified by feeling that he had employed to the best of his ability the military training of a lifetime, that he was doing the duty assigned to him by the lawfully-constituted author-ities, and that he was at all times equally ready to persevere or to be replaced.

A selfless, dispassionate, detached equanimity ruled his spirit, not only at moments of acute crisis but month after month and year after year. Inflexible, rigorously pedantic in his assertion of the professional point of view, he nevertheless at all times treated the Civil Power with respect and loyalty. Even when he knew that his recall was debated among the War Cabinet, he neither sought to marshal the powerful political forces which would have come to his aid, nor failed at any time in faithfulness to the Ministers under whom he was serving. Even in the sharpest disagreement he never threatened resignation when he was strong and they were weak. Amid patent ill-success he never in his own technical sphere deferred to their wishes, however strongly those wishes were supported by argument, by public opinion—such as it was—or by the terribly unfolding facts. Right or wrong, victorious or stultified, he remained, within the limits he had marked out for himself, cool and undaunted, ready to meet all emergencies and to accept death or obscurity should either come his way.

I had known him slightly, both in private life and in the Army since I was the youngest of subalterns and he a rising Major. At Omdurman and in South Africa we had served on horseback in the field together. We met on a different plane when I was Home Secretary and later First Lord of the Admiralty and he commanded our first and only formed Army Corps at Aldershot. Both on the Committee of Imperial Defence and at the Army Manœuvres I met him repeatedly, and we always discussed war problems. One remark he made to me at some Cavalry exercises which I was watching in 1912 has always seemed to me most revealing: 'This officer,' he said, speaking of a Brigadier, 'did not show a sincere desire to engage the enemy.' The occasion was a sham fight, but the saying was a key to his whole military outlook. Years afterwards in the height of the War, speaking to him of a Naval episode, I repeated the expression with intent. His usually placid eye lighted in a compulsive flash, and he repeated the phrase with emphatic assent. 'A sincere desire to engage the enemy.' That was Haig. That was his message.

That was the impulse which he imparted to his troops throughout his command till the last minute before eleven o'clock on the 11th of November 1918.

He presents to me in those red years the same mental picture as a great surgeon before the days of anæsthetics, versed in every detail of such science as was known to him : sure of himself, steady of poise, knife in hand, intent upon the operation ; entirely removed in his professional capacity from the agony of the patient, the anguish of relations, or the doctrines of rival schools, the devices of quacks, or the first-fruits of new learning. He would operate without excitement, or he would depart without being affronted ; and if the patient died, he would not reproach himself. It must be understood that I speak only of his professional actions. Once out of the theatre, his heart was as warm as any man's.

' A sincere desire to engage the enemy.' Woe betide the officer—Colonel, Brigadier or high General—who failed in that. Experienced, resolute men, with courage proved in the crash of battle, were sent home at an hour's notice for refusing to order—not to lead, for that would have been easier—their troops to certain destruction. Fight and kill and be killed, but obey orders, even when it was clear that the Higher Command had not foreseen the conditions ; or go, and go at once, to the rear, to England or to the devil. That was the high-tension current which flowed ceaselessly from the Commander-in-Chief, himself assailed on every side, through more than forty months of carnage. All along the chain of responsibility from Army to Corps, from Corps to Division, from Division to Brigade and from Brigade to Battalion, this ruthless and often inevitably blind force was continually applied. And behind it all a man, a knightly figure, modest in demeanour, humble in spirit, self-forgetting and far above vulgar ambition, just, merciful, humane— such are the mysteries of human nature !

Moreover, the fierce internal pressures, resulting from such discordance, could find no outlet in personal action.

Napoleon and the great Captains before him rode on the field amid their troops in the ardour of battle, and amid the perils of the storm. How gladly would Haig have welcomed the chance to mount his horse as he had done when a mere Corps Commander in the First Ypres, and ride slowly forward among the exploding shells ! But all this is supposed to be forbidden to the modern Commander-in-Chief. He is lucky if even an aeroplane bomb, or some long-range projectile near Headquarters, relieves at rare intervals by its physical reminder the inward stress of mind. No anodyne of danger, no relief in violent action ; nothing but anxiety, suspense, perplexing and contradictory information ; weighing the imponderable, assigning proportions to what cannot be measured, intricate staff duties, difficult personal negotiations, and the mutterings of far-distant guns.

But he endured it all ; and with such impassivity and matter-of-fact day-to-day routine that I who saw him on twenty occasions—some of them potentially fatal—doubted whether he was not insensitive and indurated to the torment and drama in the shadow of which he dwelt. But when I saw after the War was over, for the first time, the historic ' Backs to the Wall ' document written before sunrise on that fateful April morning in 1918, and that it was no product of some able staff officer in the bureau, but written with his own precise hand, pouring out without a check or correction the pent-up passion of his heart, my vision of the man assumed a new scale and colour. The Furies indeed contended in his soul ; and that arena was large enough to contain their strife.

*   *   *   *   *

Lord Haig's executors were well advised to entrust to Mr. Duff Cooper the presentation to the public of the late Field-Marshal's diaries.* He has discharged his task with simplicity and candour ; and in a manner which it is prob-

* ' Haig,' Duff Cooper. 1935.

able Haig himself would have approved. This is a manly story, told in a straightforward way. No one who has read Mr. Duff Cooper's *Talleyrand* requires other assurances of his skill in narrative or of his literary competence and quality. The reader may pass lightly over such incidents as that of General Robertson (who had never himself at any time led even a troop in action, and whose war duties involved him in no more risk than many clerks) speaking of the Cabinet as ' poltroons.' He should also take at its face value Haig's disparaging judgment of Mr. Lloyd George, to which needless publicity has been given. Neither Haig's view of Lloyd George nor Lloyd George's view of Haig are likely to be accepted by history. They will both be deemed much better men than they deemed each other.

Nevertheless, it is by no means proved that a general, or indeed a statesman, coping with tremendous affairs, is wise to write and still less to preserve a diary. The reputation of the late Sir Henry Wilson was grievously affected by his devoted widow's ill-considered publication of his night-thoughts. When events are moving at break-neck speed and upon a world-wide scale, when facts and values are changing every day, when all personal relations in official business must necessarily be affected, when the view of the diarist is subordinate or local, or both, the Commander exposes himself to an almost impossible test when he writes ' an average entry for each day of two or three typewritten foolscap pages,' which when duly bound comprise thirty-six volumes of diurnal commentary.

Douglas Haig embodied and lived up to the finest public school tradition. He was, in fact, at the time he became Commander-in-Chief of the greatest army Britain had ever achieved, the head boy and prize pupil of the military school. He had done all things requisite and proper. He had fought as a squadron leader, served in the field as a staff officer, played in the winning cavalry polo team, graduated with distinction at the staff college, held an important military appointment in India, commanded the Aldershot division before the outbreak of war, and valiantly led the First Army Corps and later the First Army for nearly eighteen months of Armageddon. He had no professional rivals at that time and none appeared thereafter during the struggle. His realization of this was a strong prop to him in the many ordeals, disappointments, and terrible disasters which he had to face and endure. He might be, he surely was, unequal to the prodigious scale of events; but no one else was discerned as his equal or his better. So it all worked down to blunt, grim, and simple duty, in the discharge of which one may indeed make many errors or suffer grievous misfortune, but which has to be done and which a man, if called on, has a solid right to do. Lastly there was a strong religious side to his character, and he had always cherished the belief that he was destined to lead the British army to victory.

Haig's mind, as one would expect from the credentials we have cited, was thoroughly orthodox and conventional. He does not appear to have had any original ideas; no one can discern a spark of that mysterious, visionary, often sinister genius which has enabled the great captains of history to dominate the material factors, save slaughter, and confront their foes with the triumph of novel apparitions. He was, we are told, quite friendly to the tanks, but the manœuvre of making them would never have occurred to him. He appeared at all times quite unconscious of any theatre but the Western Front. There were the Germans in their trenches. Here he stood at the head of an army corps, then of an army, and finally of a group of mighty armies. Hurl them on and keep slogging at it in the best possible way—that was war. It was undoubtedly one way of making war, and in the end there was certainly overwhelming victory. But these truisms will not be accepted by history as exhaustive.

If Haig's mind was conventional, his character also displayed the qualities of the average, decent man concentrated and magnified. This is only a part of a general's equipment,

but it is not necessarily an unimportant part. His behaviour did not crumple under violent external occurrences.
He was rarely capable of rising to great heights; he was
always incapable of falling below his standards. Thus the
army, which was in fact our island race, gathered from all
parts of the world, looked to him with confidence through
many costly failures; and the military hierarchy, very
complicated—almost a church—and in times of war of para-
mount importance, felt that in the Commander-in-Chief
they had someone on whom to rely. These are great
matters.

Until the summer of 1916 the British Expeditionary
Force played inevitably only a fractional role in the stupen-
dous Franco-German struggle. We dwell with pride on
Mons and Le Cateau, on the turn at the Marne, the glorious
defence of the Yser and the Lys, on Neuve Chapelle, and
upon our important contributory efforts at Loos to the
great battle in Champagne. These were times when our
fighting personnel was expanded far beyond our munitions.
We paid in blood and sorrow for the lack of cannon and
explosive. Sir John French, who is sometimes unduly
slighted by the admirers of Haig, bore the brunt of this.
We can certainly say that if the British Army had not been
upon the front, France would have been conquered. But
even at the end of 1915 we were but a sixth numerically,
and perhaps but a quarter morally, of the Allied Front. It
was not until the Somme in July 1916 that we became a
major factor in the vast land conflict. The next two years
shows the British war effort, casualties and will-to-conquer
as always equal to the French, and ultimately dominant.
It was over this period that Haig presided. No one can
say that it did not end in victory.

*   *   *   *   *

I saw and corresponded with him more frequently in the
last year of his life than at any other period; and in a way
—though I cannot pretend to intimacy with a personality

so reserved—I got to know him better than ever before. Curiously, but characteristically on his part, this arose out of my writing a book on the War which, while it recounted the great achievements of the armies he led, nevertheless constituted a sustained indictment of the 'Western School' of strategy which he embodied. I asked him whether he would like to read and comment upon the chapters dealing with his operations, adding that if so I must show him what was critical as well as what was appreciative. He accepted the suggestion readily, saying 'Never mind the criticisms. Let us get the facts right, and then people will be able to judge for themselves.' There followed a very active interchange of notes and comments, by which I was able to correct numerous commonly-accepted errors of fact. Throughout he manifested an entire goodwill, and treated the whole story from an impersonal and detached standpoint as if it dealt with events of a hundred years ago. I understood that this was because he was content with what he considered justice being done to the exploits of the British armies, especially in 1918, and that nothing affecting his own actions counted at all in the opposite scale. 'No one,' he wrote in a final letter, 'knows as well as I do how far short of the ideal my own conduct both of the 1st Corps and First Army was, as well as of the B.E.F. when C.-in-C.'

The nobility of this utterance in all the circumstances enables one to measure from yet another angle the real value of his services to the cause of the Allies.

But the greatest proof lies in the final phase of the War. The qualities of mind and spirit which Douglas Haig personified came to be known by occult channels throughout the vast armies of which he was the Chief. Disasters, disappointments, miscalculations and their grievous price were powerless to affect the confidence of the soldiers in their Commander. When in the autumn of 1918 the Government, often only too right before, doubted the possibility of early success, and endeavoured to dissuade him from what was feared would be a renewal of melancholy and prodigal slaughter; when in the most invidious manner they cast the direct responsibility upon him, he did not hesitate, and the war-worn, five-times-decimated troops responded to the will and impulse of their leader, and marched forward unswerving to the awful convulsions of victory final and absolute. The soldierly qualities of Foch, his wide range of vision, his vast and fine combinations, could not have ended the slaughter in 1918 unless they had been on several decisive occasions deflected or reinforced by the entirely separate impulsion of Douglas Haig. Foch's famous war cries, ' *Allez à la bataille,*' ' *Tout le monde à la bataille,*' would have carried no more meaning to history than a timely cheer, but for the series of tremendous drives and punches with which the British armies from Amiens to Mons and from the Somme to the Selle trampled down the fortifications and the brave resistance of the best that was left of the German military might, and spared mankind the slaughters which awaited the unfought campaign of 1919.

If there are some who would question Haig's right to rank with Wellington in British military annals, there are none who will deny that his character and conduct as soldier and subject will long serve as an example to all.

ARTHUR JAMES
BALFOUR

Keystone View Company

ARTHUR JAMES BALFOUR AS FOREIGN SECRETARY

ARTHUR JAMES BALFOUR

R AMSAY MACDONALD, paying his tribute as Prime
Minister, said of Arthur Balfour, 'He saw a great
deal of life from afar.' There was truth in this upon the
facts, and poignancy in the mood of the orator. MacDonald
had seen life at close quarters. He would have liked to
have viewed it from afar. An unconscious sense of envy,
wistful but not untinged with pride, led him to achieve this
just and pregnant remark. Struggling all his life in the
Labour-Socialist whirlpool, at times hunted out of Parliament, and almost out of the country, because of his association with anti-national forces ; always challenged, always
harassed, enjoying precarious gleams of success amid renewing storms of popular displeasure ; here to-day, gone to-
morrow ; the champion of causes for which he was sometimes
sorry to fight ; now on the tossing waves to the crest, now
to the trough ; Mr. MacDonald could not but regard with
admiring disdain the long, tranquil, Olympian career of his
fortunate yet defeated predecessor.

'He saw a great deal of life from afar.' Arthur Balfour
did not mingle in the hurly-burly. He glided upon its
surface. He was born to substantial wealth. After more
than fifty years of service he died with a reduced, but still
adequate estate, derived from ancient title. He was never
seriously worried about money ; he never had to face the
problem of earning his livelihood, or of paying the bills
for the common necessities of life. He had a beautiful
home in Scotland and a comfortable mansion in Carlton
House Terrace, maintained automatically by a solid capital.
This was his lot in life. He shared the gradual, steady im-

poverishment of the class of landed gentlefolk to which he belonged. Although he lost a good deal of his fortune by an unlucky speculation in later life, he never bothered much about it. His wants were small; his habit of life austere; he always had enough, and security for having enough.

Biographers of eminent persons are prone to ignore or slur over these harshly practical considerations. They have their value however in the career of any public man. Throughout his life the late Lord Balfour, fortunately for himself, still more fortunately for his country, was removed from vulgar necessities. He never had to make any of those compromises, increasing under modern conditions, between an entirely dispassionate outlook upon affairs and his daily bread. This was for him a great advantage and source of strength.

He was a bachelor. All that tremendous process of keeping a home together and rearing a family, which is the main preoccupation of the human race, was by a romantic tragedy far removed from his ken. Henceforward he was self-contained; he was entirely independent. His thought was national, his interests were world-wide. That Britain should be powerful and prosperous, that the Empire should gather more closely around her, that she should be the champion of right and peace; that her own ambitions and aspirations should fit harmoniously into the requirements of an ever-widening and strengthening Cosmopolis, and that he should play a worthy part in all this, was his life's aim.

He was in fact a lay-priest seeking a secular goal. He acquired and possessed from earlier life profound and definite conceptions; and by a marvellous gift of comprehension and receptivity he was able to adjust all the new phenomena and the ever-changing currents of events to his solidly-wrought convictions. His interest in life, thought and affairs, as Mr. MacDonald observed, was as keen at eighty as it was at twenty: but his purpose, his foundation, and his main theme were obstinate, obdurate and virtually unchanged throughout the memorable times in which he lived, played his part, and even ruled. He was a man to whom without commonplace extravagance one might apply the word 'Statesman.' His aversion from the Roman Catholic faith was dour and inveterate. Otherwise he seemed to have the personal qualifications of a great Pope. He had that composed, detached, uplifted mental and moral vision combined with the art of dexterous and practical management requisite for those who guide the course of permanent societies. To the defence of his principles and prejudices he summoned every resource of conduct, oratory and dialectic. But he knew when to change, and not only when to change, but how to change, in accordance with the pressures of events. Holding to his own convictions, steering always by the same stars, diverging only so far as was inevitable under the thrust of adverse winds, he moved with the times, and lived in the fore-front of nearly three generations. He was never stranded ; he was never out-of-date. He loved youth and accepted, nay, encouraged its demands. In mind he was always young, and yet he inspired the feeling that he possessed the wisdom of the ages.

A taste most truly refined, a judgment comprehensively balanced, an insight penetrating, a passion cold, long, slow, unyielding—all these were his. He was quite fearless ; but he had no reason to fear. Death was certain sooner or later. It only involved a change of state, or at the worst a serene oblivion. Poverty never entered his thoughts. Disgrace was impossible because of his character and behaviour. When they took him to the Front to see the war, he admired with bland interest through his pince-nez the bursting shells. Luckily none came near enough to make him jump, as they will make any man jump, if they have their chance. Once I saw a furious scene in the House of Commons when an Irish member, rushing across the floor in a frenzy, shook his fist for a couple of minutes within a few inches of his face. We young fellows behind were all ready to spring to his aid upon a physical foe; but Arthur Balfour, Leader of the House, regarded the frantic figure with no more and no less than the interest of a biologist examining through a microscope the contortions of a rare and provoked insect. There was in fact no way of getting at him. Once during the War when we were rather dissatisfied with the vigour of Sir Edward Grey's policy, I, apologizing for him, said to Mr. Lloyd George, who was hot, ' Well, anyhow, we know that if the Germans were here and said to Grey, " If you don't sign this Treaty, we will shoot you at once," he would certainly reply, " It would be most improper for a British minister to yield to a threat. That sort of thing is not done." ' But Lloyd George rejoined, ' That's not what the Germans would say to him. They would say, " If you don't sign this Treaty, we will scrag all your squirrels at Fallodon." That would break him down.' Arthur Balfour had no squirrels. Neither on the big line nor on the small line, neither by dire threats nor by playing upon idiosyncrasies, could anyone overcome his central will or rupture his sense of duty.

Such was the main impression made upon me by this remarkable man whom I knew, and whose friendship, across the vicissitudes of politics, I enjoyed in a ripening measure during thirty years. We must now come a little closer to him and meet him in the small events of life.

The Wykehamists have the motto, ' Manners makyth Man.' If this be so, Arthur Balfour was the most perfect of men. He was the best-mannered man I ever met—easy, courteous, patient, considerate, in every society and with great and small alike. But this urbane and graceful air, which was entirely natural to him and effortless, was the least part of his manners, which were equal to every situation, pleasant or awkward. Not only was he never embarrassed or at a loss himself, but he seemed to impart this gift in large measure to any company while he was among them. He put everyone at their ease and sailed with them smoothly through the most disconcerting and painful situations. Whatever had to be said, he knew how to say it ; and when others blundered into foolish or offensive remarks, he knew how to defend himself or retaliate with point, justice or severity. At the right time and in the right place he could and did say with dignity and suavity any hard things which were necessary. Such occasions were rare. He was always the most agreeable, affable and amusing of guests or companions ; his presence was a pleasure and his conversation a treat.

He possessed and practised the art of always appearing interested in any subject that was raised, or in any person with whom he was talking. He had not perhaps in conversation the vivid, vibrant qualities of John Morley, nor the brilliance, often disconcerting, of Rosebery ; but he excelled both in the pleasure he gave. His contribution was less positive. He allowed the talk to flow as his companion wished, appreciating in the most complimentary manner anything that was said in good will, taking up every point, and lifting the discussion step by step—yet often himself speaking very little. All who met him came away feeling that *they* had been at their very best, and that they had found someone who, whether he agreed or differed, understood their point of view. Very often they remembered the things they had said to him, which he had welcomed or seemed to agree with, better than what he had said to them. He loved general conversation, and knew exactly how to rule it, so that no one was left out, and it never degenerated into ' damned monologue.'

Politics, philosophy, science in all its branches, art, history, were themes upon which he embarked as readily as small-talk. He seemed to draw out all that was best in his companion. Put him next to a political opponent, a disaffected supporter, a young lady in her teens, a schoolboy, a sea-captain, an explorer, an inventor, or a learned professor of any kind, and in a few minutes one observed an animated conversation, rippling along with increasing zest and interest on both sides. No one escaped his attraction. Everyone produced his most valued mental treasures, and became proud and delighted to have them so generously admired by a man of such distinction. Yet he was swift to mark by some judicious and upsetting question any departure from truth, sense or taste as he conceived them. He would very soon have put Socrates in his place, if that old fellow had played any of his dialectical tricks on him. When I go to Heaven, I shall try to arrange a chat between these two on some topic, not too recondite for me to follow.

All his life he dwelt in circles of admiring friends. He was for many years the mainspring of a society of brilliant men and women known as ' The Souls,' who dined together, travelled together and stayed constantly in each other's delightful houses. He accepted besides, invitations from all sorts of people, never broke an engagement for something more tempting, and left behind him a trail of satisfaction and even happiness.

But underneath all this there was a cool ruthlessness where public affairs were concerned. He rarely allowed political antagonism to be a barrier in private life ; neither did he, any more than Asquith, let personal friendship, however sealed and cemented, hamper his solutions of the problems of State. Had his life been cast amid the labyrinthine intrigues of the Italian Renaissance, he would not have required to study the works of Machiavelli. Had he lived in the French Revolution, he would, when it was found absolutely necessary, have consigned a dangerous enemy of his Government or party or even an erring colleague to the guillotine with much complacency. But he would have done it in a thoroughly polite and completely impersonal manner.

It was thought by many students of politics that this side of his character presented itself in his treatment of George Wyndham. Wyndham was one of his greatest friends. For many years they were bound together by every tie of social intercourse and political comradeship which could unite an older and a younger man. But the day came when Wyndham as Irish Secretary had carried a flirtation with the Home Rulers to a point which compromised the political basis of the Conservative party. It seemed to the public that Balfour, as Prime Minister, made it clear that he required his resignation, and that he let him go into political extinction without turning a hair or lifting a finger.

But this widely-accepted impression is contradicted by the weight of first-hand evidence. Those nearest and dearest to George Wyndham declare that the Prime Minister backed him with the whole of his strength, that he refused time after time to allow him to resign, and that it was only when in the end Wyndham's health and nerves completely broke down under the varied stresses, and at the entreaty of his wife and family, heavily backed by the doctors, that Balfour finally accepted his resignation. Certain it is that Wyndham remained until the day of his death Balfour's devoted friend, and that his adoring mother, Mrs. Percy Wyndham, never harboured for a moment a sense of reproach.

* * * * *

Another much-discussed episode occurred at Mr. Chamberlain's resignation in the autumn of 1903. Chamberlain had roused the long-slumbering but always living issue of Protection in the guise of Imperial preference, and had thrown the Conservative party into a most violent schism. Balfour held it ' the unforgivable sin ' to split his party. He was wont to dwell with censure upon Sir R. Peel's action in 1846 and Mr. Gladstone's forty years later, apart altogether from the merits of those controversies. He therefore tried, as other leaders have done since, to keep the party together upon some central policy and formula which would enable Protectionists and Conservative Free Traders to remain united in one organization. He set forth his views in a pamphlet called ' Insular Free Trade,' which broadly-speaking accepted tariffs for negotiation and retaliation, but did not close the door upon the adoption of the more full-blooded policy, if the feeling in the party should gradually come to warrant it. But passions ran too high. The whole country was agog. No one would talk of anything else. The old text-books on Free Trade were taken down from the shelves, and a hurricane of disputation raged through the land. The Liberals found themselves completely united in their opposition. An election was not far distant, and threatened in these circumstances to be disastrous.

The Free Trade Ministers, Mr. Ritchie, then Chancellor of the Exchequer, Lord George Hamilton and Lord Balfour of Burleigh, felt themselves being drawn on from point to point into positions contrary to their beliefs. They took counsel together, and examined in some detail the possibilities of an alternative administration and another Prime Minister. The Duke of Devonshire, who counted for more than all the others, and was the only possible successor to Balfour, was in general agreement with them; but he moved with characteristic slowness, and from motives of delicacy had abstained from all discussions about Cabinet-making. Balfour was well-informed about the respective attitudes of all the dissentients. He considered that, apart from Devonshire, they had ' caballed' against him.

On September 9 Mr. Chamberlain wrote secretly to Balfour asking to resign his office in order to have full freedom in explaining and popularizing his Protectionist policy. He had in the ensuing days several conversations with the Prime Minister when it was agreed that for the sake of keeping the party together his resignation should be accepted. On this basis therefore, known only to Chamberlain and Balfour, the Cabinet met on September 14 and 15. The militant Free Traders who considered that Balfour was definitely on the side of Chamberlain, tendered their resignations, and understood, rightly, that these would be accepted. Devonshire remained silent, but they assumed that he was acting with them.

It has hitherto been widely believed that Balfour deliberately concealed from the Free Trade Ministers the all-
important fact that Mr. Chamberlain 'had also resigned,
and that his resignation was definitely accepted; that he
allowed a whole day's delay to intervene for the resignation
of his three colleagues involved in the Cabal to become
effective; and that only thereafter did he summon Devonshire to his room, tell him that Chamberlain had gone, and
invite him to stay. By this method, it was supposed, that
he separated the Duke from his other colleagues, and was
able to persuade him to remain in the Government, and help
to counteract Mr. Chamberlain's full Protectionist policy.
Such was the story.

This version should find no place in history. First of all,
Chamberlain actually resigned at the Cabinet—that is to
say, he said something to the effect that ' it would be better
for him to go '; or that ' he must go.' His son Austen
wrote as follows to a friend of mine. ' . . . I returned
from a short holiday abroad the evening before the critical
Cabinet meeting, and did not see my father until I met
him in Cabinet. I had, therefore, no knowledge of his
letter to Balfour, or of his intention to resign. *I heard him
announce that intention at Cabinet,** and I drove back with
him to Prince's Gardens when the Cabinet was over, and
reproached him with having taken this decision without a
word to me, but added that as he was resigning, I should certainly do the same.'

No one can doubt such testimony. It often happens
however that when a certain amount of conversation is going
on between gentlemen, everyone present does not derive the
same impression from it. Especially is this so when some
are naturally preoccupied about their own positions. The
Free Trade Ministers certainly all left the Cabinet room
without the slightest idea that Chamberlain had resigned,
and that his resignation had been accepted.

Balfour deemed it imperative to the unity of the party

* Author's italics.

to shed both Protectionist and Free Trade blood on the same day. He knew quite well that none of the Free Trade Ministers would have resigned had they known that the arch-champion of Protection was himself going into the wilderness. On the contrary, they would have rejoiced to stay in and keep him out there. But this was not Balfour's plan. He supposed that they had heard Chamberlain's statement and had tendered their resignations in the light of this essential fact. He did not make sufficient allowance for the fact that what Chamberlain said had a different significance to him, with his unique knowledge, than to his dissentient colleagues. He did not feel bound to inform those who had, as he deemed it, caballed against him, of his own position. He reserved for himself the right to deal as he chose with the various resignations which threatened him. Whether he should try to persuade anyone to stay, rested in his opinion with him alone. But then there is the question of the delay in telling the Duke of Devonshire. On this point there is a complete explanation.

The Duke came away from the Cabinet perhaps under the impression that Chamberlain had offered to resign in a half-hearted way, but that his offer had been refused. Lord Derby, then Lord Stanley, from whom I have this account, was at that time a Junior Minister, Financial Secretary to the War Office. He was the Duke's step-son-in-law, and very intimate with him. They drove down together to dine with Mr. Leopold de Rothschild in the suburbs of London at Gunnersbury. Whilst they were at dinner a red Cabinet box arrived. The Duke turned to Lord Stanley and said, ' I have left my Cabinet key in London, lend me yours.' Stanley of course was not yet entitled to possess a Cabinet key, and said so. The box therefore remained unopened, and it came back late that night to London.

The next morning Lord Stanley went into the Whips' room at No. 12 Downing Street, and was told that Chamberlain had resigned and that the Prime Minister had accepted his resignation. At luncheon Lord Stanley met by chance a friend who told him that the Duke was very lonely and very anxious, that his wife was away, that he had nobody to talk to, and that he would like to receive a visit from him.

' I went ' [writes Lord Derby] ' to the Duke's house, and found him walking about his room. He said, " Of course I have written to resign." I asked him what he had given as his reason, and he said that he could not remain in the same Cabinet as Joe Chamberlain. My answer was, " But as Joe has resigned that is no excuse at all." He jumped as if he had been shot, and said, " I know nothing about it." It then struck me that the red box the night before had contained the information and that—so like him—he had never even opened the box. He did it then, and found, as I thought he might do, a letter from Balfour telling him that Joe had resigned and hoping that he would stay.

' He was then in a great fix because he had already sent his letter of resignation to Balfour by hand. I volunteered to go down and see Balfour. At first he would not see me and was annoyed at being interrupted, as he told me he was writing a letter to the Duke saying how much he regretted his resignation, etc. I told him he need not write the letter, as the Duke was ready to withdraw his resignation, which had been sent under a misapprehension. A. J. B. then asked me to go and get the Duke to come and see him. This I did. The Duke and I dined together in the evening and he told me then everything had been satisfactorily arranged.'

These facts, stated, I believe, for the first time, show the transaction in its true light.

When, on the 18th, Chamberlain's letter of the 9th and Balfour's answer of the 16th were published, the Free Trade Ministers, whose resignations had been tacitly accepted, and who had heard nothing more since the Cabinet, considered that they had been unfairly treated by the Prime Minister and also by the Duke. Public opinion at the time was general that they ought to have been made plainly aware that the Prime Minister had Chamberlain's letter of resignation in his possession, and that he had accepted it. Even the neutral and colourless account in the Annual Register speaks of ' a widespread impression that the Free Trade element in the Cabinet had been reduced to conditions hardly compatible with that mutual confidence which was assumed to characterize the relations between ministerial colleagues.' This is no doubt true ; but it may be claimed on Balfour's behalf, first, that he had heard Chamberlain mention his resignation in the Cabinet, and secondly, that he treated Devonshire as the leader of the Free Trade Group. He informed him in writing immediately after the Cabinet of the decisive fact, viz. that Chamberlain's resignation had been offered, and more than that, accepted ; and he left it to him, if he saw fit, to tell the others. The Duke, however, could not open his red box that night, and forgot about it the next morning, and so the resignation of the three Free Trade Ministers became effective. This was, no doubt, what Balfour wished, though he had not contrived it, and could not have foreseen it. He would not in any case have made it easy for them to withdraw their resignations, even if they had desired to do so.

For the moment, the Prime Minister had achieved by management and by accident all his objects. He had got rid at a stroke of the extremists on both sides of his Cabinet. He had maintained his central rallying-ground for all the faithful confided to his care, and he had kept the impressive and ponderous Duke. The Free Trade ex-ministers in due course complained in their published letters of resignation that they never knew of Chamberlain's resignation, whereas it had in fact been accepted some days before the Cabinet meeting. They now, of course, reproached the Duke with having made a separate peace for himself upon terms not communicated to the colleagues to whom he was bound. The Duke, who cared nothing for office, but everything in the world for his personal good faith, was consternated. He had been flustered by the muddle about the red box, for which he felt himself to blame. Now however he had pledged himself to stay with the Prime Minister, and had agreed with him upon the men and measures of the reconstituted Government. He sought sanctuary, as Godolphin was wont to do, at Newmarket. Here he received a series of letters from the Free Traders. They were furious. They considered, not without reason, that he had treated them ill. Lord Derby writes to me :

' He showed me a letter from . . . You never saw such a letter in your life. It accused him of every crime under the sun—breach of faith, dishonesty, every sort of thing. It upset the old Duke very much indeed. He said to me, " To think I have gone through all my life, and then at the end of it to have these sort of accusations levelled at my head." '

Thus assailed, the Duke did not know which way to turn. For ten days he suffered acute distress. Then the Prime Minister made a speech upon the Fiscal question. Never did a grand Inquisitor scrutinize more searchingly the utterance of a suspected heretic than did this able yet simple old man his leader's speech ; and to his immense relief he found a phrase in it which went beyond, at least in some of its implications, the formula to which he had bound himself. He literally hurled in his resignation, and almost rolled with joy upon Newmarket heath. All Arthur Balfour's well-meant house of cards fell to the ground ; and the Conservative Party drifted hopelessly forward to shattering defeat.

*   *   *   *   *

It is impossible here to dwell upon Balfour's part in the complex and even more fateful Cabinet convulsion which resulted in the substitution of Lloyd George for Asquith in the crisis of December 1916. But nothing is more instructive than to follow the dispassionate, cool, correct and at the same time ruthless manner in which Balfour threaded the labyrinth without reproach. He passed from one Cabinet to the other, from the Prime Minister who was his champion to the Prime Minister who had been his most severe critic, like a powerful graceful cat walking delicately and unsoiled across a rather muddy street.

I must present a few blades from my sheaf of Balfouriana. A comment upon a speech : ' Asquith's lucidity of style is a positive disadvantage when he has nothing to say.' A retort on another occasion. ' In that oration there were some things that were true, and some things that were trite : but what was true was trite, and what was not trite was not true.' And again: ' There were some things in it meant seriously which were humorous, and there were others meant humorously which were serious.' Here is a remark which when pessimists are prating I have often found helpful: ' This is a singularly ill-contrived world; but not so ill-contrived as that.' Of a supporter somewhat over-ripe, ' He pursues us with malignant fidelity.' At a luncheon Mr. Frank Harris, wishing to shine, blurted out, ' All the evil in the world is due to Christianity and Journalism.' Arthur Balfour, contemplating this proposition for a moment, replied, ' Christianity of course, but why Journalism ? ' Once when I was very young I asked him whether he ever prepared his perorations. ' No,' he said, ' I say what occurs to me, and sit down at the end of the first grammatical sentence.'

After the fall of his Government in 1905 he used to come occasionally to small dinners of his young friends and former House of Commons colleagues who had left him, some of whom had attacked him fiercely in all the horseplay of English politics. He had been swept from power by an enormous vote of the nation. He had scarcely a hundred followers in the House of Commons, and of these three parts were rabid protectionists who owed him a grudge. He was always at his best on these occasions. Although outside, the fiercest storms of Party faction blew, no one would have supposed, as the talk ran on, that we were not all members of the same Party or even colleagues in the same Government. We touched one night upon the topic of whether public men should read newspaper comments about themselves, and in particular whether they should subscribe to a press-cutting agency. I said I always did this : one need not read the flattery, of which there was none too much in my experience, but now and then skimming through a bundle of press-cuttings one saw something which was useful to a departmental chief by opening his eyes to some scandal or grievance, or by warning him of some dangerous line of criticism of which he was not aware. ' I have never,' said ' A. J. B.,' (to use the famous initials by which he was so often named) ' put myself to the trouble of rummaging an immense rubbish-heap on the problematical chance of discovering a cigar-end.' For a long time he made it his boast that he never read the newspapers ; and for a long time this was accounted to him as a virtue. But the newspapers won in the end. He lived to enter upon the age when almost the only robustly-assertive institution in our society was the Press. At length he was scolded for not keeping in touch with public opinion ; in the end he had to read the newspapers ; but he read them as little as he could.

He had many habits which conserved his vigour. He never answered an invitation except by telegram. People were glad to have an answer quickly, and regarded a telegram as a mark of consideration. Thirty years ago the arrival of the pale orange envelope made our fathers and mothers sit up ; if it did not contain bad news, they took it as a compliment ; so all was well at that end. On the other hand, you could dictate a telegram instead of having to write *with your own hand* a ceremonious letter.

He very rarely rose before luncheon. He rested in bed, unapproachable, transacting business, reading, writing, ruminating, and at week-ends appeared, whatever the crisis, composed and fresh shortly after one p.m. His work for the day was done ; he seemed care-free, even at the head of a tottering Government, even in the darkest hours of the War. He would sit and talk gaily for a half-hour after luncheon ; he hoped to be able to play a round of golf or in later years lawn tennis. Uninstructed persons who saw him thus in private life, while the newspapers growled in double-headed columns about the political situation, were surprised and even scandalized. They thought he did not care or did not reck. But he had often been at his affairs since dawn. He was never excited, and in the House of Commons was very hard indeed to provoke. I tried often and often, and only on a few occasions, which I prefer to forget, succeeded in seriously annoying him in public debate.

In the main the House of Commons was his world. There lay the practical interests and movement of his life. For more than a quarter of a century he led the Government or the Opposition. No Minister in charge of a Bill ever worked harder, or was more thoroughly conversant with all the essentials of the legislation he was proposing. He never floundered in detail, for he had minutely and patiently studied every aspect and possible pitfall of any measure for the conduct of which he was responsible. As Leader it was his custom to wind up almost every important debate himself. He spoke usually for an hour, having perhaps four or five points with their subheads, embodied in thirty or forty words, jotted down upon two long envelopes. Within these limits he allowed his thought to flow. Often he paused to choose the word which fitted his meaning best. At such times the assembly joined him sympathetically in the search. It was as if he had dropped his eyeglasses when reading an important despatch. Everyone, friend and foe, was anxious to recover them for him. All were delighted when he found them himself in his top right-hand waist-coat-pocket. Out came the right word, amid loud cheers or loud howls and general satisfaction. This faculty of enlisting the whole audience, both sides alike, in the delivery of his speech was a potent gift ; and as far as speech can influence opinion or votes, he swayed the House of Commons.

Curiously enough this most easy, sure and fluent of speakers was the most timid, laborious of writers. He would go to a meeting of ten thousand people when every kind of consequence hung upon his words and their reception, with a preparation often completed by a conversation upon important points in the cab that drove him there. Once he saw in his mind's eye a reasoned proposition, he was certain he could unfold it intelligently and with distinction ; but when he took up the pen, ' he came all over of a tremble,' and crossed out and transposed and re-wrote to an amazing extent. He would spend hours upon a paragraph and days upon an article. This was a strange inversion. The spoken word, uttered from the summit of power, gone beyond recall, had no terrors for him ; but he entered the tabernacles of literature under a double dose of the humility and awe which are proper. He was sure of the movement of his thought ; he was shy in the movement of his pen. The history of every country abounds with brilliant and ready writers who have quailed and faltered when called upon to compose in public, or who have shrunk altogether from the ordeal. Balfour was the reverse example, and in this lies a considerable revelation of his character. His was a mind to weigh and balance, to see both sides, especially all the flaws and all the faults in his own case. The emergency and compulsion of public speech forced upon him at a high rate of speed the exposition of his thought. His mind was in action and every second he had to take mental decisions ; but in his bedroom with his writing-pad on his lap and fountain-pen poised judicially over the blank sheet of paper, a score of arguments against every case and against every phrase and almost every word paraded themselves and marched and counter-marched before his speculative gaze. Everything he wrote was upon a high level ; but its excellence was purchased by inconceivable labour.

It followed that in politics he decided more easily upon great matters than upon small. He was more effective upon large general issues, than upon the definite administrative decisions required from high executive officers in a continuous stream during periods of disturbance. He was not good at giving orders ; and there are times when the giving of many orders, clearly expressed, harmoniously related, is a desirable gift in a ruler. He abhorred plunging; but in wartime, at any rate, chiefs often have to plunge. He hated committing himself without full and thorough knowledge; but in violent times many most important things have to be done on imperfect and uncertain information, and flair based on previous study is often the safest guide. One day in 1918 when the Supreme Council of the Allies sat at Versailles in sound and almost in range of the German guns, he spoke for ten minutes upon a difficult question, and when he had finished, old Clemenceau turned his twinkling eyes upon him and abruptly inquired, ' Pour ou contre ? ' His type of mind found itself at home in choosing principles and judging the proportions of world affairs. He expected to have at his disposal competent persons of a lower grade who were able to translate his almost invariably sound conceptions into practical action.

*　　*　　*　　*　　*

This is not the place in which to deal with the many memorable acts of policy for which he was largely responsible, and I will merely select a few of the chief. All his early life was spent in resisting Home Rule for Ireland. As Irish Secretary and afterwards as leader of the House of Commons, he laboured to govern Ireland justly, firmly and beneficently. His overthrow in 1905 left Ireland more politically acquiescent, and her people better off in every way, than ever before or since. From the moment, however, that Ulster was established as a self-governing province, he concerned himself much less with the fortunes and destiny of Southern Ireland. Indeed I think he would not have been distressed had the Irish Free State been excluded altogether from the British Empire. He always regarded such exclusion as the final resource at the disposal of Great Britain.

When the United States declared war on Spain over the prolonged disturbances in Cuba, Balfour happened to be temporarily in charge of the Foreign Office. The friendship of Great Britain and Spain was old and valued. No dispute of any kind had separated the two countries which had fought side by side against Napoleon. Balfour's root-conviction, perhaps his strongest conviction, was that the English-speaking peoples of the world must stand together. He therefore in a single night reversed the mild Spanish sympathies of the Foreign Office and transformed cold neutrality into a markedly friendly attitude towards the United States. The Spaniards have long memories, and I was not at all surprised when, in the Great War, they showed themselves extremely frigid towards a combination which included the descendants of the Napoleonic invaders, the United States who had stripped them of the last vestiges of their colonial Empire, and Great Britain with whom no Spanish friendship seemed to them to count, and who still held Gibraltar. Nevertheless Balfour's decision has stood the test of time.

In the black week of the South African War, which seemed in those days quite a serious crisis, Balfour was fully equal to the occasion. He was the only Minister in London when Sir Redvers Buller's telegram arrived proposing to abandon the relief of Ladysmith, and that this town with its important garrison should fire off its ammunition and capitulate. Without waiting to consult his uncle, the Prime Minister, or his colleagues, he curtly told Buller to persevere in the relief of Ladysmith or hand over the command of the army and come home. Ladysmith was relieved.

I played some part in the events which brought him to the head of the Admiralty in the Great War. After he had ceased to be Leader of the Conservative Party in 1911, and while the shadow of approaching danger hung over us, I induced the Prime Minister, Mr. Asquith, to make him a permanent member of the Committee of Imperial Defence. I felt intensely the need of his judgment upon the life-and-death naval and military questions of those anxious years. I wished to be able to talk over with him every aspect of the German Peril with that freedom in secret matters which can only spring, and ought only to spring, from a public, official connexion. When the War broke out I associated him as much as possible with the progress of Admiralty affairs, and as everyone knows he was a convinced supporter of the enterprise against the Dardanelles. Therefore I was very glad, when I had to leave the Admiralty myself, that this operation, then in its throes, should be pursued by him. He resolutely persevered.

Still, an administrative and directly executive post like the Admiralty was not the sphere best suited to his nature and habit of mind. It was when he was transferred to the Foreign Office that his memorable share in the struggle began. His visit to Washington, when the United States entered the War, revealed him at his very best. Never has England had a more persuasive or commanding ambassador and plenipotentiary. After the War, he rescued the Peace Conference from sinking into voluble fatuity during those critical weeks when both President Wilson and Mr. Lloyd George were recalled home by the exigencies of domestic politics. For the rest, there is the Zionist declaration and the Balfour note upon Inter-Allied debts. These decisions, from which he never departed, are still too much in the area of current controversy for a final or impartial judgment to be attempted.

Amid universal goodwill and wide-spread affection he celebrated triumphantly his eightieth birthday. But thereafter hungry Time began to revenge itself upon one who had so long disdained its menace. He became an invalid. His body was stricken ; but his mind retained, almost to the very end, its clear, tranquil outlook upon the human scene, and its inexhaustible pleasure in the processes of thought.

I had the privilege of visiting him several times during the last months of his life. I saw with grief the approaching departure, and—for all human purposes—extinction, of a being high-uplifted above the common run. As I observed him regarding with calm, firm and cheerful gaze the approach of Death, I felt how foolish the Stoics were to make such a fuss about an event so natural and so indispensable to mankind. But I felt also the tragedy which robs the world of all the wisdom and treasure gathered in a great man's life and experience, and hands the lamp to some impetuous and untutored stripling, or lets it fall shivered into fragments upon the ground.

HITLER
AND HIS CHOICE

Central Press Photos Ltd

THE FÜHRER

HITLER AND HIS CHOICE

IT is not possible to form a just judgment of a public figure who has attained the enormous dimensions of Adolf Hitler until his life work as a whole is before us. Although no subsequent political action can condone wrong deeds, history is replete with examples of men who have risen to power by employing stern, grim, and even frightful methods, but who, nevertheless, when their life is revealed as a whole, have been regarded as great figures whose lives have enriched the story of mankind. So may it be with Hitler.

Such a final view is not vouchsafed to us to-day.* We cannot tell whether Hitler will be the man who will once again let loose upon the world another war in which civilization will irretrievably succumb, or whether he will go down in history as the man who restored honour and peace of mind to the great Germanic nation and brought it back serene, helpful and strong, to the forefront of the European family circle. It is on this mystery of the future that history will pronounce. It is enough to say that both possibilities are open at the present moment. If, because the story is unfinished, because, indeed, its most fateful chapters have yet to be written, we are forced to dwell upon the darker side of his work and creed, we must never forget nor cease to hope for the bright alternative.

Adolf Hitler was the child of the rage and grief of a mighty empire and race which had suffered overwhelming defeat in war. He it was who exorcized the spirit of despair from the German mind by substituting the not less baleful

* Written in 1935.

261

but far less morbid spirit of revenge. When the terrible German armies, which had held half Europe in their grip, recoiled on every front, and sought armistice from those upon whose lands even then they still stood as invaders ; when the pride and will-power of the Prussian race broke into surrender and revolution behind the fighting lines ; when that Imperial Government, which had been for more than fifty fearful months the terror of almost all nations, collapsed ignominiously, leaving its loyal faithful subjects defenceless and disarmed before the wrath of the sorely-wounded, victorious Allies ; then it was that one corporal, a former Austrian house-painter, set out to regain all.

In the fifteen years that have followed this resolve he has succeeded in restoring Germany to the most powerful position in Europe, and not only has he restored the position of his country, but he has even, to a very large extent, reversed the results of the Great War. Sir John Simon said at Berlin that, as Foreign Secretary, he made no distinction between victors and vanquished. Such distinctions, indeed, still exist, but the vanquished are in process of becoming the victors, and the victors the vanquished. When Hitler began, Germany lay prostrate at the feet of the Allies. He may yet see the day when what is left of Europe will be prostrate at the feet of Germany. Whatever else may be thought about these exploits, they are certainly among the most remarkable in the whole history of the world.

Hitler's success, and, indeed, his survival as a political force, would not have been possible but for the lethargy and folly of the French and British Governments since the War, and especially in the last three years.* No sincere attempt was made to come to terms with the various moderate governments of Germany which existed under a parliamentary system. For a long time the French pursued the absurd delusion that they could extract vast indemnities

* 1932-35.

from the Germans in order to compensate them for the devastation of the War. Figures of reparation payments were adopted, not only by the French but by the British, which had no relation whatever to any process which exists, or could ever be devised, of transferring wealth from one community to another. To enforce submission to these senseless demands, French armies actually reoccupied the Ruhr in 1923. To recover even a tenth of what was originally demanded, an inter-allied board, presided over by an able American, supervised the internal finances of Germany for several years, thus renewing and perpetuating the utmost bitterness in the minds of the defeated nation. In fact, nothing was gained at the cost of all this friction; for, although the Allies extracted about one thousand million pounds' worth of assets from the Germans, the United States, and to a lesser extent Great Britain, lent Germany at the same time over two thousand millions. Yet, while the Allies poured their wealth into Germany to build her up and revive her life and industry, the only results were an increasing resentment and the loss of their money. Even while Germany was receiving great benefits by the loans which were made to her, Hitler's movement gained each week life and force from irritation at Allied interference.

I have always laid down the doctrine that the redress of the grievances of the vanquished should precede the disarmament of the victors. Little was done to redress the grievances of the treaties of Versailles and Trianon. Hitler in his campaign could point continually to a number of minor anomalies and racial injustices in the territorial arrangements of Europe, which fed the fires on which he lived. At the same time, the English pacifists, aided from a safe distance by their American prototypes, forced the process of disarmament into the utmost prominence. Year after year, without the slightest regard to the realities of the world, the Disarmament Commission explored innumerable schemes for reducing the armaments of the Allies, none of which was pursued with any sincerity by any country except Great Britain. The United States, while preaching disarmament, continued to make enormous developments in her army, navy and air force. France, deprived of the promised United States guarantee and confronted with the gradual revival of Germany with its tremendous military population, naturally refused to reduce her defences below the danger-point. Italy, for other reasons, increased her armaments. Only England cut her defences by land and sea far below the safety level, and appeared quite unconscious of the new peril which was developing in the air.

Meanwhile the Germans, principally under the Brüning Government, began their great plans to regain their armed power. These were pressed forward by every channel. Air-sport and commercial aviation became a mere cloak behind which a tremendous organization for the purposes of air war was spread over every part of Germany. The German General Staff, forbidden by the treaty, grew year by year to an enormous size under the guise of the State guidance of industry. All the factories of Germany were prepared in incredible detail to be turned to war production. These preparations, although assiduously concealed, were nevertheless known to the intelligence departments both of France and Great Britain. But nowhere in either of these governments was there the commanding power either to call Germany to a halt or to endeavour to revise the treaties, or better still both. The first course would have been quite safe and easy, at any rate until the end of 1931, but at that time Mr. MacDonald and his colleagues were still contenting themselves with uttering high-sounding platitudes upon the blessings of peace and gaining the applause of well-meaning but ill-informed majorities throughout our island. Even as late as 1932 the greatest pressure was put by the British Government upon France to reduce her armed strength, when at the same time the French knew that immense preparations were going forward in all parts of Germany. I explained and exposed the follies of this process repeatedly and in detail in the House of Commons.

Eventually, all that came out of the Disarmament conferences was the Re-armament of Germany.

While all these formidable transformations were occurring in Europe, Corporal Hitler was fighting his long, wearing battle for the German heart. The story of that struggle cannot be read without admiration for the courage, the perseverance, and the vital force which enabled him to challenge, defy, conciliate, or overcome, all the authorities or resistances which barred his path. He, and the ever-increasing legions who worked with him, certainly showed at this time, in their patriotic ardour and love of country, that there was nothing they would not do or dare, no sacrifice of life, limb or liberty that they would not make themselves or inflict upon their opponents. The main episodes of the story are well known. The riotous meetings, the fusillade at Munich, Hitler's imprisonment, his various arrests and trials, his conflict with Hindenburg, his electoral campaign, von Papen's tergiversation, Hitler's conquest of Hindenburg, Hindenburg's desertion of Brüning—all these were the milestones upon that indomitable march which carried the Austrian-born corporal to the life-dictatorship of the entire German nation of nearly seventy million souls, constituting the most industrious, tractable, fierce and martial race in the world.

Hitler arrived at supreme power in Germany at the head of a National Socialist movement which wiped out all the states and old kingdoms of Germany and fused them into one whole. At the same time, Nazidom suppressed and obliterated by force, wherever necessary, all other parties in the State. At this very moment he found that the secret organization of German industry and aviation which the German general staff and latterly the Brüning Government had built up, was in fact absolutely ready to be put into operation. So far, no one had dared to take this step. Fear that the Allies would intervene, and nip everything in the bud, had restrained them. But Hitler had risen by violence and passion ; he was surrounded by men as ruthless as he. It is probable that, when he overthrew the existing constitutional Government of Germany, he did not know how far they had prepared the ground for his action; certainly he has never done them the justice to recognize their contribution to his success.

The fact remains that all he and Goering had to do was to give the signal for the most gigantic process of secret re-armament that has ever taken place. He had long proclaimed that, if he came into power, he would do two things that no one else could do for Germany but himself. First, he would restore Germany to the height of her power in Europe, and secondly, he would cure the cruel unemployment that afflicted the people. His methods are now apparent. Germany was to recover her place in Europe by rearming, and the Germans were to be largely freed from the curse of unemployment by being set to work on making the armaments and other military preparations. Thus from the year 1933 onwards the whole available energies of Germany were directed to preparations for war, not only in the factories, in the barracks, and on the aviation grounds, but in the schools, the colleges, and almost in the nursery, by every resource of State power and modern propaganda; and the preparation and education of the whole people for war-readiness was undertaken.

It was not till 1935 that the full terror of this revelation broke upon the careless and imprudent world, and Hitler, casting aside concealment, sprang forward armed to the teeth, with his munition factories roaring night and day, his aeroplane squadrons forming in ceaseless succession, his submarine crews exercising in the Baltic, and his armed hosts tramping the barrack squares from one end of the broad Reich to the other. That is where we are to-day, and the achievement by which the tables have been completely turned upon the complacent, feckless, and purblind victors deserves to be reckoned a prodigy in the history of the world, and a prodigy which is inseparable from the personal exertions and life-thrust of a single man.

It is certainly not strange that everyone should want to know ' the truth about Hitler.' What will he do with the tremendous powers already in his grasp and perfecting themselves week by week ? If, as I have said, we look only at the past, which is all we have to judge by, we must indeed feel anxious. Hitherto, Hitler's triumphant career has been borne onwards, not only by a passionate love of Germany, but by currents of hatred so intense as to sear the souls of those who swim upon them. Hatred of the French is the first of these currents, and we have only to read Hitler's book, *Mein Kampf*, to see that the French are not the only foreign nation against whom the anger of rearmed Germany may be turned.

But the internal stresses are even more striking. The Jews, supposed to have contributed, by a disloyal and pacifist influence, to the collapse of Germany at the end of the Great War, were also deemed to be the main prop of communism and the authors of defeatist doctrines in every form. Therefore, the Jews of Germany, a community numbered by many hundreds of thousands, were to be stripped of all power, driven from every position in public and social life, expelled from the professions, silenced in the Press, and declared a foul and odious race. The twentieth century has witnessed with surprise, not merely the promulgation of these ferocious doctrines, but their enforcement with brutal vigour by the Government and by the populace. No past services, no proved patriotism, even wounds sustained in war, could procure immunity for persons whose only crime was that their parents had brought them into the world. Every kind of persecution, grave or petty, upon the world-famous scientists, writers, and composers at the top down to the wretched little Jewish children in the national schools, was practised, was glorified, and is still being practised and glorified.

A similar proscription fell upon socialists and communists of every hue. The Trade Unionists and liberal intelligentsia are equally smitten. The slightest criticism is an offence against the State. The courts of justice, though allowed to function in ordinary cases, are superseded for every form of political offence by so-called people's courts composed of ardent Nazis. Side by side with the training grounds of the new armies and the great aerodromes, the concentration camps pock-mark the German soil. In these thousands of Germans are coerced and cowed into submission to the irresistible power of the Totalitarian State. The hatred of the Jews led by a logical transition to an attack upon the historical basis of Christianity. Thus the conflict broadened swiftly, and Catholic priests and Protestant pastors fell under the ban of what is becoming the new religion of the German peoples, namely, the worship of Germany under the symbols of the old gods of Nordic paganism. Here also is where we stand to-day.

What manner of man is this grim figure who has performed these superb toils and loosed these frightful evils ? Does he still share the passions he has evoked ? Does he, in the full sunlight of worldly triumph, at the head of the great nation he has raised from the dust, still feel racked by the hatreds and antagonisms of his desperate struggle ; or will they be discarded like the armour and the cruel weapons of strife under the mellowing influences of success ? Evidently a burning question for men of all nations ! Those who have met Herr Hitler face to face in public business or on social terms have found a highly competent, cool, well-informed functionary with an agreeable manner, a disarming smile, and few have been unaffected by a subtle personal magnetism. Nor is this impression merely the dazzle of power. He exerted it on his companions at every stage in his struggle, even when his fortunes were in the lowest depths. Thus the world lives on hopes that the worst is over, and that we may yet live to see Hitler a gentler figure in a happier age.

Meanwhile, he makes speeches to the nations, which are sometimes characterized by candour and moderation. Recently he has offered many words of reassurance, eagerly lapped up by those who have been so tragically wrong about Germany in the past. Only time can show, but, meanwhile, the great wheels revolve ; the rifles, the cannon, the tanks, the shot and shell, the air-bombs, the poison-gas cylinders, the aeroplanes, the submarines, and now the beginnings of a fleet flow in ever-broadening streams from the already largely war-mobilized arsenals and factories of Germany.

GEORGE NATHANIEL
CURZON

Graphic Photo Union

GEORGE NATHANIEL CURZON 1920

GEORGE NATHANIEL CURZON

FEW careers in modern British politics are more worthy
of examination than that of George Nathaniel Curzon,
and few records more suggestive than those he has left behind him. Here was a being gifted far beyond the average
level: equipped and caparisoned with glittering treasures
of mind and fortune; driven forward by will, courage and
tireless industry; not specially crossed by ill luck; not
denied a considerable span: and yet who failed to achieve
the central purpose of his life. Why did he fail, and how
did he fail? What were the causes personal and external
which robbed this very remarkable man, placed throughout
in such a strong position, of the prize which it was his life's
ambition to gain? Surely in this limited sphere no inquiry
could be more rich in instruction.

George Curzon was born with all the advantages of
moderate affluence and noble descent. A stately home,
beautiful surroundings, ancestral trees, every material
ministration nurtured his youth. But at the same time a
strict Miss Paraman and a stern Mr. Campbell, his governess
and private schoolmaster respectively, applied disciplinary
spurs and corrections in a most bracing and even severe
degree. A rigorous and pious upbringing proceeded in an
atmosphere of old-world dignity and on the basis of adequate
funds. Shot like a long-range projectile from this domestic
gun, the youth arrived in the early seventies at Eton. No
less than ten years were lavished upon his education. He
writes of the six he spent at Eton as the most enjoyable
of his life. Certainly they were years of constant and
almost unbroken triumph. He stood out at once beyond

273

his contemporaries as one endowed with superabundant powers. He rose rapidly in the school. He rose eventually to be virtually head of the school. He captured a record number of prizes of every kind. Latin, French, Italian, history and, above all, English prose and English verse came to him with precocious facility. At Eton he was the best and most industrious scholar of his day. But to all these achievements he added a strong, rebellious and scornful temper which made him at once admired and feared by his teachers. Armed with his terrific powers of work and easy swiftness of assimilation, he repulsed all favour and loved to excel in despite. He quitted the classes of the French, Italian and historical professors in order by private exertions to win the prizes from their most cherished pupils.

But with all this, his charm, his good looks, his fun and his natural ascendancy won him without question the acceptance of the boys and extorted the respect of the scored-off masters. He was certainly not the model pupil, but far and away the most proficient. He matured at an uncanny speed. Before he was seventeen his vocabulary became abundant, his sentences sonorous, and his taste in words polished. His entries in the record of events kept by the ' Captain of the Oppidans ' are a school legend for amplitude and magniloquence. His ideas and stock of knowledge kept pace with his fluency of speech and writing. He animated and inspired the Eton Debating Society, and led Mr. Gladstone, at the height of his career, a docile captive, to address it. Everyone remarked his present eminence and predicted his future fame.

His four years at Oxford were not less conspicuous. He focused his main attention directly upon politics. His academic studies took a second place in his interest and gained him only a Second Class in the examination. But he swiftly rose to be the leader of youthful Tory opinion. He sustained the Chatham and Canning Clubs. He became President of the Union. He wrote voluminously and spoke continually. He infused energy into everything he touched. His infant reputation spread beyond the University and throughout the aristocratic circles which in those days dominated the political scene. He was at twenty-one notorious as ' The Coming Man.'

The word ' notorious ' is used advisedly, for with all this early glitter there mingled an innocent but none the less serious tarnish. His facility carried him with a bound into prolixity ; his ceremonious diction wore the aspect of pomposity ; his wide knowledge was accused of super-ficiality ; his natural pre-eminence was accompanied by airs of superiority. Nevertheless, all these were but the under-currents to a tide that flowed strongly and hope-fully forward.

It was easy in those days—indeed it is fortunately still easy—for a young man of such parts and influence to enter the House of Commons as the freely-chosen repre-sentative of a large constituency. But here for the first time he came in contact with a set of tests to which his gifts were not wholly suited. The House of Commons of the late eighties was very different in its social levels from the assemblies of our day. But it was then, as now, the most competent and comprehending judge of a man. It found something lacking in Mr. Curzon. It was certainly not information nor application, nor power of speech nor attractiveness of manner and appearance. Everything was in his equipment. You could unpack his knapsack and take an inventory item by item. Nothing on the list was missing, yet somehow or other the total was incomplete. Making every allowance each way for youth and for excep-tional gifts, the House considered him from the earliest day of his membership as a light weight. He aroused both admiration and envy, but neither much love nor much hatred. He could expound a case with precision and deliver a rejoinder with effect. He wielded the Parlia-mentary small sword with style and finish ; and he worked and travelled and read and wrote (one book alone on Persia of thirteen hundred pages), and did all that was appointed without being able to sway opinion or shift events. Simpler people with rugged force within them and convictions quarried by experience made homely halting speeches which counted for more than his superfine performances. In the House of Commons he met his match ; and compared with the great Parliamentary figures of that time he was never regarded, even on his day, as an equal combatant or future rival. On paper, and if only it could have been settled by an examination, he had much in common with the younger Pitt. In fact, however, he was brushed aside.

The Conservative Party had been in office continuously for five years before he was accorded an Under-Secretaryship. Lord Salisbury's defeat in 1892 offered Curzon the spacious opportunities of the Opposition front bench. It may be safely said that no first-rate Parliamentarian with all the advantage of being an ex-Minister and in the absence of any definite disqualification could have failed in three years to establish a claim to Cabinet rank on the return of his Party to power. Nevertheless, in 1895 Lord Salisbury had no doubts about offering, and Mr. Curzon no doubts about accepting, the important, though none the less subordinate, office of Under-Secretary of State for Foreign Affairs. We must conclude that for all his perfectly-turned speeches, his painstaking thoroughness, his ready command of phrase and epigram, his social connections and unblemished character, he was definitely defeated in the House of Commons. This was an enduring decision.

It is only fair to say that he never of his own will gave up the struggle. He wished to fight and camp, and fight again in the House of Commons. He saw with resentment and alarm the approaching shadow of an inherited peerage. To avoid this melancholy fate he tried to legislate. Joined with two other scions of noble houses, he pressed a measure upon the House granting Members liberty to refuse or to defer unwelcome elevation. When eventually appointed Viceroy of India, he took an Irish title so as to keep the door of the House of Commons open to him on his return. Therefore no one has a right to say with certainty that he would not, like Disraeli, have succeeded in the end. He at any rate always counted his eventual exclusion from the House of Commons as one of the decisive misfortunes of his life.

I first cast an admiring, measuring eye upon him at the time of his second appointment as Under-Secretary, and was instantly attracted by the geniality, candour and fullness of his conversation. I saluted him at the Devonshire House reception which celebrated in the summer of 1895 the return of the Conservatives to power. A year later I was several times his guest as a subaltern officer when he was Viceroy of India. He had, or at any rate practised, that admirable habit, in which politicians excel, of treating quite young men on absolutely equal terms in conversation. At his table in Calcutta I hugely enjoyed his sprightly and none too merciful chaff of his close friend, my late Harrow Headmaster, Bishop Welldon, then Bishop Metropolitan of India. 'I presume,' he said to me, 'it will not be long before we hear you declaim in the House of Commons.' Though greatly hampered by inability to compose at the rate necessary for public speaking, I was strongly of the same opinion myself.

The contradictory qualities which dwell in the characters of so many individuals can rarely have formed more vivid contrasts than in George Curzon. The world thought him pompous in manner and in mind. But this widespread and deep impression, arising from the experience and report of so many good judges, was immediately destroyed by the Curzon one met in a small circle of intimate friends and equals, or those whom he treated as equals. Here one saw the charming, gay companion adorning every subject that he touched with his agile wit, ever ready to laugh at himself, ever capable of conveying sympathy and understanding. It seemed incredible that this warm heart and jolly, boyish nature should be so effectually concealed from the vast majority of those he met and with whom he worked. Most difficult in all small matters of business, disputing pettifogging details of private life to the point of quarrel with well-proved friends, he none the less was never happier or seen to better advantage than when he dispensed the splendid hospitalities of his various palatial homes. Helpful with comfort and sympathy on every occasion of sickness or sorrow in his wide circle, unpopular with most of those who served him, the master of scathing rebuke for subordinates, he seemed to sow gratitude and resentment along his path with evenly lavish hands. Bespangled with every quality that could dazzle and attract, he never found himself with a following. Majestic in speech, appearance and demeanour, he never led. He often domineered ; but at the centre he never dominated.

Curzon's Viceroyalty of India was his greatest period. For nearly seven years he reigned imperially over the vast Indian scene. He brought to that task intellectual powers never yet surpassed by his successors. Everything interested him, and he adorned nearly all he touched. A sincere love for all the peoples of India, a resolute championship of their essential dignities and rights, a deeply-informed knowledge of their monuments and art, a prodigious industry, a biting and tireless pen exercised upon interminable files, a magnificent ceremonial—these were among the contributions which over this extended period he made to the British Government of Hindustan. An essentially pacific frontier policy carrying with it a definitely anti-militarist outlook, immense schemes of reproductive public works, a liberal-minded and humanitarian tendency manifest in every branch of the administration, combined to make the Curzon Viceroyalty a memorable episode in Anglo-Indian history.

Yet it closed in sorrow and anger. A first-class quarrel developed between the Viceroy and the Commander-in-Chief, Lord Kitchener. On the merits there is, I believe, at this distance of time no question that Curzon was right.

But in craft, in slow intrigue, in strength of personality, in doubtful-dangerous manœuvres, the soldier beat the politician every time. Lord Kitchener established his own secret contacts with the Home Government and with the Secretary of State. He had his own agents and channels of communication. He selected the fighting positions with Lloyd Georgian skill. In the climax the Government of Curzon's own friends and the Secretary of State, Mr. Brodrick, almost his best friend, pronounced against him, and pronounced against him in error.

He resigned in just indignation. He returned to England with his sword drawn against his former colleagues, and chiefly against his two most intimate friends, Mr. Balfour and Mr. Brodrick. But the redoubtable conflict never took place. Curzon arrived home from India to find the long Conservative regime in virtual dissolution. Mr. Chamberlain's Tariff Reform campaign absorbed the public mind. The Conservative Government was swept out of existence at the General Election of 1906 ; and all its eminent and remarkable personalities were relegated to a limbo of shattered Opposition from which they escaped only after nine years and through the convulsions of the Great War. Their private quarrels therefore ceased to be of public significance. They slumbered, but they smouldered. It was many years before Curzon spoke to Brodrick again. Their friendship, dating from school days, had ceased for ever. As for Mr. Balfour, his calm was Olympian, his courtesy and kindness were unfailing, and his impressions ineffaceable. Here again was a fact of cardinal importance to Lord Curzon's public career.

*   *   *   *   *

We now come forward into Armageddon. In this phase Curzon came into contact with a personality almost exactly the opposite of his own. You could hardly imagine two men so diverse as Curzon and Lloyd George. Temperament, prejudices, environment, upbringing, mental processes were utterly different and markedly antagonistic. There never of course was any comparison in weight and force between the two. The offspring of the Welsh village whose whole youth had been rebellion against the aristocracy, who had skipped indignant out of the path of the local Tory magnate driving his four-in-hand, and revenged himself at night upon that magnate's rabbits, had a priceless gift. It was the very gift which the product of Eton and Balliol had always lacked—the one blessing denied him by his fairy godmothers, the one without which all other gifts are so frightfully cheapened. He had the 'seeing eye.' He had that deep original instinct which peers through the surfaces of words and things—the vision which sees dimly but surely the other side of the brick wall or which follows the hunt two fields before the throng. Against this, industry, learning, scholarship, eloquence, social influence, wealth, reputation, an ordered mind, plenty of pluck, counted for less than nothing. Put the two men together in any circumstances of equality and the one would eat the other. Lloyd George used Curzon for his purposes, rewarded him handsomely when it suited him to do so, flattered him frequently, but never admitted him to the inner chambers of his decisions.

* * * * *

George Curzon was a wonderful letter-writer. The toil of caligraphy was a pleasure to him. He could drive a quill or a steel nib in fine style faster and longer than anyone I have known. He must have written letters for many hours a day and far through the night into the new day. Propped up in the steel corsets which sustained his spine, he would write and write, charming, weighty, magnificent letters, often about not much. It was a relief to him, and perhaps unconsciously a counter-irritant to his almost constant pain or discomfort.

I remember in 1903 during his Viceroyalty in India going to see the first Lady Curzon, formerly Miss Leiter—(' the Leiter of Asia,' as the wags said)—one of the most beautiful, delightful women of her day, when she was recovering in

England from the first attack of her ultimately fatal illness. She showed me a letter from her husband in India. It was a hundred pages long! She showed me the numbers on the pages. All was written in his graceful legible flowing hand. But a hundred pages!

When I left the Cabinet, because I saw what was coming, and went out to France at the end of 1915, Curzon and I had been in close collaboration to prevent the evacuation of the Dardanelles. He wrote me a letter of certainly twenty pages, describing in vivid style the whole of the struggle within the Cabinet on that grievous issue and deploring my absence—'You who have always led us'—from the discussion. I was in the line when this rather deadly document reached me. A little later he was much concerned to retrieve it. But although I have hardly ever lost an important letter in my life, I have never been able to find it or find out what happened to it. However if it turns up now, it no longer matters.

One of Curzon's characteristic weaknesses was that he thought too much about stating his case, and too little about getting things done. When he had written his cogent dispatch, or brought a question before the Cabinet in full and careful form with all his force and knowledge, he was inclined to feel that his function was fulfilled. He had done his best. Events must take their course. He was too much concerned with what might be said about things, and too little with the things themselves.

* * * * *

I had only one public dispute with him. When Mr. Baldwin was planning the overthrow of Mr. Lloyd George's Coalition government in 1922, and the crisis approached in the autumn, there were several dinner-meetings at my house at which Lloyd George and I discussed the increasing difficulties with Austen Chamberlain, Balfour, Curzon and Birkenhead, trying to find a solution. The issue turned upon whether it was fair to ask for a Dissolution without either calling Parliament together, or waiting for the impending meeting of the National Union of Conservative Associations. It was of course understood that Mr. Lloyd George would not continue as Prime Minister after the election, unless predominant Conservative party-feeling desired it. We Liberal members of the Coalition stood on good ground because we had some months before offered in writing to resign and support a purely Conservative administration. I remember so well how, in the presence of everyone, Curzon got up from his chair to leave saying ' All right, I'm game '. This meant that he would go with us in an appeal to the country.

When the crucial meeting at the Carlton Club took place some weeks later we were somewhat surprised that Curzon threw his weight against us, that he retained the Foreign Office under the new government, and hit us as hard as he could. No doubt he hated Lloyd George. But then there was his cordial promise to us all. This defection brought a tone of acerbity into our election speeches. Curzon took the field with the statement that the dispatch to the Dominions inviting them to stand by us at Chanak against a Turkish re-invasion of Europe, had been framed and published without his being consulted as Foreign Secretary. I had undergone a few days before a severe operation for appendicitis, but I could not let this pass. So I wrote at large to say ' in spite of the momentous situation Lord Curzon had left London on Friday night for one of his country seats, and did not propose to return till Tuesday. On Sunday Lord Curzon was definitely requested by Mr. Lloyd George and Mr. Chamberlain [i.e. the Prime Minister and his own party leader] to return to London. He replied that he was remaining in the country because his house in London was not properly prepared for his reception. He was finally induced to return on Monday. To this day I do not know how the problem of his lordship's accommodation in the metropolis was ultimately solved.' He did not like this : he was not meant to like it. He replied in the *Times* that my statement was characterised by copious inaccuracy and no small malevolence, and gave a lengthy explanation of how ill he had been. We had not heard of this illness before. I contended that he had admitted the points made against him.

It was not for nine months that I saw him again. We met at a large private dinner in London. He was a leading minister and we were knocked out, so I did not press myself upon him. But as the ladies left the dining-room he came round to me and threw out his hand in a most magnificent, compulsive gesture which swept everything away. Here was the real man.

*　　*　　*　　*　　*

In the spring of 1923, Mr. Bonar Law's health broke down. A cruise in the Mediterranean failed to rally his strength, and he resolved to resign the Premiership.

Several questions of Constitutional usage and propriety arose. When a Party is in opposition, and its leadership becomes vacant, it makes its free choice among the various personalities available. But if the Party is in office, the Sovereign's choice may anticipate, and in a certain sense forestall the decision of the Party. The prerogative is absolute. It is not for any Party to offer a Prime Minister to the Sovereign. Once a Minister has the commission to form a Government, he is free to do so if he can. Nevertheless, it is perhaps more in harmony with the spirit of the Constitution that the King should allow the dominant party to choose its own leader, before committing himself to any particular man. It is inherent in the British political system that the Crown should not be drawn into a potentiaally controversial decision, except when, owing to a deadlock or an emergency, there is no escape. A needless shock would be sustained by the Crown if, for instance, the new Prime Minister was not accepted as the leader of the party possessing the majority in the House of Commons. Even if out of deference to the Royal decision, but somewhat against its natural inclination, a Party accepted as its leader the nominated Prime Minister, it might well be that the Prime Minister's position would be difficult, and the Government short-lived. It costs nothing for the Crown to wait a few days, and allow disputed claims to settle themselves. The Crown would then act upon an ascertained fact, rather than upon an estimate however well-informed.

It is customary, of course, for the outgoing Prime Minister, who is, presumably, the head of the stronger party, and of the majority in the House of Commons, to advise the King who should be his successor. Thus, the risks of the Crown making an unacceptable choice are greatly diminished, and in any case, whatever happens, the Sovereign is protected by the fact that he has acted upon responsible advice. If trouble arises, the outgoing Prime Minister is there to bear the brunt. In the majority of cases, the advice is obvious. But there are occasions when the matter is doubtful. This was one of them. Moreover, Mr. Bonar Law had only a few weeks earlier come to the conclusion that Curzon would not do. The incident which determined him must be mentioned.

A promoter wishing to start an enterprise in Turkey before the conclusion of a formal peace with Mustapha Kemal, had applied to Mr. Bonar Law. The Prime Minister, about to depart upon his melancholy, almost despairing, voyage in search of health, referred the matter to the Foreign Office in a brief letter. Lord Curzon found in this an occasion to write back with acerbity. He criticised in scathing terms the character of the promoter, and in his most lecturing manner dwelt upon the inconveniences which arise when persons are led to suppose they can apply to No. 10, Downing Street upon questions within the province of the Foreign Office. Such a practice, he remarked, would only revive one of the worst traditions of the late regime. The Prime Minister who had done nothing to deserve this rebuke, was too ill to be angry : but undoubtedly he became acutely conscious of the difficulties which would arise in a government, and in a party, if they fell into the hands of one who could write on such a small pretext so hectoring an effusion.

Mr. Bonar Law's malady was gaining daily upon him, and he did not feel himself justified in pronouncing. All he was sure of was that he would not recommend Curzon. He therefore wrote to Lord Curzon on May 20, ' I understand that it is not customary for the King to ask the Prime Minister to recommend his successor in circumstances like the present, and I presume he will not do so ; but if, as I hope, he accepts my resignation at once, he will have to take immediate steps about my successor.' This, of course, recognized the priority of Curzon's claim, but was non-committal.

Mr. Bonar Law was now too ill even to take leave of the King personally. Two of his closest friends travelled to Windsor with his resignation. King George after expressing his sorrow at the news asked whom he would advise him to send for. The two gentlemen said that he was already too ill to take the responsibility of advising ; so the King then asked that the Prime Minister should merely advise him to which other Minister in the Cabinet he should have recourse for advice. Mr. Bonar Law when this was brought to him, was at first inclined to offer as an adviser the name of Mr. Neville Chamberlain of whose good sense and judgment he had formed the highest opinion. As Mr. Chamberlain was only the Postmaster General and was new to the Cabinet, he put this aside, and sent the reply that Lord Salisbury should assume the duty. Lord Salisbury, apprised of this, repaired immediately to London. But in the meanwhile the King, fearing that he might in calm weather be called upon not only to choose a Prime Minister for himself, but in fact decide the leadership of the Conservative party, took other steps. He sought counsel with other elder statesmen of independent position, in order that the high function of the Crown should be discharged in harmony with the public mood and interest.

*　　*　　*　　*　　*

On Monday, May 21, 1923, Lord Curzon was at Monta-
cute House in Somersetshire, where he was spending the
Whitsun recess. The morning post brought Mr. Bonar
Law's letter. The moment then at which his life had
aimed, had come. Curzon surveyed the political scene,
and could discern no serious rival. Of the great figures
of Conservatism there was none likely to dispute his
claims. Lord Balfour was in his seventy-fifth year. Mr.
Austen Chamberlain and Lord Birkenhead had not yet been
forgiven for their loyalty to Mr. Lloyd George. Of Curzon's
colleagues in the Bonar Law administration only one was
a possible competitor, and it is doubtful whether Curzon
ever considered him. Nor was this unreasonable. In
official experience, in mental calibre, in Parliamentary rank
and reputation, he far surpassed the only conceivable rival.

Mr. Baldwin was at that time a new and almost unknown
figure. He had only been six months Chancellor of the
Exchequer, and scarcely three years in the Cabinet. He
had never made a noticeable speech in Parliament or elsewhere. Curzon on the other hand was Leader in the House
of Lords. He had filled a prominent position in the public
eye for a quarter of a century, and at the moment he
occupied the Foreign Office with his customary distinction.
All Monday Lord Curzon waited for the summons that was
sure to come. At last it arrived. Towards evening a telegram from Lord Stamfordham was delivered, calling the
Secretary of State to London. The journey to town on
Tuesday was filled with the making of plans. There was
no doubt in Curzon's mind—nor indeed should there have
been—as to the meaning of the summons.

He was to become Prime Minister.

But as the inquiries of the King had proceeded, what
may at first have seemed the obvious choice appeared in
a new and doubtful light. Lord Balfour's great influence
was thrown into the scales against the former Viceroy. He
was summoned specially from Sheringham in Norfolk where
he lay ill of phlebitis. The doctors protested that travelling

would be dangerous. Balfour was undeterred. He felt he had a duty to perform. Arrived at the Palace, he expressed with conviction the view that in these days a Prime Minister must be in the House of Commons. He confined himself strictly to this point. He was careful to use no other argument. It was enough. When late that night Balfour returned to his sick-bed at Sheringham after his fatiguing journey, he was asked by some of his most cherished friends who were staying with him, ' And will dear George be chosen ? ' ' No,' he replied placidly, ' dear George will not.'

While Curzon was journeying to London, debating what he should do with No. 10, Downing Street, the King sent for Mr. Baldwin. When, that afternoon, Lord Stamford-ham was announced at Carlton House Terrace, it was only to tell him that Mr. Baldwin was already at Buckingham Palace. The blow was bitter, and for the moment overwhelming.

The course of history was thus sharply deflected by the choice of the Crown. The Conservative party would certainly have accepted Curzon as their leader if he had received the King's Commission. The untimely dissolution of 1923 would have been avoided. The Parliament newly-elected would have lived the greater part of its normal life ; the Socialists would not have come into power in the autumn upon a minority vote ; the General Elections of 1923 and 1924 with their great strain upon the Parliamentary personnel, and their injury to public economy and administration, would have been avoided. The principle that a Prime Minister in the Lords is an anachronism, was, as it were, recognized by the Crown. Actually, it is a question which only Parliament can settle in presence of the personalities and circumstances of the occasion.

Now that these matters can be viewed in the afterlight, opinion has declared itself, that the right choice was made. It is more doubtful whether it was made in the right way. But had Curzon been able to foresee events, his personal fortunes might yet have been retrieved. The new Prime Minister was deeply anxious to retain his services. No sooner did Mr. Baldwin receive the commission than his first visit was made to Curzon to ask him to remain at the Foreign Office. Curzon agreed at once. He had no wish to give up the Foreign Office. He did not allow his grief to distort his action. He did not give way to pique. He played his part loyally in the new team. This right and public-spirited conduct, though creditable to his character, was finally fatal to his ambitions. If he had stood aside from the Government, there can be little doubt that after the electoral disaster which befell the Conservative party six months later, he would have been in a position of greater strength than ever before. Baldwin was judged to have blundered. Curzon, uncompromised by the miscalculation, and representing the Free Trade policy now again perforce adopted by the Conservatives, might well have been the indispensable man. When therefore at the end he lost the game, it was because he played it fairly and like a man. This was one of those cases in which virtue is not its own reward.

A final disillusionment for Curzon resulted from the next turn of Fortune's wheel; and when the Government of 1924 was formed, he yielded the Foreign Office to another.

These heavy reverses were supported after the initial shocks with goodwill and dignity. But undoubtedly they invested the long and strenuous career with ultimate disappointment. The morning had been golden; the noontide was bronze; and the evening lead. But all were solid, and each was polished till it shone after its fashion.

PHILIP
SNOWDEN

Elliott & Fry, Ltd
PHILIP SNOWDEN, CHANCELLOR OF THE EXCHEQUER

PHILIP SNOWDEN

WHAT sort of picture does the average man and woman make of the political figures of the present day ? How far is it removed from the truth ? How far is it a caricature ? Do the millions form their opinions from the cartoons and comments of the newspapers ? Or have they some deep instinct which enables them to discern the real character and worth of their public men ?

Undoubtedly when politicians, or statesmen as they like to be called, have been long on the stage, their fellow-countrymen have a pretty shrewd idea of their quality and value. About new people, suddenly lifted by the Press or the Caucus, or both, to national prominence, the average man or woman (we always have to say ' or woman ' now they have the vote) may easily be misled and is rightly distrustful. That is why our vast electorate, like its smaller predecessors, likes to be governed by well-known person-alities or even by well-known names. They like to act upon an impression of a man gathered, shall we say, across a quarter of a century. They feel that on such a survey, taking the rough with the smooth, they can form a clear like or dislike, a definite agreement or opposition.

It would be wrong to think of Mr. Snowden as the spiteful, vindictive Death's-head of his caricatures ; as a sworn tormentor who used the Rack, the Thumbscrew, and the Little Ease of taxation with gusto upon his victims. He was really a tender-hearted man, who would not have hurt a gnat unless his party and the Treasury told him to do so, and then only with compunction. Philip Snowden was a remarkable figure of our time. He was among the chief architects of the Labour-Socialist Party. He was the first and so far the only Socialist Chancellor of the Exchequer. He played a decisive part in the political convulsion which hurled the Socialists from power in 1931, and inaugurated the National Government regime twice acclaimed by enormous majorities.

For nearly forty years Philip Snowden steadily and consistently built up the Socialist party. He faced all its misfortunes, swallowed and reproduced most of its follies; and he held an indisputable right to share its years of prosperity. The first quality that the British nation approved in Philip Snowden was that they knew where he stood.

He was no more a doctrinaire Socialist than Ramsay MacDonald, but he revolted from Socialism at a different angle. MacDonald liked the Tory atmosphere and tradition; the glamour of old England appealed to him. Snowden viewed the Socialist creed with the blistering intellectual contempt of the old Gladstonian Radical. To him Toryism was a physical annoyance, and militant Socialism a disease brought on by bad conditions or contagion, like rickets or mange. His heart was filled with an equal measure of disgust and pity when he contemplated the true-blue Conservative or the green-eyed Socialist.

There are few survivors now. Gladstonian Radicals are a very arrogant brood. To begin with they are quite sure they know all about everything. For them the world might have much to do, but it had nothing to know after the days of Queen Victoria. Adam Smith and John Stuart Mill wrote it all out quite plainly. Cobden, Bright, and with some backsliding due, as they opine, to his bad early environment, Mr. Gladstone, expressed it with admirable eloquence. The solitary new teacher whom they will admit very suspiciously to their mental parlours is Mr. Henry George—(not Mr. Lloyd George by any manner of means!). Henry George with his Land Taxation impinged roughly upon the Victorian Radicals. There was a leak, it seemed, in the diving-bell in which they dwelt. It was an undoubted leak. It might be deplored, but had to be faced ; otherwise not a chink, crack or crevice had been opened in their system of thought by half a century of shock and change.

Snowden's rigidity of doctrine was otherwise impenetrable. Free imports, no matter what the foreigner may do to us ; the Gold Standard, no matter how short we run of gold ; austere repayment of debt, no matter how we have to borrow the money ; high progressive direct taxation, even if it brings creative energies to a standstill ; the ' Free breakfast-table,' even if it is entirely supplied from outside the British jurisdiction ! Their one weakness, their one indulgence, their one relish,—the exceptional taxation of the value of the land, which, as has been often mentioned, ' God gave to the people.' For the rest, resistance to all wars, even the most inevitable, and dour, cold aversion from all imperial possessions and assets, even those from which large numbers of cottage homes gain the employment which gives them their daily bread. As for those who cannot understand or will not believe these doctrines, it were better for them that a millstone were bound about their neck, and that they were cast out into the Primrose League, or into the Independent Labour Party.

We must imagine with what joy Mr. Snowden was welcomed at the Treasury by the permanent officials. All British Chancellors of the Exchequer have yielded themselves, some spontaneously, some unconsciously, some reluctantly to that compulsive intellectual atmosphere. But here was the High Priest entering the sanctuary. The Treasury mind and the Snowden mind embraced each other with the fervour of two long-separated kindred lizards, and the reign of joy began. Unhappily a lot of things cropped up which were very tiresome. First of all the Chancellor of the Exchequer had to go on pretending he was a Socialist, the wordy champion of the class war and so on. This was awkward when a ' statesmanlike ' speech had to be made to the Bankers, or an appeal made to the public to buy Saving Certificates. Then the finances had been left in such a shocking state by that profligate Mr. Churchill, that the new Chancellor of the Exchequer in his difficulties had to adopt just the same kind of devices he had blamed so harshly in his predecessor. Economy, too, was very baffling when the Tories had kept the military services at the minimum, and all the Socialists put their trust in the Dole as the last hope of Party salvation. Upon these incongruities there is no need to dwell.

I have of course no sympathy with the cause which Snowden championed. The destruction of Liberalism by the Labour movement, and the ranging of the less-contented and less-prosperous millions of our countrymen under the foreign and fallacious standards of Socialism, has been a disaster to the British people, the consequences of which are only gradually becoming apparent. It has been attended with a decline in the progress of democracy, with a marked discrediting of universal suffrage, and with the decay of the parliamentary institutions by which the liberties of England were won. A crudeness and dullness has been brought into the discussion of every question, which can already be sharply contrasted with the tenseness of Victorian debates, and the strict control then exerted by the House of Commons over the Executive.

The promulgation by great organized parties of a programme of nationalizing all the means of production, distribution, and exchange, coupled with the cosmopolitan, anti-patriotic mood, has produced in Europe violent reactions towards the extremes of nationalism and the tyrannies of dictatorship. If in our island these results have not yet become apparent, it is only because Socialists, when they become Ministers, largely abandon in practice the doctrines and principles by preaching which they have risen to power. It was undoubtedly a grave mischief and injury not only to the working people but to the whole nation, to found a class party affianced to visionary principles which could only be translated into action by desperate civil commotion and the ruin of British freedom and greatness.

After thirty years of faithful, tireless labour in building up this new party Philip Snowden found himself compelled by public duty to turn the whole of his vitriolic eloquence and propagandism against his own creation, and chose to end his political life as a Viscount in the hereditary Assembly which he had so long laboured to destroy. The apparent contradiction of spending a life-time in creating the Socialist Party and then striking it with unconcealed relish its fatal blow does not, when all is considered, expose him to any charge of instability or inconsistency of purpose. All his life he sincerely hated Toryism, Jingoism, Vested Interests, and what are called ' The Upper Classes.' On the other hand, he never had the slightest intention of taking part in any revolutionary movement, nor would he in any circumstances have become responsible for a state of laxity and demoralization, financial or political, which would endanger the solid foundations of the established monarchical, parliamentary and capitalist system. On the contrary, confronted with the imminence of a breakdown in the existing order of things and national bankruptcy, he not only withstood his own friends and colleagues, but fell upon them with a whole-hearted ferocity which astounded the public and delighted the greater part of it.

A distinction must be drawn between his conduct and that of Mr. Ramsay MacDonald. In the hour of national emergency Snowden quitted and at the same time almost destroyed the party he had made. But as soon as the crisis had passed he sought occasion to break with his new allies, and become again the lively exponent of the ideas he had championed all his life. He did not dream of continuing in his office as a quasi-Conservative Minister. Whether if he had been the head of the Government, he would have acted differently, cannot be known. The pleasures and pomps of Ministerial life, such as they are, the amenities of elegant and opulent society, made no appeal to him. Nothing that could be offered by the ruling forces in our Commonwealth swayed his judgment or his action.

The crisis surmounted, he shook off his new friends with the same thorough-paced vigour as he had his old. The violence of his denunciations of the Socialists in 1931 was matched by the terms in which he upbraided the National Government in 1935. This apparent catholicity of animosities gave him the appearance of a kind of fierce dog who would bite anyone and everyone for biting's sake. Actually it arose from an extreme integrity of personal conviction from which only a supreme emergency justified a temporary departure. Such a man, had he been a Spaniard, might have saved Spain the horrors of civil war by upholding democratic and parliamentary government with an iron hand. Such a man was the German Socialist Noske who saved Germany from Communism in 1919. Snowden knew exactly how far he meant to go, and when pushed beyond that limit reacted with a violence at once salutary and astonishing.

The story which he has written of his early life makes us all not only respect his character, but also admire the free, tolerant Constitution of England under which he rose from a humble cottage in a Yorkshire village to be Chancellor of the Exchequer in the richest country in the world and —if that be promotion—a Viscount among its ancient aristocracy. The tale reveals to us the dignity and spaciousness of an English cottage home. He displays the riches of poverty when sustained by strict principles, by religious faith, and by a keen interest in social evolution. We hear discussions between his father and his uncle upon predestination, election, and hell-fire, and the decisive summing-up of his mother :

' You say that God loves us as we love our own children. Do you think I would put one of my children into hell-fire ? No ! not how bad he'd been.'

We see this little row of cottagers, who drew their water from a well in the adjoining field, rising in physical revolt against the attempt of the landowner's agent to make a charge for its use. Who can wonder at the bent given to a child's mind by such a spectacle and such an experience ?

Philip was a clever boy and soon top of the village school. To those to whom his crippled figure was so familiar it is strange to learn that no one could beat him at running and jumping. He became a pupil teacher. He passed the pre- scribed examination for a lower grade of the Civil Service, and became a ' gauger and surveyor of Inland Revenue ' in the Treasury, of which he was afterwards twice to be the Ministerial chief.

But it is the third phase of his life which most powerfully commands sympathy. Hopelessly crippled by an affection of the spine which followed a slight accident, he was forced to leave the Civil Service. His father had died. He re- turned with his mother to his native village of Ickornshaw, now noted in the Peerage. For ten years he traversed the length and breadth of the island, as a Socialist lecturer and agitator. To say that these were years of struggle against poverty would be altogether to misconceive their quality. Philip Snowden vanquished poverty from the outset by the simple process of reducing his own wants to so rigorous a compass that upon thirty shillings a week, which was all that he would take for his lectures, he was able to pursue a great world issue and lead a life of proud independence. He was a preaching friar with no Superior to obey but his intellect. In this latter-day period when riches count so much and the fear of poverty haunts so many, there are moral lessons of the highest value for all classes in this modest account.

I first met him many years ago when I was a young Liberal Minister and he one of the small band of Independent Labour men who nevertheless found themselves forced to conform to the main policy of the Asquith Government. We travelled for four hours together to Lancashire. Then for the first time I saw beneath this apparently bitter and even spiteful spirit and regard something of the appeal and kindliness of his nature. His face, though in a way twisted by pain, ill-health and the mood of revolt, was lighted by a smile truly disarming, comprehending and delightful.

Afterwards it fell to my lot for seven years to wrangle with him about finance as Chancellor of the Exchequer, or in opposition to his Chancellorship, and we hit each other as hard as we could within the wide rules of Order. But never have I had any feeling towards him which destroyed the impression that he was a generous, true-hearted man.

The Marxian aberration never obsessed his keen intelligence. One who knew him well said to me, ' No one will ever know what a Labour Government will be like till they see one without Snowden at the Exchequer.' Arrived at this post, he confronted his colleagues with a resistance to wild and sloppy extravagance, however popular, which staggered them. Although overborne on many points, he continued to fight for what he regarded as the essential principles of sound finance, and the friction of this conflict roused him to the fury and even hatred with which he eventually assailed his friends and colleagues.

The British democracy should be proud of Philip Snowden. He was a man capable of maintaining the structure of Society while at the same time championing the interests of the masses. His long life of effort, self-denial, and physical affliction was crowned by honourable success. His fearlessness, his rectitude, his austerity, his sobriety of judgment, his deep love of Britain and his studiously-concealed, but intense, pride in British greatness, distinguish him as one of the true worthies of our age. His life of privation, of affliction, of self-discipline, of war-time odium, had a grand culmination. The history of Parliament will not ignore the scene when the House of Commons rose to their feet in enthusiasm as he recited the famous lines :

' All our past proclaims the future : Shakespeare's voice
    and Nelson's hand,
' Milton's faith and Wordsworth's trust in this our chosen
    and chainless land,
' Bear us witness . . .
    Come the world against her, England yet shall stand ! '

CLEMENCEAU

Central Press Photos Ltd

GEORGES CLEMENCEAU IN RETIREMENT

CLEMENCEAU

MANY futile lamentations have been printed about the quarrel between Clemenceau and Foch. The reading world has been invited to deplore the mutual reproaches of these twin saviours of France in her extremity. Both disputants were old men, covered with glory and nearing the grave. They belong to history; and a deathless page of history belongs to them. Why should they tear that page? Even if Clemenceau did treat Foch roughly, and did brush him from the political arena as soon as the victory was won, or if Foch had sent earlier a plaster bust of himself to Clemenceau, hoping to procure patronage, surely, it is urged, these tales might well have been left untold. Everything should be presented decorously to future generations. Litter should not be allowed to gather around the monument upon which only the good and great things that men have done should be inscribed.

I cannot agree. The Muse of History must not be fastidious. She must see everything, touch everything, and, if possible, smell everything. She need not be afraid that these intimate details will rob her of Romance and Heroworship. Recorded trifles and tittle-tattle may—and, indeed, ought—to wipe out small people. They can have no permanent effect upon those who have held with honour the foremost stations in the greatest storms. A generation or two—a century, certainly—will present these two men in their true proportions. The judgment of our descendants will be unruffled by their final disputations. We are the richer rather, that Foch flings the javelin at Clemenceau from beyond the tomb, and that Clemenceau, at the moment of descending into it, hurls back the weapon with his last spasm.

We are certainly the richer by the possession of Clemenceau's remarkable book ' Grandeurs et Misères de la Victoire.' Quick and shallow writers have been prone to treat this work as the morose incoherences of an aged mind. They have hastened to apologize for it. Common sense and fairness, we are told, forbid us to attach importance to the fierce mumblings of a moribund octogenarian. I, on the contrary, regard this book as a magnificent contribution to the history of the Age and of the Crash. On every page it contains sentences and phrases which illuminate and make plain to future times not only the character of Clemenceau, but the story of the War and its causes. Foch's rank among the world's great generals may be disputed, but it is already certain that Clemenceau was one of the world's great men. And here we have his image hewn by himself —a rugged masterpiece, unfinished and in parts distorted, but for all time a revelation.

The truth is that Clemenceau embodied and expressed France. As much as any single human being, miraculously magnified, can ever be a nation, he was France. Fancy paints nations in symbolic animals—the British Lion, the American Eagle, the Russian double-headed ditto, the Gallic Cock. But the Old Tiger, with his quaint, stylish cap, his white moustache and burning eye, would make a truer mascot for France than any barnyard fowl. He was an apparition of the French Revolution at its sublime moment, before it was overtaken by the squalid butcheries of the Terrorists. He represented the French people risen against tyrants—tyrants of the mind, tyrants of the soul, tyrants of the body; foreign tyrants, domestic tyrants, swindlers, humbugs, grafters, traitors, invaders, defeatists —all lay within the bound of the Tiger; and against them the Tiger waged inexorable war. Anti-clerical, anti-monarchist, anti-Communist, anti-German—in all this he represented the dominant spirit of France.

There was another mood and another France. It was the France of Foch—ancient, aristocratic; the France whose grace and culture, whose etiquette and ceremonial has bestowed its gifts around the world. There was the France of chivalry, the France of Versailles, and, above all, the France of Joan of Arc. It was this secondary and sub-merged national personality that Foch recalled. In the combination of these two men during the last year of the War, the French people found in their service all the glories and the vital essences of Gaul. These two men embodied respectively their ancient and their modern history. Between the twain there flowed the blood-river of the Revolution. Between them towered the barriers which Christianity raises against Agnosticism. But when they gazed upon the inscription on the golden statue of Joan of Arc: ' La pitié qu'elle avait pour le royaume de France ' and saw gleaming the Maid's uplifted sword, their two hearts beat as one. The French have a dual nature in a degree not possessed by any other great people. There is nothing like this duality in Great Britain or the United States, or even in Germany. It is an unending struggle which goes on continually, not only in every successive Parliament, but in every street and village of France, and in the bosom of almost every Frenchman. Only when France is in mortal peril does the struggle have a truce. The comradeship of Foch and Clemenceau illustrates as in a cameo the history of France.

* * * * *

Clemenceau's story is familiar to most of us. A life of storm, from the beginning to the end; fighting, fighting all the way; never a pause, never a truce, never a rest. His blade was forged and tempered in the fires and chills of half a century. He was Mayor of Montmartre amid the perils of the Commune. His assault upon the crumbling Empire and his resistance to the excesses of the revolutionaries; his vain attempt to save the lives—almost at the cost of his own

—of Generals Clément Thomas and Lecomte, concentrated upon him the malice both of extremists opposed in their atrocities, and of reactionaries victorious and seeking the punishment of those who had stirred the mob, and could no longer lead it. He struggled long and arduously to earn his daily bread as a doctor, as a teacher, as a journalist. All these trials were but the early morning of his long and long-threatened life. When he entered Parliament another series of conflicts began. The unswerving Radical-Republican ; the destroyer of Ministers and Ministries ; the Parliamentary Tiger whom all politicians feared ; the iconoclast, the duellist, the merciless assailant of men who were building the new French Colonial Empire, gathered against him foes on every side. He followed Gambetta and repudiated him. He was duped by Boulanger and became his greatest enemy. The existence of the Republic hung for years by a thread. In Clemenceau, at least, the thread had one unsleeping guardian.

But what a tumult of animosities followed in his wake ! Everyone had felt the lash of his tongue and of his pen, and not a few had faced his sword or pistol. Deep forces, wide-spread interests, sacred traditions had been affronted—nay, wounded, injured, hampered. A dozen statesmen of first-class eminence remembered that he had been the ruin of their ambitions and of their plans. Sometimes their plans were good. Jules Ferry, denounced and driven from power as ' the Tonkinner,' tripled by his labours and his sacrifices the extent of the French Colonial possessions. His fall was due to Clemenceau more than to any other man. Another field opened, an old, historic field for France. The English invited French co-operation in restoring solvency and order to Egypt. Fear of Clemenceau was a recognizable factor in the momentous decision which made the French Fleet steam supinely from the scene of the impending bombardment of Alexandria. Clemenceau had not been able to stop France acquiring Tunis, Tonkin, or Indo-China. But he had broken the man who did the work ; and he had, in fact, kept her out of Egypt. The new Colonial Empire of France had its contribution of bayonets to make in the fighting lines of 1914. No one had checked or prevented the acquisition of that Empire so much as Clemenceau. Surely, in after years, this reflection must have caused him many a pang. It certainly brought him many a reproach.

There is in French politics an intensity, an intricacy, and a violence unequalled in Great Britain. It reached its extreme in the eighties and nineties. All the elements of blood-curdling political drama were represented by actual facts. The life of the French Chamber, hectic, fierce, poisonous, flowed through a succession of scandals and swindles, of exposures, of perjuries, forgeries, and murders, of plottings and intriguings, of personal ambitions and revenges, of crooking and double-crossing, which find their modern parallel only in the underworld of Chicago. But here they were presented upon the lime-lit stage of the most famous of the nations before an audience of all the world. The actors were men of the highest ability, men of learning and eloquence, men of repute and power ; men who proclaimed the noblest sentiments, who lived in the public eye ; men who directed armies, diplomacy and finance. It was a terrible society, grimly polished, loaded with explosives, trellised with live electric wires. Through the centre of it, turning to make a front now here, now there, and beating down opponents with his mace, Clemenceau long strode, reckless, aggressive and triumphant.

Let me merely mention the four major scandals which convulsed France in the last quarter of the nineteenth century. The Grévy affair, in which the President's son-in-law was convicted of the wholesale bartering of honours, costing President Grévy his place and fame : the vain Boulanger craze, which came within an ace of destroying the Republic under pretext of cleansing and rehabilitating it. These were the first two. Greater and worse were to follow : the cesspool of Panama must be drained : the torture of Dreyfus must run its course. Let the reader remember that each of these astounding episodes, ready-made dramas of actual life, took place in a country already riven internally by memories of revolution and civil war, divided into the unforgiving factions of Royalists, Bonapartists, Republicans and Socialists ; in a State where nothing was secure or unchallenged ; a State newly-defeated in the field, and dwelling always under the shadow of the German power. They took place among a people whose history for a century had been one of external wars ending in disasters, and internal feuds culminating in massacres and proscriptions. Thrice had foreign armies entered Paris to dictate a peace. Four or five *coups d'état* or revolutions had erected or overthrown Sovereigns, Constitutions, Governments and Laws. As recently as 1871 the suppression of the Commune had been attended by thousands of executions. On every side, in every party, blood and the stains of blood were visible—unconcealable by elegant manners, culture, or intellectual glory. There was nothing like it in modern Europe before the War. There never has been so polite and civilized a society, nursing such hideous wounds.

Clemenceau gave no quarter and could expect none. He had overturned a series of Governments by taking every advantage, fair or unfair. He had been pitiless in the Grévy scandal. He had the political scalps of a dozen Ministers nailed upon his door. He had been at all times ready to go all lengths—including armed action—against General Boulanger and the patriotic forces which gathered blindly behind that man of straw. So far, he had been the ruthless attacker. But with Panama the boot seemed on the other leg. The pestilence of suspicion tainted him with its infecting breath. The two greatest scoundrels in the Panama frauds, the two chief corrupters of public men, were Cornelius Herz and Baron Reinach. Clemenceau was intimate with both. The former had given financial aid to his newspaper *Justice* ; he had, with characteristic courage, escorted the latter to see the Minister of the Interior on the very night of Reinach's death-agony. The conduct of one hundred and forty deputies was in question. Many were known to be involved in the coils of corruption. On every side reputations were broken or assailed. Each falling man strove to drag down others. In the delirium of such days the slightest contact with the guilty was held to compromise a public man. Clemenceau's contacts had not been slight : nor was the explanation which he vouchsafed particularly exhaustive. Should he, then—he, who had been so unsparing of others—escape ? Was not this the moment for his foes to unite and crush him once for all ?

In full Assembly the passionate Déroulède declared that Herz's rise to influence and honour in France could only be due to the aid of some man of exceptional influence and power. ' This serviceable, devoted, indefatigable intermediary—so active, so dangerous—you all know him. His name is on the lips of all, but there is not one among you who would name him ; for he has three things you fear—his sword, his pistol and his tongue. I defy all three, and I will name him. It is M. Clemenceau ! '

And, again :

' Cornelius Herz is an enemy agent. It is right that his accomplices should suffer. Meanwhile, let us mark out for public vengeance the most formidable, the guiltiest of those who served him.'*

No country is free from such episodes. The savings of the thrifty have been squandered, public money has been pilfered or shamefully misapplied. Members of the legislature, or even ministers, have received bribes or benefits, or have come under obligations to great interests ; and it can be presumed or alleged that their votes or speeches have been corrupt. Mixed up with those actually guilty are many who, though not criminals, are compromised by imprudent conduct or unsavoury association. Mixed up again with these are men whose completely innocent transactions or friendships seem to class them with the guilty. Once the

* ' The Tiger, Georges Clemenceau, 1841–1929,' by George Adam.

hue and cry is raised, once motives are impugned, once lists of names are circulated by rumour, and suspicion spreads on all sides, thoroughly legitimate actions or connections may be profoundly dangerous to a public man. But there is always one sure defence for confident integrity : a modest, austere mode of living, domestic accounts which can be laid before the whole world, a proud readiness to exhibit every source of income. Such was the defence which Clemenceau was able to make. ' My life is an open book,' he said to his constituents, ' and I defy anyone to find any other luxury in it than a saddle-horse whose upkeep costs me five francs a day, and a five-hundred-franc share in a shoot.'

But further charges were in store. Repulsed upon Panama, Clemenceau's many foes returned to the attack with new weapons. Documents purporting to come from the British Foreign Office were produced with the connivance of the French Ministry to prove that he was in the pay of England. These documents were obviously forgeries, and the direct attack in the Chamber broke down ignominiously ; but the tale was spread far and wide. ' Now,' it was said, ' we know why he opposed our Colonial expansion ; now we know why he kept us out of Egypt and nearly did us out of Tunis.' Hateful cries ' A-oh yes ! ' and ' Spik Ingleesh ! ' saluted him at every meeting. He was defeated in his constituency of the Var, and quitted its bounds under the taunts and insults of the mob. Rarely was a public man in time of peace more cruelly hounded and hunted. Dark days, indeed, and the leering triumphs of once-trampled foes !

> ' The desolator, desolate ;
> The victor overthrown ;
> The arbiter of others' fate,
> A suppliant for his own.'

No, not suppliant : never that. Defiant, unconquerable, he faced the infuriated French world alone.

Excluded from the Chamber, his voice could no longer be heard. Never mind ! He had another weapon. He had a pen. His biographer says that Clemenceau's journalistic output could not be contained in a hundred substantial volumes. He wrote for bread and life : for life and honour ! And far and wide what he wrote was read. Thus he survived. He survived not to recover only, but to assault : not to assault, but to conquer. The worst of all the scandals had yet to come. Clemenceau became the champion of Dreyfus. Here he had to fight, to him the most sacred thing in France—the French Army. The Church, Society, High Finance, the Press—these, as before, were ranged against him. But now, in addition, was that splendid organization upon whose bayonets the liberties of Europe were soon to depend. ' Destroy confidence in the Army chiefs, and you will have imperilled the safety of the country ! ' exclaimed the generals in chorus. ' Is it to a butchery you wish us to lead your sons ? ' cried General de Pellieu at one of the Dreyfus trials. But after all, the question at issue was whether Dreyfus was a traitor or not. And he was innocent. The whole nation took sides. Friendships were ruptured and families divided. But the genius of France was not darkened. Truth and Justice marched forward : and along the path which he had helped to clear for them, Clemenceau came back into his own. He even became for a space Prime Minister.

*　　*　　*　　*　　*

Such was the man who, armed with the experience and loaded with the hatreds of half a century, was called to the helm of France in the worst period of the War. Many of the French generals were discredited, and all their plans had failed. Widespread mutinies had been with difficulty suppressed at the front. Profound and tortuous intrigues gripped Paris. Britain had bled herself white at Paschendaele, the Russians had collapsed, the Italians were at the last gasp, and the Americans were far away. The giant enemy towered up, brazen, and so far as we could see, invulnerable. It was at this moment, after every other conceivable combination had been tried, that the fierce old man was summoned to what was in fact the Dictatorship of France. He returned to power as Marius had returned to Rome ; doubted by many, dreaded by all, but doom-sent, inevitable.

It was at this time that I first began to know him. I had met him several times before, but only in a casual way. My work as Minister of Munitions brought me frequently to Paris, and involved me constantly with French Ministers. My close association with Mr. Lloyd George afforded addi-tional intimate contacts. I was with Clemenceau for half an hour on the morning when he was forming his Ministry. I listened to his opening speech in the Chamber. My friend, colleague, and opposite number, Albert Thomas, had only a day or two before lost office in the ministerial earthquake. We had been drawn so closely together in the details of business, that I ventured an appeal to the Tiger not to disturb a cross-channel combination that was working smoothly. I thought I had made an impression ; but meanwhile Thomas, supported by the Socialists, had declared that Clemenceau as Premier ' was a danger to national defence.' This of course was mortal.

I also heard Clemenceau's reply in the Chamber. It is very difficult for a foreigner with only a superficial know-ledge of the language and only an indirect sensing of the atmosphere, to judge such oratorical performances. Cer-tainly Clemenceau reproduced more than any other French Parliamentarian I have heard, the debating methods of the House of Commons. The essence and foundation of House of Commons debating is formal conversation. The set speech, the harangue addressed to constituents, or to the wider public out of doors, has never succeeded much in our small wisely-built chamber. To do any good you have got to get down to grips with the subject and in human touch with the audience. Certainly Clemenceau seemed to do this ; he ranged from one side of the tribune to the other, without a note or book of reference or scrap of paper, barking out sharp, staccato sentences as the thought broke upon his mind. He looked like a wild animal pacing to and fro behind bars, growling and glaring ; and all around him was an assembly which would have done anything to avoid having him there, but having put him there, felt they must obey. Indeed it was not a matter of words or reasoning. Elemental passions congealed by suffering, dire perils close and drawing nearer, awful lassitude and deep forebodings, disciplined the audience. The last desperate stake had to be played. France had resolved to unbar the cage and let her tiger loose upon all foes, beyond the trenches or in her midst. Language, eloquence, arguments were not needed to express the situation. With snarls and growls, the ferocious, aged, dauntless beast of prey went into action.

In this fashion did the death-grapple with Germany begin. It was to last for a whole year. Cruel aspersions and injuries were inflicted on eminent Frenchmen. The execution of proved traitors was but the symbol of a potential terrorism which would have sent, if the need or the mood had required it, men guilty of no more than intellectual vagaries, men who had held the highest office in the State, to face a firing-party at Vincennes. Mere opposition or association with friends previously considered lukewarm or defeatist was sufficient to expose statesmen of the highest standing at least to the danger of arrest. Clemenceau inspired on all sides a terror ; but no one had so much reason to complain of it as the Germans.

As a foreigner he allowed me sometimes to say things to him he would have tolerated from few Frenchmen. ' Surely it would be wise to get them all around you now, and to forget old quarrels. Distinguished people get into positions which they cannot get out of by themselves. In England we often help them to get down off awkward perches. We make many muddles, but we always keep more or less together.' His eye twinkled, he wagged his head, his droll comprehending smile lit up the seared Mongol-like visage.

One day he said to me, ' I have no political system, and I

have abandoned all political principles. I am a man dealing with events as they come in the light of my experience,' or it may be it was ' according as I have seen things happen.' I was reminded of Monsieur de Camors' letter to his son: ' All principles are equally true or equally false, according to circumstances.' Clemenceau was quite right. The only thing that mattered was to beat the Germans.

Presently came the supreme crisis. The Germans were again on the Marne. From the heights of Montmartre the horizon could be seen alive with the flashes of artillery. The Americans were pitchforked in at Château-Thierry. I had important munition and aeroplane factories all around Paris: we had to prepare to move them and to improvise shelters farther south : so I was much in the French capital. Before a war begins one should always say, ' I am strong, but so is the enemy.' When a war is being fought one should say, 'I am exhausted, but the enemy is quite tired too.' It is almost impossible to say either of these two things at the time they matter. Until the Germans collapsed, they seemed unconquerable ; but so was Clemenceau. He uttered to me in his room at the Ministry of War words he afterwards repeated in the tribune: ' I will fight in front of Paris ; I will fight in Paris ; I will fight behind Paris.' Everyone knew this was no idle boast. Paris might have been reduced to the ruins of Ypres or Arras. It would not have affected Clemenceau's resolution. He meant to sit on the safety-valve, till he won or till all his world blew up. He had no hope beyond the grave ; he mocked at death ; he was in his seventy-seventh year. Happy the nation which when its fate quivers in the balance can find such a tyrant and such a champion.

*   *   *   *   *

When the victory was won, France to foreign eyes seemed ungrateful. She flung him aside and hastened back as quickly as possible to the old hugger-mugger of party politics. In principle one cannot blame the French ; but they might have behaved more politely. The Clemenceau of the Peace was a great statesman. He was confronted with enormous difficulties. He made for France the best bargain that the Allies, who were also the world, would tolerate. France was disappointed; Foch was disappointed, and also offended by personal frictions. Clemenceau, unrepentant to the end, continued to bay at the Church. The Presidency passed to an amiable nonentity, who soon tumbled out of a railway-carriage. The Tiger went home, as everyone thought to die. But he lived for years and years in the fullest possible physical and mental vigour. At any moment he was fit to grasp the helm and steer the ship. Of course he felt it. Proud as Lucifer, he wrapped himself in his deathless record and formidable prestige. ' What are you going to do ? ' they asked him when he returned from his tour in India. ' I am going to live until I die,' he replied obdurately.

Whenever I visited Paris on public business, whatever the Government in power, I made a point of calling on him. ' I invite no one here,' he said, ' but whenever you come, you will be welcome.' He even on one occasion went to the point of saying in ' an unforgettable manner ' to his eldest daughter, from whom I have it, ' Mr. Winston Churchill is very far from being an enemy of France.' I have my last picture of him a year before he died. The little house in the Rue François : a small library-sittingroom. It is winter, and the room seems to be unheated. There is a large fireplace ; but it is piled full of books. Evidently no fires this year ! I wish I had kept on my overcoat. The old man appears, in his remarkable black skull-cap, gloved and well wrapped-up. None of the beauty of Napoleon, but I expect some of his St. Helena majesty ; and far back beyond Napoleon, Roman figures come into view. The fierceness, the pride, the poverty after great office, the grandeur when stripped of power, the unbreakable front offered to this world and to the next—all these belong to the ancients.

'Mr. Churchill, I always admired the English love of horses. I have found out why they love horses. Look at their cavalry horses ; look still more at their artillery horses. Never were such horses so beautifully kept. I will tell you why the English love horses. They are sailors ; they live on the sea in ships. Only in their holidays do they come back to land ; and there they love animals, especially horses, because they never see them when they are on the seas.' And again :

'When I was in India I saw some things your people do not see. I used to go to the bazaars and to the fountains. I had a good interpreter, and lots of people came to me and talked. Your English officers are rough with the Indians ; they do not mingle with them at all ; but they defer to their political opinions. That is the wrong way round. Frenchmen would be much more intimate, but we should not allow them to dispute our principles of Government.'

'Mr. Lloyd George, he is now an enemy of France. He told me himself the English will never be friends with France, except when she is weak or in danger. I am angry with him, but all the same I am glad he was there while those things were going on.'

I mentioned the name of a French statesman. 'No, I cannot discuss French politics with a foreigner. You will excuse me, there are some names I do not pronounce. Come whenever you will '—at the doorway ' Good-bye.'

*　　*　　*　　*　　*

I received from his daughter the following note :

'There is a legend gathered round the memory of my father, which was already linked with my grandfather, Benjamin Clemenceau, that he wished to be buried standing upright. If he had desired it, his wish would have been carried out, with the immense respect for everything which remains of his—everything that he has touched, particularly by myself his eldest daughter, who had worked so close to him, so close, in so many daily contacts, who had known his intimate thoughts. Anyway he himself arranged even with meticulous and detailed care all that concerned his last resting-place. If you go one day to visit this grave, nameless, and without any inscription, I think that you will be moved in that simple and lonely place, where one only hears the wind in the trees and murmuring of a brook in the ravine. But he had wished to return alone to his father's side, to the land whence his ancestors came, *les Clemenceau du Colombier*, from the depths of the woodlands of La Vendée, centuries ago.'

KING GEORGE V

Graphic Photo Union

HIS MAJESTY KING GEORGE V

KING GEORGE V

THE reign of King George V will be regarded as one of the most important and memorable in the whole range of English history and that of the British Empire. In no similar period have such tremendous changes swept across the world; in none have its systems, manners and outlook been more decisively altered; in none have the knowledge, science, wealth and power of mankind undergone such vast and rapid expansion. Indeed, the speed at which the evolution of society has taken place baffles all comparison. These great shocks and disturbances have been fatal to most of the empires, monarchies and political organizations of Europe and Asia. A large part of the globe which in Victorian times lay in the mild sunshine of law and tranquillity is now scourged by storms of anarchy. Mighty nations which gained their liberties in the nineteenth century, and hopefully erected parliaments to preserve them, have fallen, or yielded themselves, to the sway of dictatorships. Over immense regions inhabited by the most gifted and educated races, as well as in barbarous countries, all enjoyment of individual freedom, all assertion of the rights of the individual against the State, has utterly lapsed. Democracy has incontinently cast aside the treasures gained by centuries of struggle and sacrifice. With a savage shout, not only the old feudalisms, but all liberal ideals have been swept away.

Still there is one great system in which law is respected and freedom reigns, where the ordinary citizen may assert his rights fearlessly against the executive power and criticize as he chooses its agents and policies. At the heart of the

British Empire there is one institution, among the most ancient and venerable, which, so far from falling into desuetude or decay, has breasted the torrent of events, and even derived new vigour from the stresses. Unshaken by the earthquakes, unweakened by the dissolvent tides, though all be drifting, the Royal and Imperial Monarchy of Britain stands firm. An achievement so remarkable, a fact so prodigious, a fact contrary to the whole tendency of the age, cannot be separated from the personality of the good, wise and truly noble King whose work is ended.

The late King's father died at a moment of severe political excitement and constitutional crisis. The Great Council which at St. James's Palace recognized and acclaimed George V as King, saw before them a man humble in the presence of the responsibilities which the hereditary lawful succession of a thousand years had cast upon him. There were few who did not feel compassion and sympathy for the unproved inheritor of such anxious glories. Some there were—many perhaps—who had misgivings for the future. Yet at that moment no one could foresee the terrible and shattering catastrophes towards which Europe and the whole world were hurrying. The fortunes even of our own land were loaded with difficulty and quarrel. The parties raged against each other. All men were agog about the veto of the Lords, about Home Rule for Ireland, about the rise of Socialism. Little did they dream that Armageddon was upon them.

We must descend to particulars. The Lords had rejected the Budget passed by a great Liberal majority in the House of Commons. They had challenged, as it seemed, the slowly built-up prescription of generations about money Bills. Upon appeal to the voters at a General Election on this direct issue the same Government had been returned by an adequate majority. It seemed that the creation of four or five hundred peers would be necessary to give effect to the so-called will of the people, if a second election returned the same political forces to power.

Here was the first problem of the new reign. It is easy, now that all these matters have settled themselves, have passed from life into history, to underrate its poignant character. One day, many years after, I ventured to ask His Majesty which was the worst time he went through. Was it this constitutional crisis, or was it the Great War? ' For me,' he said, ' the most difficult was the Constitutional crisis. In the War we were all united, we should sink or swim together. But then, in my first year, half the nation was one way and half the other.' One may imagine that most of the King's personal friends, the Services, and the social circles in which he had moved, resented bitterly the monstrous, yet possibly inevitable, creation of hundreds of new peers. A precedent there was from the reign of Anne, but only for the creation of a dozen, and only for the purpose of carrying through a definite policy. Now there was to be a manufacture of hereditary nobles upon a scale certainly fatal to the whole institution of the peerage. Nevertheless the Constitution must be made to work, and if no House of Commons could be found to submit any longer to the unlimited veto of the Lords, this lamentable expedient must be faced.

Towards the end of 1910, the Prime Minister, Mr. Asquith, asked the King for a dissolution—the second within the year—and, in addition, for a guarantee that if the new House of Commons—the third in succession—were of the same mind upon the limitation of the veto, he would consent to swamp the House of Lords and bear down its enormous Conservative majority by a host of new peerages. There is no doubt that the King suffered the deepest distress. He felt most keenly that the Prime Minister did not come to him alone, but brought with him also the Ministerial leader of the House of Lords, Lord Crewe. Mr. Asquith did this, no doubt, because Lord Crewe was a personal friend of the King, and he thought the painful discussion would be easier. Eventually the King gave the guarantee. Had he not done so, the Ministry would have resigned, and there is little doubt that at the ensuing election they would have been supported by the majority of the voters. His consent, of course, remained secret between himself and his chief Ministers.

The General Election followed. The new House of Commons passed the Parliament Act by a majority of 150. The House of Lords prepared to resist stubbornly, and the King, at a certain moment, allowed it to be stated in debate that he would consent to the overwhelming creation. Upon this intimation the Lords gave way, and the Parliament Act received the Royal Assent. It was the prelude, and meant to be the prelude, to the Home Rule Bill for Ireland.

Looking back, we must conclude that this most decided action of the King's upon a matter admittedly at the extreme fringe of the Constitution was wise and right. The Parliament Act is still the law of the land. Successive large Conservative majorities have hitherto refused to touch the new constitutional relation established by it between the two Houses. Ireland, by paths eventually far more disastrous than those which then seemed open, has gained the power to manage or mismanage her own affairs, and lost the power to manage or mismanage those of the Empire.

I have dealt precisely with this historic transaction because it must be regarded as one of the most important exercises, if not the most important, of the personal discretion of the Sovereign in interpreting the Constitution ; because it was imposed upon him at the very outset of his reign ; and because it proves the sagacity and faithfulness with which he observed the spirit of the British Constitution at a time when its letter formed no complete guide. We next entered upon a period of violent political strife. Ulster threatened armed resistance to any plan, however safe-guarded, of associating her with the Parliament in Dublin. The Covenant was signed by the Ulstermen, arms were procured from abroad, military organizations were set on foot in the North.

Counter-preparations were made in Nationalist Ireland. The factions of Orange and Green, exasperated by the antipathies of Protestant and Catholic, faced one another in menacing attitude; and the sympathy of the powerful Conservative Party and most of the rank, wealth and leadership of the British nation was passionately cast into the Ulster scale. Nay, even their aid was promised. The misunderstanding about the movements of Royal Regular Forces led, as has been described, to wholesale resignation of their commissions by the officers of the regiments immediately affected. Though it was not mutiny in any base sense, but rather an act of conscientious passive resistance, this episode has descended to us under the name of 'The Curragh Mutiny.' One may imagine the grief of the King, the head of the Army.

Side by side with these grievous events and driftings towards the rending of our national life marched other manifestations of unrest. The Women's Suffrage movement took a violent turn. Militancy became the order of the day. The streets and public meetings were the scene of frantic struggles, with women transported beyond themselves. The gaols saw them forcibly fed in hundreds. One unhappy creature cast herself to death under the hoofs of the horses on Derby Day. Labour agitation proceeded ceaselessly, heralding and accompanying the rise of the Socialist Party, and strikes and industrial disturbances were rife in all parts of the land. And then on the top of all sounded the awful warnings and mutterings which announced the approach of foreign peril and of a world war.

It was in these years that the institution of the Monarchy and the growing regard for the person of the King preserved unity, in measures of defence and foreign policy, in a nation otherwise torn by the fiercest political strife and even, as it sometimes seemed, drawing near to the verge of civil war. Amid this domestic turbulence and growing foreign danger the King experienced his keenest anxieties and sorrows. He had not then the commanding influence which he had gathered to the Crown and to his person by the end of his long reign ; but he adhered unswervingly to the Constitution. He strove to mitigate the fury of parties and to preserve intact the grand common inheritance of the British people. Quietly and patiently he strengthened himself, and steadily he mounted in the esteem and confidence of all classes of his subjects. Steadily also grew to power and preparedness that splendid Navy, then unquestionably the strongest in the world, in which his early life had been spent, whose ships he had commanded, with whose rough and seamy side he was familiar, and whose officers and men he knew.

Then suddenly, out of what, to ordinary folk, appeared to be a summer sky, rushed the thunderbolts of world war.

This is not the place to argue whether a more precise declaration by Great Britain might have postponed the German onslaught. It must have been with much compunction that King George, by the advice of Sir Edward Grey, signed his non-committal reply to the impassioned appeal of President Poincaré. Certainly he understood as well as any of his Ministers the vital need of bringing the British Empire unitedly into the struggle. Certainly also that love of peace—though not peace at any price—which his whole reign evinced, led him to avoid the formidable danger of moving in such a terrible business in advance of public opinion. The reserve, and even apparent hesitancy, of Britain were part of the price we had to pay for being a free Constitutional Democracy. But we gained it back tenfold by the surge of national and Imperial resolve and inflexible determination, wearing down the will-power of every antagonist, lasting unquenched over fifty-two fearful months, with which the nation once convinced entered the struggle.

We saw the King on the eve of Armageddon using all the influence he had so far been able to gather to bring about the settlement of the Irish problem, and to make Britain united in an hour so big with fate. His Buckingham

Palace conference could have been only the beginning of negotiations between the parties out of which a settlement, for which statesmen on both sides were striving, might have emerged. But the War swept all this for the time being into limbo.

The King and his devoted Queen threw themselves into every form of war work and set an example to all. Tirelessly the King inspected and reviewed the growing armies, alas for many months without weapons. Day by day he encouraged and assisted his Ministers in their various tasks. As soon as his eldest son reached the minimum age he allowed him to go to the Front, where that Prince—afterwards King Edward VIII—was repeatedly under shell and rifle fire in the trenches as a junior officer of the Guards. ' My father has four sons,' he said, ' so why should I be fettered ? ' But his second son, now King George VI, was also in danger. He served afloat and was present at the Battle of Jutland, the largest of all naval encounters. King George himself frequently visited the war zone, and the photographs of him in his steel helmet attest the numerous occasions when he came under or within the fire of the enemy. On one of these visits of inspection an unlucky accident occurred. His horse, startled by the loud cheers of the troops, reared up and fell backwards, crushing and mangling the King in a most grievous manner. When some months afterwards I took leave of him, on resigning from the Cabinet, I was shocked at his shattered condition and evident physical weakness, which had of course been hidden from the world.

The agony of the War continued. Governments and Ministers were worn out by its strains. The King was ever at hand to aid in forming new combinations designed to liberate and express more freely the indomitable war resolve of his people and Empire. All stood firm, not a link in the chain broke ; but the holding-ground in which all the anchors of British strength were cast was the hereditary Sovereign and the function of Monarchy which he so deeply comprehended. Victory came at last. Victory absolute, final, unquestionable; a triumph in arms rarely surpassed in completeness and never in magnitude. All the kings and emperors against whom he had warred, fled or were deposed. Once again Buckingham Palace was beset by an enormous concourse. It was no longer the loyal, ardent, but inexperienced enthusiasm of August, 1914. With a haggard joy, with indescribable relief and profound thankfulness, his people and Empire acclaimed the Sovereign whose throne, founded upon law and freedom, had withstood so gloriously the most formidable assaults and frightful hazards.

The shadow of victory is disillusion. The reaction from extreme effort is prostration. The aftermath even of successful war is long and bitter. The years that followed the Great War, and such peace as the infuriated democracies would allow their statesmen to make, were years of turbulence and depression. Shrill voices, unheard amidst the cannonade and the hum of national exertion, were now the loudest notes. Subversive processes, arrested by the danger, resumed their course. Weak peoples, protected by the shield of Britain from conquest or invasion, used their nursed-up and hoarded strength against their successful guardians. But the King preserved his sense of proportion. When Mr. Lloyd George returned from Paris with the Treaty of Victory, he took the unprecedented course of himself meeting his deserving subject at Victoria Station and driving him in his own carriage to Buckingham Palace. History will not overlook the significance of this act.

The main feature of our domestic politics since the War has been the devouring of the Liberal Party by the Socialists, and the presentation as an alternative Government of this powerful but strangely-assorted force, with their dissolvent theories, with their dream of a civilization fundamentally different from the only one we have been able to evolve by centuries of trial and error. George V's relations with Mr. Ramsay MacDonald and the Socialists form an important chapter in his Kingcraft. Here again the Constitution and workings of Parliamentary Government were alike his guides and his instruments. He was determined from the outset to show absolute impartiality in the Constitution to all parties, irrespective of their creed or doctrine, who could obtain a majority in the House of Commons. Indeed, if the balance were to be swayed at all, it must be on the side of the new-comers, and they must be given help and favour by the Crown.

The King, uplifted above class-strife and party-faction, has a point of view unique in our society. To be the Sovereign of all his people can be his only ambition. He must foster every tendency that makes for national unity. All law-abiding subjects must have the chance, by Constitutional process, to exercise the highest duties under the Crown. Every political leader who commands a majority in the House of Commons, or even through the division of other parties can maintain himself in that Assembly, is entitled to the fullest, most generous measure of the Royal countenance and aid. Well might the King re-echo the old saying ' Trust the people.' Never did he fear, never did he need to fear, the British Democracy. He reconciled the new forces of Labour and Socialism to the Constitution and the Monarchy. This enormous process of assimilating and rallying the spokesmen of left-out millions, will be intently studied by historians of the future. To the astonishment of foreign countries and of our American kinsmen, the spectacle was seen of the King and Emperor working in the utmost ease and unaffected cordiality with politicians whose theories at any rate seemed to menace all existing institutions, and with leaders fresh from organizing a General Strike.

The result has been to make a national unity upon Constitutional fundamentals which is the wonder of the world. Such an evolution, which might well have occupied a tumultuous century, and perhaps in its process wrecked the continuity and tradition of our national life, was achieved by

George V in the compass of his reign. In so doing he revived the idea of Constitutional Monarchy throughout the world. He drew upon himself and his country the envious admiration of many lands. He revivified the national spirit, popularized hereditary Kingship, and placed himself upon an eminence where, as a true servant of the State, he commanded not only the allegiance, but the affection, of all sorts and conditions of men.

Ireland was another sphere in which the hand of the King can be discerned without prejudice to the direct responsibility of Ministers. At grave personal risk he undertook to open the first Parliament of Northern Ireland. On this solemn occasion he asked his Ministers that words should be put in his mouth which would appeal to all his Irish subjects, appeal not only to the North but to the South. The effect of these words was electrical For good or for ill—I still believe, at last for good—the Irish settle‑ ment proceeded irresistibly towards its conclusion. On the morning after the Treaty was signed the King summoned his Ministers concerned to Buckingham Palace, was photo‑ graphed in their midst, and in the most marked and public manner associated himself personally with their action. All this policy still lies in controversy, and bitter have been the disappointments of those who signed the Treaty.

The most disputable political action which the King took was during the financial and economic crisis of 1931. There is no doubt that he used his personal influence, now become so great, to bring about the formation of a national, or so-called national, Administration, to save the country from unnecessary collapse and unwarrantable bankruptcy. But in no way did his action go beyond the boundaries of the Royal function. The entire responsibility, moral and practical, was borne by Mr. Ramsay MacDonald, the Prime Minister, and by Mr. Baldwin. These Ministers advised the King, and are accountable for their advice. Though that advice was in accordance with his own feelings and wishes, it in no way deranged the constitutional position.

The formation of a National Government and the over-whelming endorsement which it received from the largest electorate that has ever voted in our country, inaugurated a period of economic recovery and political quiet the like of which no other State can show during these eventful and difficult years. That it has been obtained at a serious cost to the vigour and vitality of our political life and perhaps even to the effectiveness of our government may be argued. But the impressive advantages were eagerly grasped by the people, and four years later they recorded once again their decisive approval of what had been done. The last phase of the King's reign thus saw the fruition of his heart's desire.

What a contrast were these last four years to the four stormy years in which it had opened! He found his country convulsed with furious party struggles. He left it tranquil and in the main united. He surmounted the greatest war ever known. He presided over the fortunes of the British Empire in years of hideous and mortal peril. He saw it emerge without the diminution by one single inch of his vast dominion. He saw the power of the Crown and of the Sovereign strengthened to an unmeasured extent, while at the same time the loyalty of the whole Empire and the rights and freedom of his subjects were established upon an ever-broader basis. He saw the Crown, which to ignorant and unthinking minds and also to many intellectuals of an earlier century had become a mere symbol, now the indis-pensable modern link upon which alone the entire British Empire or Commonwealth of Nations holds together. In-deed, by a movement contrary to the tendencies of our own past and of the age, the Crown has been placed in direct relation with all the self-governing Dominions, and their Ministers are found willing in high constitutional matters to deal personally with the Sovereign and with the Sovereign alone.

Many were the changes which he saw in our habits, cus-toms and moods. Women have acquired complete political enfranchisement and exercise enormous political power. The motor car has replaced the horse, with all that that implies. The wealth and well-being of every class has advanced, upon a giant scale. Crime, brutal violence, drunkenness, and the consumption of liquor, have diminished. We are a gentler and a more decent people. The thriving free Press has become a faithful guardian of the Royal Family. The broadcast has enabled the Sovereign to speak to all his peoples. In a world of ruin and chaos King George V brought about a resplendent rebirth of the great office which fell to his lot.

A singular completeness and symmetry dignifies his reign. The Silver Jubilee gave expression to the slowly gathered, pent-up affection of his subjects in all quarters of the world. Reverence for the Crown was fortified by honour and love for the Monarch. We saw him receiving the addresses of his Parliament in Westminster Hall, his four sons at his side. We heard his voice giving his simple heartfelt message of good cheer to all the men and women in all the lands that owned his sway. When the allotted span of life had run out, and when no climax of his reign remained, he passed swiftly and silently from our midst. Upon the verge of eternity, with failing hand, he attempted to sign the necessary commission for a Council of Regency; and he died surrounded by his loved ones, amidst the respect of mankind and the grief of all his subjects. In harness to the last, he left behind him an example and an inspiration to all concerned in the government of men. Duty, public and private, faithfully, strictly, untiringly, unostentatiously, and successfully performed, and a calm, proud humility at the summit of majestic affairs, are characteristics which will for ever illumine his fame.

LORD FISHER
AND HIS BIOGRAPHER

Elliot & Fry, Ltd.

LORD FISHER

LORD FISHER AND HIS BIOGRAPHER

IN these days ten years is a long time to wait for the posthumous biography of an eminent man. The task of writing the life of Lord Fisher has been attempted by more than one accomplished journalist. The two substantial volumes which now see the light are the work of his old friend and trusted agent, Admiral Bacon.* They will be read with the interest inseparable from Fisher's strange, dynamic personality. But it is a pity that Admiral Bacon should have discharged his mission in a spirit and method so calculated to revive the animosities and quarrels which hung around the great old sailor's neck. Most of his contemporaries were prepared to take the rough with the smooth and to let bygones be bygones. To import a mood of hatred and spiteful controversy into the discussion of the memorable transactions with which Lord Fisher was concerned, was to render no true service to his memory. His friends can only hope that these rather hurriedly slung-together records will not be the final appreciation which his own time will make of ' Jacky ' Fisher.

As I am involved in these matters, I will first say a word or two about Admiral Bacon. Bacon was an energetic, ambitious and highly competent Captain closely associated with Lord Fisher in the great revival of gunnery in the British Navy which was achieved at the beginning of the century. When Lord Fisher was First Sea Lord of the Admiralty, Captain Bacon, as he then was, commanded a ship in the Mediterranean Fleet. From this station he wrote to his intimate friend and patron, the First Sea Lord,

---

[1] *Life of Lord Fisher*, by Admiral Sir Reginald Bacon.

333

a series of vigorous and favourable accounts of the reception of the new Fisher reforms by the Fleet. As Lord Charles Beresford who was in command was hostile to these changes, Bacon's accounts, although perhaps privileged by their private and personal character, constituted, if they should become public, a divergence from his immediate Chief, and a special relationship with the First Sea Lord.

Fisher was so delighted with these letters, and thought they illustrated so powerfully the policy which he was quite rightly developing and enforcing, that he had them printed in his own arresting typography by the Admiralty Printing Press, and then after some time had passed circulated them fairly freely throughout professional and political circles. One copy was conveyed to the Editor of the *Globe* Newspaper, now defunct, and Bacon immediately found himself denounced for disloyal and unprofessional conduct towards his superior officer. The details of this extinct controversy need not concern us here. Bacon was exonerated by the Board of Admiralty of having written anything improper. He was offered further employment, but in view of the atmosphere created he decided to retire from the Service ; and shortly afterwards Lord Fisher himself resigned his position as First Sea Lord. Bacon was then in the prime of life and equipped with immense and precious technical knowledge. The expansion of the Royal Navy which preceded the Great War required largely increased facilities for making big cannons and turrets for battleships. Bacon became the manager of the Coventry Ironworks, newly devoted to naval purposes. Here he smouldered energetically from 1907 till the outbreak of the Great War.

He now appears from his writings to be inspired by a strong sense of personal grievance and of antipathy to me. But this is quite undeserved, and I will briefly set forth my relations with him. When the war broke out I had occasion to see him about the cannons and turrets he was making. He then declared that all the existing fortresses in Europe could be smashed up by heavy howitzers capable of being transported into the field. This was before the fall of Liége and Namur, and seeing his judgment and impressions vindicated by events, I directed him to make a dozen 15-inch howitzers, which he undertook to achieve in six months. These were of course the largest weapons of their kind till then ever designed. To stimulate his efforts I promised him that if the contract was completed within the specified time he should himself command them at the front. This road back into the fighting line was of course the dearest prize that could be set before an officer who had left the Service amid some disputation.

Lord Fisher at my instance was brought back to the Admiralty in the winter of 1914 as First Sea Lord. In March, 1915, Captain Bacon had made good his undertaking. Two of his enormous howitzers were already firing in France under his personal direction. The command of the Dover Patrol, one of the most important key posts in our naval war front, happened to be vacant. I knew that Lord Fisher would like to have his old subordinate and scapegoat back in the Navy. I knew also that he would be shy of proposing this himself, and I thought that Bacon with his extraordinary mechanical ingenuity and personal drive would be the very man for the Dover Cordon. I therefore proposed his appointment to Lord Fisher. The old man was profuse in expressions of gratitude, and Captain Bacon became the Admiral in charge of the Straits of Dover.

In his life of Lord Fisher Bacon complains repeatedly of a civilian as First Lord of the Admiralty, a mere politician, having the power to pick and choose naval officers for the highest commands. He specially animadverts upon my appointment of Lord Beatty some years before to the battle-cruiser squadron. How shocking to think that these sacred matters should be disposed of by a personage of purely political status ! But I must demurely observe that it was this same civilian influence to which alone he owed, first his re-entry into the fighting service and secondly the greatest opportunity of his life. No Board of Admirals, judging in a spirit of strict professionalism, would in those times have considered even for a moment the somewhat pathetic appeal of a retired officer mouldering on the beach, whose record was in their eyes smirched by disloyalty to his Commander-in-Chief.

For two years Admiral Bacon did his work, as far as I can measure it, extremely well, but in 1917 when the full force of the renewed German submarine campaign fell upon us, it became apparent that far too many enemy submarines were making their way through the Straits of Dover to prey upon our transports and convoys in the English Channel. In the dire pressure of events Bacon was deprived of his command and Sir Roger Keyes appointed in his stead. Within a few weeks of the change the British grip upon the Straits of Dover was restored, and within a few months no less than nine German submarines attempting to make a passage were destroyed. At this time I had long ceased to be responsible for the Admiralty. After serving in France or out of office for nearly two years, I had become Minister of Munitions. I was therefore in a position to know the facts, and I had no doubt that whatever Bacon's usefulness might have been in his first year, he was far too deeply absorbed in technical research and had lost touch with the dominant military aspect of his duties. However, knowing his abilities of research and invention, I was glad to find him further employment in the technical branches of my wide-ranging department. In this he discharged his duties to my satisfaction till the end of the war. Thus three times running I offered him a prized opportunity of serving his country actively at the moment of her greatest need.

Now that I have set all these matters down I am conscious that they may imply a certain criticism upon my own choice of men. I do not think this criticism would be just, because in every one of his employments Admiral Bacon rendered most valuable service. The fact that he was a technician rather than a tactician no doubt made his removal from the Dover command necessary. That in no way derogates from his usefulness in other spheres and functions. But whatever strictures may be made upon civilian influence in Naval appointments in peace or war, Admiral Bacon is surely himself the last man to make them. We may leave him thus, lucky without knowing it, consumed by a grievance which cannot interest the public, and in his sombre moods finding no hand to bite but the only one that fed him.

This digression upon Admiral Bacon is necessary to make the reader understand the kind of atmosphere in which Lord Fisher moved and the extremely able but at the same time often somewhat questionable train he gathered around him. The Bacon facet reflects a flash of the light that flowed from the old man himself. There was always something foreign to the Navy about Fisher. He was never judged to be one of that 'band of brothers' which the Nelson tradition had prescribed. Harsh, capricious, vindictive, gnawed by hatreds arising often from spite, working secretly or violently as occasion might suggest by methods which the typical English gentleman and public-school boy are taught to dislike and avoid, Fisher was always regarded as the 'dark angel' of the Naval service. The old sailor would not have recoiled from or even perhaps resented this description; on the contrary he gloried in it. 'Ruthless, relentless and remorseless' were the epithets he sought always to associate with himself. 'If any subordinate opposes me,' he used to say, 'I will make his wife a widow, his children fatherless and his home a dunghill.' He acted up to these ferocious declarations. 'Favouritism,' he wrote brazenly in the logbook of the *Vernon*, 'is the secret of efficiency.' To be a 'Fisherite' or, as the Navy called it, to be in 'the Fish pond' was during his first tenure of power an indispensable requisite for preferment. On the whole his vendettas and manœuvres were inspired by public zeal and conduced, as I hold, markedly to the public advantage. But behind him and his professional progeny, the bloodhounds followed sniffing and padding along, and now and then giving deep tongue.

My bringing Fisher back to the Admiralty in 1914 was one of the most hazardous steps I have ever had to take in my official duty. Certainly, so far as I was personally concerned, it was the most disastrous. Yet looking back to those tragic years I cannot feel that if I had to repeat the decision with the knowledge I had at that time, I should act differently. Fisher brought to the Admiralty an immense wave of enthusiasm for the construction of warships. His genius was mainly that of a constructor, organizer and energizer. He cared little for the Army and its fortunes. That was the affair of the War Office. He delighted to trample upon the Treasury wherever spending money was concerned. To build warships of every kind, as many as possible and as fast as possible, was the message, and in my judgment the sole message, which he carried to the Admiralty in the shades of that grim critical winter of 1914. I, concerned with the war in general and with the need of making British naval supremacy play its full part in the struggle, was delighted to find in my chief naval colleague an impetus intense in its force but mainly confined to the material sphere. I therefore gave him the freest possible hand and aided him to the best of my ability. When in 1917, two years after he and I had left the Admiralty, the main German submarine warfare reopened and the very foundations of our naval power were called in question, we had good reason to rejoice that all these ships and masses of small craft were crowding into the water. This was Fisher's achievement and contribution. It was so great and decisive that so far as I can measure, it makes amends for all.

His biographer is at pains to prove him an audacious naval strategist and war leader. We are reminded that he had a wonderful plan for forcing an entry into the Baltic with the British fleet, for securing command of that sea, cutting Germany from the Scandinavian supplies, and

liberating Russian armies for an amphibious descent upon
Berlin. It is quite true that Lord Fisher frequently talked
and wrote about this design, and that we together authorized
the building of a number of steel-protected flat-bottomed
boats for landing troops under fire. I do not however
believe that at any moment he had framed a definite or
coherent plan of action. Still less do I believe that he had
the resolution which, after the long and comparatively easy
stages of preparation were completed, would inevitably
have been required. He was very old. In all matters
where naval fighting was concerned he was more than
usually cautious. He could not bear the idea of risking
ships in battle. He settled down upon a doctrine widely
inculcated among our senior naval officers, that the Navy's
task was to keep open our own communications, blockade
those of the enemy, and to wait for the Armies to do their
proper job. Again and again, orally and in writing, I
confronted him with the issue ' Before you can enter the
Baltic you must first block up the Elbe. How are you
going to do this ? Are you ready to take the islands and
fight the fleet action necessary to block the Elbe ? Can
you divide the fleet and enter the Baltic with a part while
the Germans are free to sally out with their whole strength
from either end of the Kiel Canal ? ' Deep and sometimes
fiercely intimate as was our association, courageous as he
was in thought, brutally candid as he was in discussion, he
never would face this pretty obvious question. I must
record my conviction that he never seriously intended to
dare the prolonged and awful hazards of the Baltic operation, but that he talked vaguely and impressively upon
this project, which in any case was remote, with a view to
staving off demands which he knew I should make upon
him, (which indeed all the allied. Governments including
markedly President Wilson and the United States made
upon their Admiralties), to use the naval forces more
directly in the main shock of the war.

I have narrated at length in my memoirs the facts which

led to Fisher's brief regime and his resignation in May, 1915. Since I wrote *The World Crisis* several important new facts have been exposed. I did not know for instance that Lord Fisher, while working on terms apparently of the closest comradeship with me, was in secret contact with the leaders of Parliamentary opposition. I had never read, until Mr. Asquith sent it to me, the astounding ultimatum which he presented after his exodus from the Admiralty to His Majesty's Government. I had always been content to treat his behaviour at this climax as the result on the whole of a nervous breakdown. I still believe that such a mental and moral collapse is the main explanation, and by far his most serviceable excuse.

But Admiral Bacon forces us to remind ourselves of what he actually did. He was working on terms of honourable confidence and warmly-professed friendship with a political chief to whom, as he repeatedly stated, he was under important personal obligations. He agreed with that chief, with the full approval of the War Council, to carry out the operations against the Dardanelles. For three months or more he signed and sent every order to the Fleet attacking the Dardanelles. He added important vessels to it upon his personal initiative. When after the fall of the Outer Forts success seemed possible and even probable, he offered to go out and take command himself of the decisive effort that must be made to force the passage. When things began to go wrong, he set himself to stint the campaign and put obstacles in the path of action. He resisted the dispatch of the most necessary supplies, apparatus and reinforcements. By this time an army had been landed and twenty thousand men killed or wounded. The Army was clinging on to the dearly-won positions by tooth and nail. He had advocated the sending of this army. But he dissociated himself from all responsibility for its fortunes. His political chief was now exposed to ever-increasing criticism, and the Dardanelles operation was widely condemned.

At this moment, reckless of consequences to Fleet and Army, repudiating his own responsibility for the course on which events had been launched, he resigned his executive office at a moment's notice and on a frivolous pretext. A couple of submarines, we are assured by his biographer, more than he had bargained for were included in the proposed reinforcement of the fleet at the Dardanelles. He resigned, he refused to discharge the most necessary duties —even pending the appointment of a successor. He retired to his house, he pulled down the blinds, and advertised the fact that he had gone on strike. He communicated secretly with the leaders of the Opposition. Ordered by the Prime Minister in the King's name to return to his duty, he continued obdurate. He formulated no case, he declined all discussion. Meanwhile we were at war. We were in fact at one of its climacterics. In France our armies were repulsed. At the Dardanelles they were in jeopardy. German submarines menaced the fleet in the Mediterranean ; and the whole German High Sea Fleet steamed out of its harbours into the North Sea. Every preparation was made by me without any First Sea Lord for what might have been a supreme naval battle. Both fleets were moving towards each other ; but the responsible naval officer still withheld his aid. And a few days later, when a great political crisis had developed, he wrote an ultimatum to the Prime Minister prescribing in insulting detail the terms upon which he should be made Naval Dictator, adding that these terms must of course be published to the Fleet.

These are unhappily incontestable facts. Admiral Bacon drags them all nakedly into the light of day, and endeavours not indeed to justify, for that he admits to be impossible, but to excuse them at my expense. Their mere recital in his pages is blasting to Fisher's name and reputation.

I for my part, as I have said, have always adopted the hypothesis of a nervous breakdown. The strain of the war at this moment was more than his aged nerves could bear.

Hysteria rather than conspiracy is the true explanation of his action. Although he did his best to ruin an operation which might well have halved the duration of the war, and although incidentally he destroyed my power to intervene decisively in its course, I have always tried to take a charitable view and to make the best case which was possible. I knew his weakness as well as his strength. I understood his extravagances as much as I admired his genius. In sheer intellect he stood head and shoulders above his naval fellows. I am sure he was not so black as his clumsy biographer has painted him. There is always, as was well said, more error than design in human affairs. I felt for him in the bitter years of exclusion that followed his desertion of his post. I even advocated his re-employment. I am sorry that Admiral Bacon should force me to anticipate, however casually, the grievous inquest of history.

CHARLES STEWART PARNELL

National Gallery, Dublin

CHARLES STEWART PARNELL
by Sidney Prior Hall

CHARLES STEWART PARNELL

IT is difficult, if not in some ways impossible, for the present generation to realize the impressive and formidable part played by Mr. Parnell in the later decades of the reign of Queen Victoria. Modern youth now sees Home-Rule Ireland a sullen, impoverished group of agricultural counties leading a life of their own, detached from the march of Britain and the British Empire, incapable of separate appearance in any but the small and discordant rôles upon the world stage. But in the days of which we write, Ireland and the Irish affairs dominated the centre of British affairs, while Britain herself was universally envied and accepted as the leader in an advancing and hopeful civilization. For two generations after Catholic Emancipation had cast its healing influence upon the politics of the United Kingdom, the Irish parliamentary party lay quiescent in the lap of Westminster, and sought but rarely to influence events. Those were the days when Mr. Isaac Butt with his mild academic dreams of constitutional Home Rule by good will all round led the Irish members with a much admired, but little repaid, decorum. ' Gentlemen first, Irishmen second ' was said to have been in those days a motto for Irish representatives.

In the seventies, however, a new figure appeared upon the Irish benches whose character, manner and method seemed to contradict all the ordinary traits of Irishmen. Here was a man, stern, grave, reserved, no orator, no idealogue, no spinner of words and phrases ; but a being who seemed to exercise unconsciously an indefinable sense of power in repose—of command awaiting the hour. When the House of Commons became aware of Parnell's growing influence with the Irish Party, nearly all of whom were Catholics, it was noted with surprise that the new or future leader of Ireland was a Protestant and a delegate to the Irish Church Synod. It was also said, ' He is the most English Irishman ever yet seen.' Indeed, during the seventies it was upon English politics that Parnell chiefly laid his hand at Westminster. He became the ally and to some extent the spear-point of English Radicalism, then rising sharp and keen into prominence. To him perhaps more than anyone else the British army owes the abolition of the cruel and senseless flogging then considered inseparable from effective military discipline. In every movement of reform, now achieved and long surpassed, Parnell brought the Irish parliamentary party to the aid of the most advanced challenging forces in British public life. Yet he was himself a man of Conservative instincts, especially where property was concerned. Indeed, the paradoxes of his earnest and sincere life were astonishing : a Protestant leading Catholics ; a landlord inspiring a ' No Rent ' campaign ; a man of law and order exciting revolt ; a humanitarian and anti-terrorist controlling and yet arousing the hopes of Invincibles and Terrorists.

In Ireland National leaders have often presented themselves as men of fate, and instruments of destiny. The distressful country fastened its soul almost superstitiously upon the career of every chieftain as he advanced. Men like O'Connell and Parnell appeared, not in the manner of English political leaders, but rather like the prophets who guided Israel.

An air of mystery and legend had hung about Parnell from his Cambridge days. He was the reverse of a demagogue and agitator. He studied mathematics and metallurgy. He was the heir to a landed estate. He was a Sheriff and a keen cricketer. His permanent ambition was to find the gold veins in the Wicklow mountains, and through all his political triumphs and agonies he could turn for peace and diversion to the laboratory with its scales,

retorts and test-tubes. His Irish nationalism, which persisted and grew upon this unusual background, has been
traced to his mother and her admiration for the idealistic
Fenians. Assassination he abhorred. He was too practical
to harbour Fenian dreams of insurrection against the might
of Britain. As his authority grew, Fenians and Invincibles
stayed the bloody hand for fear of a Parnell resignation.

What an authority it was! Nothing like it has ever
been seen in Ireland in recorded times. Many years ago
when I was a boy, convalescing at Brighton after a serious
accident, I there saw day by day Mrs. O'Connor, wife of
the famous ' Tay Pay,' afterwards father of the House of
Commons. From her I heard many tales and received many
vivid pictures of Parnell and his rise and fall. The Irish
members who followed him unquestioningly hardly dared
to address him. A cold nod in the lobby or a few curt
directions given in an undertone along the Benches—stern,
clear guidance in the secret conclaves—these were the only
contacts of the Irish political party with their leader.
' Can't you go and see him, and find out what he thinks
about it ? ' was the inquiry of an English politician in the
eighties to an Irish member. ' Would I dare to inthrude
upon Misther Parnell ? ' was the answer. As will be seen,
there were reasons on both sides for this caution.

When Mr. Gladstone's government of 1880 took their
seats triumphantly upon the Treasury Bench and looked
around them, they saw upon the western horizon the dark
thunderclouds of Irish storm ; an agrarian campaign backed
by outrage ; a national movement enforced by dynamite ;
an Irish parliamentary party using the weapon of Obstruction. All these processes developed simultaneously ; at
their head Parnell ! In those days the Irish question, which
now seems incredibly small, soon absorbed nine-tenths of
the political field and was destined for forty years to remain
the principal theme of British and Imperial politics. It
divided Great Britain ; it excited the United States ; the
nations of Europe followed the controversy with rapt atten-

tion. Foreign politics, social politics, defence, and Parliamentary procedure—all were continuously involved. Above all, it became the main process by which parties gained or lost the majorities indispensable to their power.

Without Parnell Mr. Gladstone would never have attempted Home Rule. The conviction was borne in upon the Grand Old Man in his hey-day that here was a leader who could govern Ireland, and that no one else could do it. Here was a man who could inaugurate the new system in a manner which would not be insupportable to the old. Parnell with his dogged tenacity and fascination over his followers became the keystone of the Home Rule arch which Gladstone tried to erect and beneath whose ruins he and his adherents fell. Parnell was the last great leader who could hold all the Irish. As a Protestant he was probably the only one who might eventually have conciliated Ulster. Lord Cowper once said that he had neither the virtues nor the vices of an Irishman. He was a great moderate who held back the powers of revolution as an unflung weapon in his hand. If he accepted Boycotting, it was only as a half-way house between incendiarism and constitutionalism. One of his followers, Frank O'Donnell, used to say Parnell talked daggers, but used none. In the first phase in 1881 Mr. Gladstone arrested Parnell and threw him into Kilmainham gaol. But the forces at work within the Liberal party were such as to compel the Prime Minister of Great Britain to parley with his political prisoner. After much difficulty an agreement was reached. Parnell was liberated with redoubled prestige.

But the fight grew more bitter. It wrecked the old liberties of the House of Commons. Obstruction was practised as a Parliamentary art, and the ancient freedom of debate was destroyed by the closure—'Clôture,' Lord Randolph Churchill always used to call it, to brand it with its foreign origin—and ever-tightening rules of order. Parnell said that he based his tactics on those of General Grant, namely, slogging away by frontal attack. He met

English hatred with obstruction, and coercion with a bitterness which destroyed the old amenities of Parliamentary debate. In Ireland, neither the Church nor the Revolutionaries liked him, but both had to submit to his policy. He was a Garibaldi who compelled at once the allegiance of the Pope and of the *Carbonari* in the national cause. When taunted with stimulating outrage and even murder, he thought it sufficient to reply, ' I am answerable to Irish opinion, and Irish opinion alone.'

This is not the place to recount the history of those times. The barest summary will suffice. The Liberal Government incorporated all that remained of the once great Whig Party now borne forward to its extinction upon the crest of energetic democracy. The Whigs were as violently offended by agrarian warfare and the violation of Parliamentary tradition as their Tory opponents. Mr. Gladstone, the champion of freedom and national movements in every foreign country, the friend of Cavour and Mazzini, the advocate of Greek and Bulgarian independence, now found himself forced by duress to employ against Ireland many of the processes of repression he had denounced so mercilessly (and we will add so cheaply) in King Bomba and the Sultan of Turkey. His own chief secretary for Ireland was murdered in the Phœnix Park. Explosions shook the House of Commons. The Habeas Corpus was suspended over the greater part of Ireland. Defence of evictions, riots and occasional fusillades darkened the columns of Liberal newspapers hitherto so forward in blaming foreign tyrants. All this was horribly against the grain with Mr. Gladstone and detestable to the new electorate he had called into being. Always at the back of his mind he nursed the hope of some great conciliation, some act of faith and forgiveness which should place the relations of the sister islands upon an easy, sure and happy foundation. While he denounced Parnell and the Irish Nationalists as ' marching through rapine to the disintegration of the Empire,' in his heart there rose the solemn thought which he afterwards in 1886 embodied

349

in his most memorable peroration. ' Ireland stands at the bar and waits. She asks for a blessed act of oblivion, and in that act of oblivion our interests are even greater than hers.'

In this sort of mood the Liberal Government battered its way through the election of 1885 and still emerged the victor, though now dependent upon the Irish vote. Chamberlain, Morley, Dilke and other Radicals, the men of the new time, all looked towards a settlement. The Grand Old Man, shocked by many of their doctrines, shared their hopes, and brought to them the far stronger surge of his own inspiration. It must also be added that his power to head a government after the 1885 election depended upon an arrangement with Parnell. But the Tories, or some of them, were also bidding in the market. Lord Carnarvon, Irish viceroy in Lord Salisbury's Government, met Parnell in an empty house in London. Lord Randolph Churchill, leader of the Tory Democracy which had swept the great cities in 1885 and confronted Whigs and Radicals with the then undreamed-of spectacle of enormous crowds of enthusiastic Tory working-men, was in close and deep relation with the Irish leaders. Joseph Chamberlain, aggressive exponent of the new Radicalism, was full of plans for a deal with the Irish. Among these, Parnell probably preferred the Tory suitors. His own Conservative instincts, his sense of realism, the anger excited against Liberal coercion, led him a long way towards the Tories. After all, they could deliver the goods. Perhaps they alone could do so, for the House of Lords in those days was a barrier which none but Tories could pass. During Lord Salisbury's brief minority Government of the summer of 1885 when the Irish party in the main supported the Conservatives, both Mr. Chamberlain and Mr. Gladstone addressed themselves, through an intimate channel, to Parnell.

The love of Charles Stewart Parnell and Kitty O'Shea holds its place among the romances of political history. Since 1880 Parnell had loved Kitty, or as he called her,

' Queenie.' This lady was an attractive adventuress, bored with her husband—no wonder !—and aching for a slip in the secret brew of politics. The sister of an English Field-Marshal, she was not very deeply vowed to the cause of Ireland. She heard of Parnell as a rising portent when he was living in solitary lodgings in London. She invited him to dinner for a wager. She sent her card in to him at the House of Commons. When he appeared she dropped a red rose. He picked it up ; its shrivelled petals were buried with him in his coffin.

If ever there was a monogamist it was Parnell. Early in life he had been jilted. He had only taken to politics as an anodyne. Kitty became all-important and absorbing to him. She was at once mistress and nurse, queen and companion, and the lonely man fighting the might of Britain, afflicted by ill-health, drew his life from her smile and presence. By a strange telepathy he could tell whenever she entered the Ladies' Gallery in the House. In her strange book she describes the life they lived together, first at Eltham and then at Brighton. It was a mixture of secrecy and recklessness. From a very early stage the complaisance of the husband was indispensable. Collision with Captain O'Shea passed swiftly into collusion. O'Shea accepted the position. He even profited by it, though not in the base way sometimes represented. He too was under the spell of the great man. By Parnell's support O'Shea was returned as an Irish Nationalist for Galway, although all the other leading Home Rulers thought him but a poor champion of the Irish cause. When murmurs broke out in the election at the advancement of this lukewarm, unsuitable candidate, Parnell silenced them with an imperious gesture. ' I have a Parliament for Ireland in my hand. Forbear to dispute my will.'

Thus we see Parnell and Kitty living as man and wife year after year in love none the less true because illicit ; while the Captain following the Irish leader enjoyed the opportunities of being a go-between with Chamberlain, with

Dilke, and with other prominent men in the great world of London. But always in his heart lurked the spirit of revenge. Often he writhed and cursed, and then subsided. As long as the supreme political interest held, he endured. We have the incident in O'Shea's triangular household of Parnell finding him in Kitty's bedroom, a conjuncture forbidden by their unwritten law. Instead of kicking out O'Shea, Parnell slung Kitty on to his shoulder and carried her off to another room. It was said of Parnell that he was himself a volcano under an ice-cap. He certainly lived upon the brink of a geyser which might at any moment erupt in scalding water. The public knew nothing of all this secret drama, but as early as the Kilmainham Treaty it became a matter of knowledge to the Cabinet. Parnell hastened from the gaol to visit her, and received their dead child in his arms. Sir William Harcourt as Home Secretary informed the Cabinet that the Kilmainham Treaty had been engineered by the husband of Parnell's mistress. Kitty played a vital part in Parnell's action. She prevented him from abandoning politics after the Phœnix Park murders. She was always the intermediary between him and Mr. Gladstone. O'Shea has been as bitterly blamed by his countrymen as anyone in Irish history. There is no doubt that he was thrilled to see his wife adjusting enormous State issues between Parnell and the Prime Minister. His own relations with Chamberlain, of whom he was a frequent attendant, made a compulsive appeal to his sense of self-importance and even to his pride. The story was neither so simple nor so contemptible as it has been painted.

Parnell was so early interwoven with the O'Sheas that there was no time in the eighties in which he could have disentangled himself. Before Gladstone cast him into Kilmainham Gaol he was deep in their toils and enchantments. Mrs. O'Shea's book pretends that she continued to deceive O'Shea, but there is no doubt that from 1881 onwards he was fully apprised. The opening of letters by close friends in the party had made them aware of the intrigue, and both

Healy and Biggar repeatedly warned Parnell that the O'Sheas would be his ruin. Parnell cared nothing for this. His was a love stronger than death, defiant of every social ordinance, scornfully superior not only to worldly ambitions, but even to the Cause entrusted to his hands.

Meanwhile national history unfolded. Mr. Gladstone embraced Home Rule. He broke with the Whigs. By what he always regarded as a strange, inexplicable eddy he found himself confronted by ' Radical Joe.' Lord Randolph Churchill led the Tories of Birmingham to the support of the candidates they had fought a few months before. Lord Salisbury was returned to power. Chamberlain became a pillar of the Unionist administration. Gladstone had re-united himself with all the sentimental forces which made nineteenth-century Liberalism so great but so transient a factor in European history. For reasons which have no part in this tale Lord Randolph Churchill resigned from Lord Salisbury's Government. Tory Democracy was dumb-founded and discouraged. The Unionist Government plodded on dully and clumsily without much illumination, but with solid purpose. Gradually Mr. Gladstone's strength revived. The process was stimulated by a surprising occurrence.

In 1887, *The Times* newspaper began to publish a series of articles under the heading of ' Parnellism and Crime.' Then, in order to substantiate the charges made by its correspondent, it reproduced, in what Morley calls ' all the fascination of facsimile,' a letter in Parnell's handwriting which directly connected the Irish leader with the murder campaign. The story of this letter is without compare in the annals of the Press. In 1885 there lived in dis-honourable poverty in Dublin a broken-down journalist named Richard Pigott. For years he had preyed upon a credulous public. He had raised subscriptions for the defence of the accused in Fenian trials and the relief of their wives and children, and then embezzled the moneys received. That source of income failing, he had turned to the writing of begging letters. But the wells of Christian charity yielded little to his pump. According to rumour, he was about this time supplementing their scanty flow by the sale of indecent books and photographs. And even that could not procure sufficient for his moderate needs. In this crisis of his fate there came to him a gentleman convinced that Parnell and his colleagues were parties to the crimes of the extremists. But he wanted proof, and he offered Pigott a guinea a day, hotel and travelling expenses, and a round price for documents, if he could supply the necessary evidence. Of course Pigott could supply it. And so the famous Parnell letter, and a host of other incriminating documents, came into being, and ultimately found their way to the offices of *The Times*.

The manager of *The Times*, unfortunately, did not investigate the origin of these letters. He paid, in all, over £2,500 for them. But he asked no questions. He believed that the letters were genuine because he wanted them to be genuine. And the Government took the same view for precisely the same reason. They believed that here they had a weapon of the first importance, not only against Parnell but against Gladstone. Against Lord Randolph Churchill's earnest advice, embodied in a secret memorandum, they set up a Special Commission of three Judges to investigate the connection of Parnell and his colleagues, and the movement of which they were the leaders, with agrarian political crime assassination.

It was, in effect, a State trial—but a State trial without a jury. For over a year the Judges toiled and laboured. Many of the secrets of terrorism and of counter-espionage were laid bare. Strange figures like Le Caron, in the deep-hidden employ of the British Government, told their tale of conspiracies in England, Ireland and America. The whole political world followed the case with fascination. Nothing like it had been seen since the impeachment of Sacheverell. The brilliant Irish advocate who was afterwards Lord Russell of Killowen, Lord Chief Justice of England, was principal counsel for his compatriots. He was aided by a young Radical lawyer, by name Herbert Henry Asquith. The climax was not reached until February, 1889, when Pigott was put in the box and broke down in fatal cross-examination. His exposure by Russell was complete and remorseless. He was asked to write down the words 'likelihood' and 'hesitancy' which he had misspelt in the forged letter. He repeated his misspellings. He wrote 'hesitency' as it appeared in the accusing document. Letters which he had written, begging for money, were read out, and greeted with mocking laughter from all parts of the Court. There was another day of damning exposure. The fact of forgery was established. Then, on the third day, when Pigott's name was called, he did not answer. He had fled from justice. Detectives tracked him to an hotel in Madrid, and he blew out his brains to escape the punishment of his crime.

The effect of these proceedings upon the British electorate was profound. A general election could not long be delayed, and the prospect of a sweeping Liberal victory seemed certain. Parnell was widely regarded throughout Britain as a deeply wronged man who had at length been vindicated. He had been cleared of a horrible charge brought against him by political malice. The prospects of a Home Rule victory were never so bright. Making allowance for the differences between countries, the charge against Parnell was invested with all the significance attached in France to the Dreyfus case. All the political forces were stirred by vehement passion. Then came the counterstroke. Someone detonated O'Shea. The husband who for ten years had been inert suddenly roused himself to strike a deadly blow. He opened proceedings for divorce against his wife, naming Parnell as co-respondent. Some day an historical examination will reveal what is at present disputed, namely, whether Chamberlain stirred O'Shea to this action. It must be remembered that many people sincerely believed that the life of the British Empire depended upon the defeat of Home Rule.

Both Parnell and Mrs. O'Shea were at first unperturbed by the proceedings. Parnell was sure he could hold Ireland, and even Irish Conservatism. To Kitty divorce promised the end of a false and odious situation and of a long apprehension, and she saw a sure and quick way to becoming Mrs. Parnell. If Parnell had defended the suit, he could, in the opinion of his renowned solicitor Sir George Lewis, have certainly won by proving the long collusion. But Kitty and he could never then be united before the whole world in wedlock. It must be admitted that Parnell inclined to this course. But Mrs. O'Shea's counsel, Frank Lockwood, a man of exceptional brilliancy, persuaded him to let the case go forward without resistance. In after years Lockwood said, ' Parnell was cruelly wronged all round. There is a great reaction in his favour. I am not altogether without remorse myself.'

The furious political world of the early nineties learned with delight or consternation that Parnell was adjudged a guilty co-respondent. The details of the case, published verbatim in every newspaper, fed the prudish curiosity of the public. According to one story Parnell had made his exit on one occasion from her room down the fire-escape, and this tale aroused unpitying laughter. But the reaction which followed was different from what Parnell had foreseen. Mr. Gladstone did not appear at the first blush so shocked as might have been expected from so saintly a figure. It was only when he realized the violent revolt of English Nonconformity against a ' convicted adulterer ' that he saw how grievous was the injury to his political interests and how inevitable his severance from Parnell had become. He repudiated Parnell, and Ireland was forced to choose between the greatest of English parliamentarians, the statesman who had made every sacrifice for the Irish cause, who alone could carry the victory in the larger island, and the proud chieftain under whom the Irish people might have marched to a free and true partnership in the British Empire. The choice was bitter, but the forces inexorable.

A meeting of the Irish Party was called on a requisition signed by thirty-one members. Parnell, re-elected leader only the day before, was in the chair, looking, as one of those present put it, ' as if it were we who had gone astray, and he were sitting there to judge us.' An appeal was made to him to retire temporarily, leaving the management of the Party in the hands of a Committee to be nominated by himself : then, after the excitement had died down, he could resume the leadership. Parnell said nothing. But equally strong appeals were made by other members that he should not retire. In the end, the meeting adjourned.

Parnell now fought for time. He believed that Ireland was behind him, and that if he could only delay decision long enough, he must win. But when the party meeting resumed, his opponents were taking a stronger line. Mr. T. M. Healy was leading the rebels. ' I say to Mr. Parnell his power has gone,' he declared. ' He derived that power from the people. We are the representatives of the people.' Parnell was stung to reply ; ' Mr. Healy has been trained in this warfare,' he said. ' Who trained him ? Who gave him his first opportunity and chance ? Who got him his seat in Parliament ? That Mr. Healy should be here to-day to destroy me is due to myself.' Day after day the debate went on, Parnell fighting more and more desperately to avoid a vote on the real issue, still clinging to the belief that the people of Ireland would support him against the insurgent M.P.s. But he knew that the tide was turning against him. His eyes blazed ever more fiercely in his pallid face : it was only by an intense effort that he still held himself in check. On every side tempers were taut, at the breaking-point. On the fifth day Healy quoted a speech of Parnell's, six months before, in which he had referred to an alliance with the Liberals, ' an alliance which I venture to believe will last.' ' What broke it off ? ' demanded Healy. ' Gladstone's letter,' said Parnell. ' No,' retorted Healy. ' It perished in the stench of the Divorce Court.'

The end came on the seventh day of the meeting, December

6th, 1890. There were disorderly scenes. John Redmond, who had stuck to Parnell through thick and thin, used the phrase, 'the master of the Party.' 'Who is to be the mistress of the Party ? ' cried the bitterest tongue in Ireland. Parnell rose, his eyes terrible. For a moment it seemed that he was going to strike Healy, and some of the rebels even hoped that he would. But : ' I appeal to my friend the chairman,' said one of them. 'Better appeal to your own friends,' said Parnell, ' better appeal to that cowardly scoundrel there, that in an assembly of Irishmen dares to insult a woman.' There was more barren argument, more recriminations. Finally, Justin M'Carthy rose. ' I see no further use carrying on a discussion which must be barren of all but reproach, ill-temper, controversy and indignity,' he said, ' and I therefore suggest that all who think with me at this grave crisis should withdraw with me from this room.' Forty-five members filed out silently, twenty-seven remained behind. And Ireland, Parnell was soon to discover, was with the majority.

The Catholic Church swung decidedly against him. In vain he asserted his vanished authority. In vain he fought with frantic energy at savage Irish by-elections. Another year of grim struggle at hopeless odds sapped a constitution always frail. Then in Morley's moving words, ' the veiled shadow stole upon the scene,' and Charles Stewart Parnell struggled for the last time across the Irish Channel to die at Brighton on October 6th, 1891, in the arms of the woman he loved so well.

It is forty-five years since that final scene. But Parnell's figure looms no smaller now, seen through the gathering mists of history, than it did to his contemporaries. They saw the politician ; and they saw him, of necessity, through the spectacles of faction and party prejudice. We see the man, one of the strangest, most baffling personalities that ever trod the world's stage. He never forgot. He never forgave. He never faltered. He dedicated himself to a single goal, the goal of Ireland a nation, and he pursued it unswervingly until a rose thrown across his path opened a new world, the world of love. And, as he had previously sacrificed all for Ireland, so, when the moment of choice came, he sacrificed all, even Ireland, for love. A lesser man might have given more sparingly and kept more. Most of the Irish politicians who deserted him went unwillingly. Had he accepted a temporary retirement, he might have returned, in a year or so, to all his former power. He was young enough, he was only in his forty-sixth year when he died, worn out by the struggle he might so easily have avoided. But though he could command, he could not conciliate. And so, in place of the applause that might have been his as first Prime Minister of Ireland, we have the paler but perhaps wider fame of the undying legend. In place of the successful politician, we have the man of fire and ice, of fierce passions held in strong control, but finally breaking out with overwhelming force, to destroy and immortalize him. ' It will be a nine days' wonder,' he said to a colleague, in telling of his decision not to defend the divorce action. ' Nine centuries, sir,' was the reply.

Such is the tale which comprised all the elements of a Greek tragedy. Sophocles or Euripides could have found in it a theme sufficient to their sombre taste. Modern British opinion rebels at its conclusions. Contemporary foreign opinion frankly could not understand the political annihilation of Parnell. It was ascribed to British hypocrisy. But the result was clear and fatally disastrous. The loves of Parnell and Kitty O'Shea condemned Ireland to a melancholy fate, and the British Empire to a woeful curtailment of its harmony and strength.

'B.-P.'

The Daily Mirror

LORD BADEN-POWELL

' B.-P.'

THE three most famous generals I have known in my life won no great battles over the foreign foe. Yet their names, which all begin with ' B,' are household words. They are General Booth, General Botha and General Baden-Powell. To General Booth we owe the Salvation Army; to General Botha, United South Africa; and to General Baden-Powell, the Boy Scout Movement.

In this uncertain world one cannot be sure of much. But it seems probable that one or two hundred years hence, or it may be more, these three monuments that we have seen set up in our lifetime will still proclaim the fame of their founders, not in the silent testimony of bronze or stone, but as institutions guiding and shaping the lives and thoughts of men.

I remember well the first time I saw the hero of this article, now Lord Baden-Powell. I had gone with my regimental team to play in the Cavalry Cup at Meerut. There was a great gathering of the sporting and social circles of the British Army in India. In the evening an amateur vaudeville entertainment was given to a large company. The feature of this was a sprightly song and dance by an officer of the garrison, attired in the brilliant uniform of an Austrian Hussar, and an attractive lady. Sitting as a young lieutenant in the stalls, I was struck by the quality of the performance, which certainly would have held its own on the boards of any of our music halls. I was told:

' That's B.-P. An amazing man ! He won the Kader Cup, has seen lots of active service. They think no end of him as a rising soldier ; but fancy a senior officer kicking his legs up like that before a lot of subalterns ! '

I was fortunate in making the acquaintance of this versatile celebrity before the polo tournament was over.

Three years passed before I met him again. The scene and the occasion were very different. Lord Roberts's army had just entered Pretoria, and General Baden-Powell, who had been relieved in Mafeking after a siege of 217 days, was riding in two or three hundred miles from the Western Transvaal to report to the Commander-in-Chief. I thought I would interview him on behalf of the *Morning Post* and get a first-hand account of his famous defence.

* * * * *

We rode together for at least an hour, and once he got talking he was magnificent. I was thrilled by the tale, and he enjoyed the telling of it. I cannot remember the details but my telegram must have filled the best part of a column. Before dispatching it I submitted it to him. He read it with concentrated attention and some signs of embarrassment, but when he had finished he handed it back to me, saying with a smile, ' Talking to you is like talking to a phonograph.' I was rather pleased with it, too.

In those days B.-P.'s fame as a soldier eclipsed almost all popular reputations. The other B.P.—the British Public —looked upon him as the outstanding hero of the War. Even those who disapproved of the War, and derided the triumphs of large, organized armies over the Boer farmers, could not forbear to cheer the long, spirited, tenacious defence of Mafeking by barely eight hundred men against a beleaguering force ten or twelve times their numbers.

* * * * *

No one had ever believed Mafeking could hold out half as long. A dozen times, as the siege dragged on, the watching nation had emerged from apprehension and despondency into renewed hope, and had been again cast down. Millions who could not follow closely or accurately the main events of the War looked day after day in the papers for the fortunes of Mafeking, and when finally the news of its relief was flashed throughout the world, the streets of London became impassable, and the floods of sterling cockney patriotism were released in such a deluge of unbridled, delirious, childish joy as was never witnessed again till Armistice Night, 1918. Nay, perhaps the famous Mafeking night holds the record.

Then the crowds were untouched by the ravages of war. They rejoiced with the light-hearted frenzy of the spectators of a great sporting event. In 1918 thankfulness and a sense of deliverance overpowered exultation. All bore in their hearts the marks of what they had gone through. There were too many ghosts about the streets after Armageddon.

One wondered why B.-P. seemed to drop out of the military hierarchy after the South African War was over. He held distinguished minor appointments ; but all the substantial and key positions were parcelled out among men whose achievements were unknown outside military circles, and whose names had never received the meed of popular applause.

There is no doubt that Whitehall resented the disproportionate acclamation which the masses had bestowed upon a single figure. Was there not something ' theatrical,' ' unprofessional ' in a personality which evoked the uninstructed enthusiasms of the man-in-the-street ? Versatility is always distrusted in the Services. The voice of detraction and professional jealousy spoke of him as Harley Street would speak of the undoubted cures wrought by a quack. At any rate, the bright fruition of fortune and success was soon obscured by a chilly fog, through which indeed the sun still shone, but with a dim and baffled ray.

The caprices of fortune are incalculable, her methods inscrutable. Sometimes when she scowls most spitefully, she is preparing her most dazzling gifts. How lucky for B.-P. that he was not in the early years of the century taken into the central swim of military affairs, and absorbed in all those arduous and secret preparations which ultimately enabled the British Expeditionary Army to deploy for battle at Mons !

How lucky for him, and how lucky for us all ! To this he owes his perennially revivifying fame, his opportunity for high personal service of the most enduring character ; and to this we owe an institution and an inspiration, characteristic of the essence of British genius, and uniting in a bond of comradeship the youth not only of the English-speaking world, but of almost every land and people under the sun.

It was in 1907 that B.-P. held his first camp for boys to learn the lore of the backwoods and the discipline of scout life. Twenty-one boys of every class from the East End of London, from Eton and Harrow, pitched their little tents on Brownsea Island in Dorsetshire. From this modest beginning sprang the world-wide movement of boy scouts and girl guides, constantly renewing itself as the years pass, and now well over two millions strong.

*　　*　　*　　*　　*

In 1908 the Chief Scout, as he called himself, published his book, *Scouting for Boys*. It appealed to all the sense of adventure and love of open-air life which is so strong in youth. But beyond this it stirred those sentiments of knightly chivalry, of playing the game—any game—earnest or fun—hard and fairly, which constitute the most important part of the British system of education.

Success was immediate and far-reaching. The simple uniform, khaki shorts and a shirt—within the range of the poorest—was founded upon that of General Baden-Powell's old corps, the South African Constabulary. The hat was the famous hat with the flat brim and pinched top which he had worn at Mafeking. The motto ' Be Prepared ' was founded on his initials. Almost immediately we saw at holiday times on the roads of Britain little troops and patrols of boy scouts, big and small, staff in hand, trudging forward hopefully, pushing their little handcart with their kit and camping gear towards the woodlands and park-lands which their exemplary conduct speedily threw open to them. Forthwith there twinkled the camp fires of a vast new army whose ranks will never be empty, and whose march will never be ended, while red blood courses in the veins of youth.

It is difficult to exaggerate the moral and mental health which our nation has derived from this profound and simple conception. In those bygone days the motto ' Be Prepared ' had a special meaning for our country. Those who looked to the coming of a great war welcomed the awakening of British boyhood. But no one, even the most resolute pacifist, could be offended ; for the movement was not militaristic in character, and even the sourest, crabbedest critic saw in it a way of letting off youthful steam.

*   *   *   *   *

The success of the scout movement led to its imitation in many countries, notably in Germany. There, too, the little troops began to march along the roads already trampled by the legions.

The Great War swept across the world. Boy scouts played their part. Their keen eyes were added to the watchers along the coasts ; and in the air raids we saw the spectacle of children of twelve and fourteen performing with perfect coolness and composure the useful functions assigned to them in the streets and public offices.

Many venerable, famous institutions and systems long honoured by men perished in the storm ; but the Boy Scout Movement survived. It survived not only the War, but the numbing reactions of the aftermath. While so many elements in the life and spirit of the victorious nations seemed to be lost in stupor, it flourished and grew increasingly. Its motto gathers new national significance as the years unfold upon our island. It speaks to every heart its message of duty and honour : ' Be Prepared ' to stand up faithfully for Right and Truth, however the winds may blow.

ROOSEVELT
FROM AFAR

Keystone View Company

FRANKLIN DELANO ROOSEVELT

ROOSEVELT FROM AFAR

THE life and well-being of every country are influenced by the economic and financial policy of the United States. From the cotton spinners of Lancashire to the ryots of India ; from the peasantry of China to the pawn-brokers of Amsterdam ; from the millionaire financier watching the tape machine to the sturdy blacksmith swinging his hammer in the forge ; from the monetary philosopher or student to the hard-headed business man or sentimental social reformer—all are consciously or unconsciously affected. For in truth Roosevelt is an explorer who has embarked on a voyage as uncertain as that of Columbus, and upon a quest which might conceivably be as important as the discovery of the New World. In those old days it was the gulf of oceans with their unknown perils and vicissitudes. Now in the modern world, just as mysterious and forbidding as the stormy waters of the Atlantic is the gulf between the producer, with the limitless powers of science at his command, and the consumer, with legitimate appetites which will never be satiated.

Plenty has become a curse. Bountiful harvests are viewed with dread which in the old times accompanied a barren season. The gift of well-organized leisure, which machines should have given to men, has only emerged in the hateful spectacle of scores of millions of able and willing workers kicking their heels by the hoardings of closed factories and subsisting upon charity, or as in England upon systematized relief. Always the peoples are asking themselves ' Why should these things be ? Why should not the new powers man has wrested from nature open the portals

of a broader life to men and women all over the world ? '
And with increasing vehemence they demand that the
thinkers and pioneers of humanity should answer the riddle
and open these new possibilities to their enjoyment.

A single man whom accident, destiny, or Providence,
has placed at the head of one hundred and twenty millions
of active, educated, excitable and harassed people, has set
out upon this momentous expedition. Many doubt if he will
succeed. Some hope he will fail. Although the policies of
President Roosevelt are conceived in many respects from a
narrow view of American self-interest, the courage, the
power and the scale of his effort must enlist the ardent
sympathy of every country, and his success could not fail
to lift the whole world forward into the sunlight of an
easier and more genial age.

There is therefore a widespread desire to look at this man
in the midst of his adventure. Trained to public affairs,
connected with the modern history of the United States
by a famous name, at forty-two he was struck down with
infantile paralysis. His lower limbs refused their office.
Crutches or assistance were needed for the smallest movement from place to place. To ninety-nine men out of a
hundred such an affliction would have terminated all forms
of public activity except those of the mind. He refused to
accept this sentence. He fought against it with that same
rebellion against commonly-adopted conventions which we
now see in his policy. He contested elections : he harangued
the multitude : he faced the hurly-burly of American politics in a decade when they were exceptionally darkened by
all the hideous crimes and corruption of Gangsterdom which
followed upon Prohibition. He beat down opponents in
this rough arena. He sought, gained and discharged offices
of the utmost labour and of the highest consequence. As
Governor of New York State his administration, whatever its
shortcomings, revealed a competent, purposeful personality.
He stooped to conquer. He adapted himself to the special
conditions and to the humiliations which had long obstructed

the entry of the best of American manhood into the unsavoury world of politics. He subscribed to the Democratic ticket and made himself the mouthpiece of party aims without losing hold upon the larger objectives of American public life.

World events began to move. The Hoover administration could only gape upon the unheard-of problems of depression through glut. The long ascendancy of the Republican regime was clearly drawing to its close. The Presidency of the United States awaited a Democratic candidate. Five or six outstanding figures presented themselves, in busy scheming rivalry.

In the opinion of many of the shrewdest leaders of his party, Roosevelt was the weakest of these contestants. And there were for long those who considered that in hard common sense and genuine statecraft Roosevelt's former leader, Governor Al Smith, was unquestionably the strongest. But Roosevelt pulled his wires and played his cards in such a way that Fortune could befriend him. Fortune came along, not only as a friend or even as a lover, but as an idolator. There was one moment when his nomination turned upon as little as the spin of a coin. But when it fell there was no doubt whose head was stamped upon it.

He arrived at the summit of the greatest economic community in the world at the moment of its extreme embarrassment. Everybody had lost faith in everything. Credit was frozen. Millions of unemployed without provision filled the streets or wandered despairing about the vast spaces of America. The rotten foundations of the banks were simultaneously undermined and exposed. A universal deadlock gripped the United States. The richest man could not cash the smallest cheque. People possessing enormous intrinsic assets in every kind of valuable security found themselves for some days without the means to pay an hotel bill or even a taxi fare. We must never forget that this was the basis from which he started. Supreme power in the Ruler, and a clutching anxiety of scores of millions who demanded and awaited orders.

Since then there has been no lack of orders. Although the Dictatorship is veiled by constitutional forms, it is none the less effective. Great things have been done, and greater attempted. To compare Roosevelt's effort with that of Hitler is to insult not Roosevelt but civilization. The petty persecutions and old-world assertions of brutality in which the German idol has indulged only show their small-ness and squalor compared to the renaissance of creative effort with which the name of Roosevelt will always be associated.

The President's second momentous experiment is an attempt to reduce unemployment by shortening the hours of labour of those who are employed and spreading the labour more evenly through the wage-earning masses. Who can doubt that this is one of the paths which will soon be trodden throughout the world? If it is not to be so, we may well ask what is the use to the working masses of invention and science. Are great discoveries in organiza-tion or processes only to mean that fewer labourers will produce more than is required during the same long hours, while an ever larger proportion of their mates are flung redundant upon the labour market? If that were so, surely the poor English Luddites of a hundred years ago were right in attempting to break up the new machines. Alone through the establishment of shorter hours can the wage-earners enjoy the blessings of modern mass production ; and indeed without shorter hours those blessings are but a curse.

Thus the Roosevelt adventure claims sympathy and admiration from all of those in England, and in foreign countries, who are convinced that the fixing of a universal measure of value based not upon the rarity or plenty of any single commodity, but conforming to the advancing powers of mankind, is the supreme achievement which at this time lies before the intellect of Man. But very con-siderable misgivings must necessarily arise when a campaign to attack the monetary problem becomes intermingled with, and hampered by, the elaborate processes of social reform and the struggles of class warfare. In Great Britain we know a lot about trade unions. It is now nearly a century since they began to play a part in our life. It is half a century since Lord Beaconsfield, a Conservative Prime Minister at the head of an aristocratic and bourgeois Parliament, accorded them exceptional favour before the law and protected them from being sued in their corporate capacity. We have dwelt with British trade unionism ever since. It has introduced a narrowing element into our public life. It has been a keenly-felt impediment to our productive and competitive power. It has become the main foundation of a socialist political party, which has ruled the State greatly to its disadvantage, and will assuredly do so again. It reached a climax in a general strike, which if it had been successful would have subverted the Parliamentary constitution of our island.

But when all is said and done, there are very few well-informed persons in Great Britain, and not many employers of labour on a large scale, who would not sooner have to deal with the British trade unions as we know them, than with the wild vagaries of communist-agitated and totally unorganized labour discontent. The trade unions have been a stable force in the industrial development of Britain in the last fifty years. They have brought steadily to the front the point of view of the toiler and the urgent requirements of his home, and have made these vital matters imprint themselves upon the laws and customs of our country. They have been a steadying force which has counterbalanced and corrected the reckless extravagances of the Red intelligentsia. Over and over again in thirty years we have heard employers say, ' We might easily go further than the trade union leaders and fare a good deal worse ' ; and in the Great War, the sturdy patriotism of the trade unionists and the masculine common sense of their officials gave us an invaluable and, as it proved, unbreak-

375

able basis upon which to carry forward the struggle for national self-preservation.

But when one sees an attempt made within the space of a few months to lift American trade unionism by great heaves and bounds to the position so slowly built up—and even then with much pain and loss—in Great Britain, we cannot help feeling grave doubts. One wonders whether the struggle of American industrial life—its richness and fertility, its vivid possibilities to brains and brawn, to handicraft and industry, the whole spread over so vast a continent with such sharp contrasts in conditions and climate—may not result in a general crippling of that enterprise and flexibility upon which not only the wealth, but the happiness of modern communities depends. One wonders whether the rigid and hitherto comparatively modest structure of American trade unionism will be capable of bearing the immense responsibilities for national well-being and for the production of necessaries of all kinds for the people of the United States which the power now given to them implies. If anything like a beer racket or any other racket broke in upon the responsible leaders of American trade unions, the American democracy might easily wander in a very uncomfortable wilderness for ten or twenty years. Our trade unions have grown to manhood and power amid an enormous network of counter-checks and consequential corrections; and to raise American trade unionism from its previous condition to industrial sovereignty by a few sweeping decrees may easily confront both the trade unions and the United States with problems which for the time being will be at once paralysing and insoluble.

A second danger to President Roosevelt's valiant and heroic experiments seems to arise from the disposition to hunt down rich men as if they were noxious beasts. It is a very attractive sport, and once it gets started quite a lot of people everywhere are found ready to join in the chase. Moreover, the quarry is at once swift and crafty, and therefore elusive. The pursuit is long and exciting, and everyone's blood is infected with its ardour. The question arises whether the general well-being of the masses of the community will be advanced by an excessive indulgence in this amusement. The millionaire or multi-millionaire is a highly economic animal. He sucks up with sponge-like efficiency money from all quarters. In this process, far from depriving ordinary people of their earnings, he launches enterprise and carries it through, raises values, and he expands that credit without which on a vast scale no fuller economic life can be opened to the millions. To hunt wealth is not to capture commonwealth.

This money-gathering, credit-producing animal can not only walk—he can run. And when frightened he can fly. If his wings are clipped, he can dive or crawl. When in the end he is hunted down, what is left but a very ordinary individual apologizing volubly for his mistakes, and particularly for not having been able to get away?

But meanwhile great constructions have crumbled to the ground. Confidence is shaken and enterprise chilled, and the unemployed queue up at the soup-kitchens or march out upon the public works with ever-growing expense to the taxpayer and nothing more appetizing to take home to their families than the leg or the wing of what was once a millionaire. One quite sees that people who have got interested in this fight will not accept such arguments against their sport. What they will have to accept is the consequences of ignoring such arguments. It is indispensable to the wealth of nations and to the wage and life standards of labour, that capital and credit should be honoured and cherished partners in the economic system. If this is rejected there is always, of course, the Russian alternative. But no one can suppose that the self-reliant population of the United States, which cut down the forests and ploughed up the soil and laced the continent with railways, and carried wealth-getting and wealth-diffusing to a higher point than has ever been reached by mankind, would be content for a week with the dull brutish servitude of Russia.

377

It was a prudent instinct that led Mr. Roosevelt to discard those attempts at legal price-fixing which have so often been made in old-world countries, and have always, except in time of war or in very circumscribed localities, broken down in practice. Such measures are appropriate to break monopolies or rings, but can never be accepted as a humdrum foundation for economic life. There can never be good wages or good employment for any length of time without good profits, and the sooner this is recognized, the sooner the corner will be turned.

Writing as a former Chancellor of the British Exchequer for nearly five years, I find myself very much astonished by a law recently passed in the United States that all returns of income for the purposes of taxation must be made public. Such a rule would seem highly obstructive to commercial revival, as well—though this is minor—as being objectionable in the sphere of personal relations. In Great Britain we plume ourselves on collecting effectually the largest possible revenues from wealth upon as high a scheme of graduated taxation as will not defeat its own purpose. Our income and super-tax payers have frequently been paid tributes by foreign observers for the thoroughness and punctuality with which they meet their dues. Even our own Socialist ministers have testified to this. But it has always been accepted that the relations of the taxpayer, rich or poor, are with the State and the State alone, and that neither his employees nor his trade rivals, neither his neighbours nor his creditors, neither his enemies nor his friends, should know what has passed between him and the Treasury. To ask a trader or manufacturer engaged in productive enterprise, with all the hazards attendant thereupon, to reveal not only to the collectors of the public revenue but to all and sundry his income for the year, must be an impediment to national business almost measureless in its irritation, and in its mischief. It seems to me to be only another variant of that hideous folly of prohibition from which the wisdom and virility of the United States by a patient but irresistible heave of broad shoulders so lately shook itself free.

No one could write in this sense without at the same time feeling the justification there is for the anger of the American public against many of their great leaders of finance. The revelations and exposures which have flowed in a widening stream, and even flood, during the last four years, have laid many prominent persons open to prejudice and public censure, apart altogether from the law. The passionate desire of the struggling wage-earner with a family at home and many applicants for his job, with the vultures of ill-health and bad luck hovering above him and those dear to him, is for clean hands in the higher ranks, and for a square deal even if it be only a raw deal.

A thousand speeches could be made on this. The important question is whether American democracy can clear up scandals and punish improprieties without losing its head, and without injuring the vital impulses of economic enterprise and organization. It is no use marching up against ordinary private business men, working on small margins, as if they were the officials of Government departments, who so long as they have attended at their offices from ten to four in a respectable condition, have done their job. There are elements of contrivance, of housekeeping, and of taking risks which are essential to all profitable activity. If these are destroyed the capitalist system fails, and some other system must be substituted. No doubt the capitalist system is replete with abuses and errors and inequities like everything else in our imperfect human life ; but it was under it that only a few years ago the United States produced the greatest prosperity for the greatest numbers that has ever been experienced in human record. It is not illogical to say : ' Rather than condone these faults and these abuses we will sweep this system away no matter what it costs in our material well-being. We will replace it by the only other system which enables large organizations and developments to be undertaken, namely, nationalization of all the means of production, distribution, credit and exchange.' It is, however, irrational to tear down or cripple the capitalist system without having the fortitude of spirit and ruthlessness of action to create a new communist system.

There, it seems to foreign observers, lies the big choice of the United States at the present time. If the capitalist system is to continue, with its rights of private property, with its pillars of rent, interest and profit, and the sanctity of contracts recognized and enforced by the State, then it must be given a fair chance. It is the same for us in the Old World. If we are to continue in the old leaky lifeboat amid these stormy seas, we must do our best to keep it bailed, to keep it afloat, and to steer for port. If we decide to take to the rafts of a new system, there also we are vociferously assured there is a chance of making land. But the Siberian coast is rugged and bleak, and there are long, cruel frosts in the Arctic Ocean.

It is a very open question, which any household may argue to the small hours, whether it is better to have equality at the price of poverty, or well-being at the price of inequality. Life will be pretty rough, anyhow. Whether we are ruled by tyrannical bureaucrats or self-seeking capitalists, the ordinary man who has to earn his living, and tries to make provision for old age and for his dear ones when his powers are exhausted, will have a hard pilgrimage through this dusty world. The United States was built upon property, liberty and enterprise, and certainly it has afforded the most spacious and ample life to the scores of millions that has ever yet been witnessed. To make an irrevocable departure into the Asiatic conceptions would be a serious step, and should be measured with a steady eye at the outset.

We must then hope that neither the tangles of the N.R.A. nor the vague, ethereal illusions of sentimentalists or doctrinaires will prevent President Roosevelt from testing and plumbing the secrets of the monetary problem. If he succeeds all the world will be his debtor : if he fails he will at any rate have made an experiment for mankind on a scale which only the immense strength of the United States could sustain. It would be a thousand pities if this tremendous effort by the richest nation in the world to expand consciously and swiftly the bounds of the consuming power should be vitiated by being mixed up with an ordinary radical programme and a commonplace class fight. If failure there be, which God forfend, it will be taken for a generation as proof positive that all efforts to procure prosperity by currency and credit inflation are doomed to failure.

But the President has need to be on his guard. To a foreign eye it seems that forces are gathering under his shield which at a certain stage may thrust him into the background and take the lead themselves. If that misfortune were to occur, we should see the not-unfamiliar spectacle of a leader running after his followers to pull them back. It is to be hoped and indeed believed that the strong common sense, the sturdy individualism and the cold disillusioned intelligence of the American people will protect their leader from such inglorious experiences.

However we may view the Presidency which has reached half its natural span,* it is certain that Franklin Roosevelt will rank among the greatest of men who have occupied that proud position. His generous sympathy for the underdog, his intense desire for a nearer approach to social justice, place him high among the great philanthropists. His composure combined with activity in time of crisis class him with famous men of action. His freeing the United States from prohibition and the vigour of his administrative measures of relief and credit expansion proclaim him a statesman of world renown. He has known how to gain the confidence and the loyalty of the most numerous and the most ebullient of civilized communities, and all the world watches his valiant effort to solve their problems with an anxiety which is only the shadow of high hope.

* Written in 1934.

Will he succeed or will he fail ? That is not the question we set ourselves, and to prophesy is cheap. But succeed or fail, his impulse is one which makes towards the fuller life of the masses of the people in every land, and which as it glows the brighter may well eclipse both the lurid flames of German Nordic national self-assertion and the baleful unnatural lights which are diffused from Soviet Russia.

INDEX

INDEX